William Faulkner

LITERATURE AND LIFE SERIES
(Formerly Modern Literature and World Dramatists)
Selected list of titles:

Complete list of titles in the series available from publisher on request.

WILLIAM FAULKNER

Alan Warren Friedman

UNGAR • NEW YORK

1986

Copyright © 1984 by Frederick Ungar Publishing Co., Inc.

Printed in the United States of America

Grateful Acknowledgment is made to Random House, Inc., for permission to quote from the copyrighted works of William Faulkner. Portions of "The Love Song of J. Alfred Prufrock" in *Collected Poems 1909-1962* by T.S. Eliot, copyright 1936 by Harcourt Brace Jovanovich, Inc; copyright © 1963, 1964 by T.S. Eliot are reprinted by permission of the publisher.

Library of Congress Cataloging in Publication Data

Friedman, Alan Warren.
 William Faulkner.

 (Literature and life series)
 Bibliography: P.
 Includes index.
  1. Faulkner, William, 1897-1962. 2. Novelists, American—20th century—Biography. I. Title. II. Series.
 PS3511. A86Z783265 1985 813'.52 [B] 82-40274
 ISBN 0-8044-2218-4

Contents

"This factor of involuntary repetition . . . surrounds with an uncanny atmosphere what would otherwise be innocent enough, and forces upon us the idea of something fateful and unescapable where otherwise we should have spoken of 'chance' only."

—Sigmund Freud, "The 'Uncanny' "

"In fashioning a work of art we are by no means free. . . . We do not choose how we shall make it. . . . It pre-exists us and therefore we are obliged, since it is both necessary and hidden, to do what we should have to do if it were a law of nature, that is to say to discover it."

—Marcel Proust, *Time Regained*

"Creating is living doubly. The groping, anxious quest of a Proust . . . signifies nothing else. At the same time, it has no more significance than the continual and imperceptible creation in which the actor, the conqueror, and all absurd men indulge every day of their lives. All try their hands at miming, at repeating, and at re-creating the reality that is theirs."

—Albert Camus, "Absurd Creation"

"To be an artist is to fail, as no other dare fail, . . . failure is his world and the shrink from it desertion."

—Samuel Beckett, *Three Dialogues*

Acknowledgments

My work on Faulkner has benefited from various forms of encouragement. The University Research Institute of the University of Texas provided grant support. My colleagues Evan Carton, John Slatin, and Warwick Wadlington offered excellent critical comments. In Philip Winsor I have been blessed with an extraordinarily supportive editor. My superb Faulkner Honors Seminar of Spring 1983—Kurt Bauer, Casey Cravens, Mary Farrington, Dymra Henderson, Dixie Manson, Beth Moten, Mindy Smith, Paul Smith, Eric Stimmel, Andy Troup, Melissa Truitt, and Scott Williams—graciously allowed me to inflict much of this upon them. Claude Levy of the English Department of the University of Paris, Nanterre and Edward Sherman of the University of Texas's Law School encouraged me with invitations to present versions of "Errors and Trials" to their classes (the latter on three separate occasions!). Earlier versions of "'Jest another Snopes'" appeared in *Delta* (France), III (November 1976), 125-51, and in my book, *Multivalence: The Moral Quality of Form in the Modern Novel* (Baton Rouge and London: Louisiana State University Press, 1978), 141-77. My greatest debt, one beyond recounting, is to Liz—in this and in all things.

List of Abbreviations

The Following works, further noted in the Bibliography, will be cited in the text according to the abbreviations indicated:

AA:	William Faulkner, *Absalom, Absalom!*
AILD:	William Faulkner, *As I Lay Dying.*
Blotner:	Joseph L. Blotner, *Faulkner: A Biography.*
BW:	*Big Woods: The Hunting Stories of William Faulkner.*
CS:	*Collected Stories of William Faulkner.*
ESPL:	William Faulkner, *Essays, Speeches and Public Letters.*
F in U:	*Faulkner in the University: Class Conference at the University of Virginia, 1957-1958.*
F-C:	*The Faulkner-Cowley File: Letters and Memories, 1944-1962.*
Flags:	William Faulkner, *Flags in the Dust.*
GDM:	William Faulkner, *Go Down Moses.*
H:	William Faulkner, *The Hamlet.*
LA:	William Faulkner, *Light in August.*
Letters:	*Selected Letters of William Faulkner.*
Lion:	*Lion in the Garden: Interviews with William Faulkner, 1926-1962.*
M:	William Faulkner, *The Mansion.*
Mos:	William Faulkner, *Mosquitoes.*
Nagano:	*Faulkner at Nagano.*
P:	William Faulkner, *Pylon.*
R:	William Faulkner, *The Reivers: A Reminiscence.*
RN:	William Faulkner, *Requiem for a Nun.*
S:	William Faulkner, *Sanctuary.*
S&F:	William Faulkner, *The Sound and the Fury.*
SP:	William Faulkner, *Soldiers' Pay.*
T:	William Faulkner, *The Town.*
Unv:	William Faulkner, *The Unvanquished.*
WP:	William Faulkner, *The Wild Palms.*

Chronology

1897   William Cuthbert Falkner born September 25 in New Albany, Mississippi, the oldest of four brothers.

1902   Family moves to Oxford.

1905-14   Attends Oxford Graded School and Oxford High School.

1914   Begins close relationship with Phil Stone, who becomes his mentor, critic, and friend.

1916   Attends University of Mississippi on a casual basis.

1918   Rejected by U.S. Army. Joins Royal Air Force in Canada; discharged after six months without having served overseas. Changes name from "Falkner" to "Faulkner."

1919   First published writing: poem called "L'Apres-Midi d'un Faune" in *The New Republic* (6 August). Again attends University of Mississippi unsuccessfully.

1921   Works as clerk in New York City bookstore.

1921-24   Serves as postmaster at University of Mississippi.

1922-24   Serves as scoutmaster.

1924   Removed as scoutmaster; resigns as postmaster. Meets Sherwood Anderson in New Orleans. Publishes *The Marble Faun* (poems).

1925   Lives in New Orleans; contributes to *The Double Dealer* and *The Times-Picayune*. Flies with barnstormers. In Europe for six months.

1926   *Soldiers' Pay* published. In New Orleans for four months; collaborates with William Spratling on *Sherwood Anderson and Other Famous Creoles*.

1927	*Mosquitoes* published. *Flags in the Dust* rejected for publication.
1928	In New York for three months.
1929	*Sartoris* and *The Sound and the Fury* published. Marries Estelle Oldham Franklin (June 20). Works in University power plant.
1930	*As I Lay Dying* published. Buys antebellum house and renames it "Rowan Oak."
1931	Daughter Alabama born (January 11), lives five days. *Sanctuary* and *These 13* published.
1932	*Light in August* published. Begins writing for MGM in Hollywood. Murry Falkner dies.
1933	*A Green Bough* (poems) published. Daughter Jill born (June 24). Buys first plane.
1934	*Doctor Martino and Other Stories* published. Works three weeks at Universal Studios.
1935	*Pylon* published. Brother Dean Swift killed while flying plane given him by Faulkner. Meets Meta Carpenter.
1935-37	Works at Twentieth Century-Fox a total of eighteen months.
1936	*Absalom, Absalom!* published.
1938	*The Unvanquished* published; screen rights sold to MGM.
1939	*The Wild Palms* published. Elected to National Institute of Arts and Letters.
1940	*The Hamlet* published.
1942	*Go Down, Moses* published.
1942-45	Works at Warner Brothers a total of twenty-six months.
1946	*The Portable Faulkner,* ed. Malcolm Cowley, published.

1947	Teaches six classes at University of Mississippi (April).
1948	*Intruder in the Dust* published; screen rights sold to MGM. Elected to American Academy of Arts and Letters.
1949	*Knight's Gambit* published. *Intruder in the Dust* filmed in Oxford. Meets Joan Williams.
1950	*Collected Stories of William Faulkner* published. Receives American Academy's Howells Medal for Fiction and 1949 Nobel Prize for Literature.
1951	Receives National Book Award for *Collected Stories* and Legion of Honor in New Orleans. *Requiem for a Nun* published.
1951-54	Works intermittently as scriptwriter for Howard Hawks.
1952	Travels to France, England, and Norway.
1954	Travels to Europe, Egypt, South America, and New York. *A Fable* published.
1955	Receives National Book Award and Pulitzer Prize for *A Fable*. *Requiem for a Nun* produced as play in Zurich (in Paris, 1956; Athens, 1957; New York, 1959). Spends month in Japan as cultural ambassador for State Department (see *Faulkner at Nagano*). Spends month in Europe. *Big Woods* published.
1957	Spends semester at University of Virginia as writer-in-residence (see *Faulkner in the University: Class Conferences at the University of Virginia, 1957-58*). Cultural ambassador to Athens for two weeks; receives Silver Medal of Greek Academy. *The Town* published.
1958	Spends a second semester as writer-in-residence at University of Virginia.

1959	Breaks collarbone in fall from horse. *The Mansion* published.
1960	Accepts appointment to University of Virginia faculty. Maud Butler Falkner dies.
1961	Travels to Venezuela for State Department.
1962	Makes two-day visit to U.S. Military Academy at West Point (see *Faulkner at West Point*). Receives Gold Medal for Fiction from National Institute of Arts and Letters. *The Reivers* published. Dies of heart attack (July 6).
1968	*The Faulkner-Cowley File: Letters and Memories 1944-62* published.
1973	*Flags in the Dust* (original version of *Sartoris*) published.

William Faulkner

1

William Faulkner: Failure and Repetition

William Faulkner, one of the two or three finest novelists this country has produced, was a prolific writer. During more than four decades, he wrote some twenty novels, upwards of a hundred short stories, two collections of poems, several plays, numerous essays, interviews, speeches, and public letters, and worked on many Hollywood film scripts. He was both a careful craftsman—working and reworking his material for publication, and later often revising it again to fit changing conceptions—and also a daring experimenter with narrative, chronology, structure, and tone. Along with Conrad, Kafka, Joyce, Lawrence, and Hemingway, Faulkner is one of the great short-story writers—and he wrote many more than most of them did. At least four of his books—*The Sound and the Fury, As I Lay Dying, Light in August,* and *Absalom, Absalom!*—are generally regarded as among the most powerful and innovative of twentieth-century novels, while several others—*Sanctuary, The Hamlet, Go Down, Moses*—are of nearly equal stature.

Born on September 25, 1897, in northern Mississippi, Faulkner spent most of his sixty-five years in what he called "my own little postage stamp of native soil" (*Lion,* 255), and of which, in the map he made of it for *Absalom, Absalom!,* he declared himself "Sole Owner and Proprietor." His family's

residence and prominence there went back generations: "My
great-grandfather, whose name I bear, was a considerable
figure in his time and provincial milieu. He was prototype of
John Sartoris [in *Flags in the Dust* and *The Unvanquished*]:
raised, organized, paid the expenses of and commanded the
2nd Mississippi Infantry, 1861—2, etc. . . . He built the first
railroad in our county, wrote a few books, made grand
European tour of his time, died in a duel and the county raised a
marble effigy which still stands in Tippah County. The place of
our origin shows on larger maps: a hamlet named Falkner just
below Tennessee line on his railroad" (*Letters*, 211-12).
Although Colonel William Cuthbert Falkner—"pioneer,
lawyer, soldier, railroad builder, politician, best-selling
writer"[1]—was indeed a volatile and violent man, in fact the
very stuff of myth and therefore an apt figure on which to
model one's life,[2] Faulkner's accounts about both his family
and himself generally express his fictionalizing instincts
rather than historical veracity; in this case, the duel, the effigy,
and the family's origins in the hamlet of Falkner are all more
fanciful than factual.[3]

Faulkner's paternal grandfather, John Wesley Thompson
Falkner, who was known as the Young Colonel, was the
original for Bayard Sartoris, the boy in *The Unvanquished* and
the old banker in *Sartoris/Flags in the Dust*. Though also
highly political, he lived a far less adventurous life that did his
father; his title was honorary rather than earned. He extended
his father's railroad, and became an Assistant U.S. Attorney
and president of the First National Bank of Oxford. The eldest
of his three children, Murry, married Maud Butler; they had
four sons, the eldest of whom was the novelist (Faulkner was,
in fact, at least the fourth successive generation of first-born
sons). Like his son, Murry Falkner inherited nothing and held
a variety of jobs, including running a livery stable in which
Faulkner (who restored the "u" to the family name) said "I
more or less grew up" (*Letters*, 212). In 1918 Murry became
business manager of the University of Mississippi in Oxford
("a political job," Faulkner called it [*Letters*,212]), "he served

dutifully for ten years, only to be dismissed in a political shuffle." [4] He died a broken and irrelevant man in 1932, unmourned by the wife who, on her deathbed, confessed she had never much liked him. [5] Faulkner, who claimed to have escaped his "mother's influence pretty easy" as an adolescent (*Letters*, 212), admired her for her "fierce will and enduring pride." [6] He was extremely close to her and wrote her regularly, usually weekly, when he was away and saw her almost daily when he was in Oxford. This relationship was an enduring one since she died less than two years before he did.

Faulkner's formal education was minimal—he was a high school dropout and a desultory university student—but he was an avid reader, especially under the tutelage of Phil Stone, with whom he began a close relationship in 1914 (and who later became the model for Faulkner's Gavin Stevens). Rejected by the U.S. Army during World War I because of his height (five feet, five and a half inches), Faulkner served in the Royal Air Force in Toronto—but despite a widespread belief (which Faulkner himself fostered at times), he did not serve overseas as he had desired. After he returned to Oxford, Faulkner's dandified dress and manner caused him to be dubbed "Count," while his failure to hold a steady job inspired some to extend the appellation to "Count No' Count." He summarized the immediate postwar years as follows: "Painted houses. Served as a 4th class postmaster. Worked for a New Orleans bootlegger. Deck hand in freighters (Atlantic). Hand in a Gulf of Mexico shrimp trawler. Stationary boiler fireman. Barnstormed an aeroplane out of cow pastures. Operated a farm, cotton and feed, breeding and raising mules and cattle. Wrote (or tried) for moving pictures. Oh yes, was a scout master for two years, was fired for moral reasons." [7] By the early nineteen-twenties Faulkner was committed to writing as a career. He had published a number of poems in 1919, and his first book, *The Marble Faun* (1924), was a poetry collection derivative of the French symbolist poets he read under Phil Stone's tutelage. Later, Faulkner would say, "I'm a failed poet. Maybe every novelist wants to write poetry first, finds he can't

and then tries the short story which is the most demanding
form after poetry. And failing at that, only then does he take
up novel writing" (*Lion*, 238). In 1920, he wrote a verse play,
Marionettes, that also echoes the French poets; it was not
published until 1975. Sherwood Anderson, whom he met in
New Orleans in 1924, encouraged and influenced Faulkner,
even to promising assistance in getting his first novel
published providing, if Faulkner's story can be believed, he did
not have to read it (*Lion*, 249). *Soldiers' Pay*, his first novel,
appeared in 1926, as did *Sherwood Anderson and Other
Famous Creoles* (in collaboration with William Spratling), a
parodic book that Anderson resented and never forgave.
Faulkner's second novel, *Mosquitoes* (1927), also was based on
his New Orleans experience.

Faulkner spent the second half of 1925 in Europe, mostly
writing productively in Paris, before returning to New
Orleans and then Oxford. In 1929, a pivotal year, he married
the recently divorced Estelle Oldham Franklin, whom he had
known most of his life and had unsuccessfully courted before
her first marriage, and he published the first two of his
fourteen Yoknapatawpha novels—*Sartoris* and *The Sound
and the Fury*—books that signaled his coming to maturity as a
writer and that inaugurated the remarkable seven-year period
that also saw the publication of *As I Lay Dying* (1930),
Sanctuary (1931), *Light in August* (1932), *Pylon* (1935),
Absalom, Absalom! (1936), as well as two collections of stories
and a second book of poems.

During the nineteen-thirties and forties, Faulkner spent
large periods of time away from Oxford, mostly writing in
Hollywood in order to pay his mounting bills. His hatred for
the place was unequivocal—his letters reiterate that theme
and his longing to return home. But the truth is more
complicated: he strove to return there throughout the late
thirties and early forties, a five-year period when he was
blackballed due to a drunken spree, and not just for the money.
The woman he loved was there—not in Oxford—and with
her he found something of what was missing in his loveless

marriage. Still, his life and work seemed to depend on the world he knew best—though he has said that a writer does not really write "about his environment" (*Lion*, 177)—and he spent most of his time in northern Mississippi, farming, hunting, fishing, riding, among the people whom he knew best and to whom he felt closest.

Faulkner's early novels were critically well received but sold little; *Sanctuary* was his first financial success, though for sensationalist reasons he deplored. Critical acclaim has grown steadily until it has become something of an industry, but most of his books were out of print when he won the Nobel Prize in 1950. He garnered honor and fame abroad long before he did at home, and much of his life was a saga of debts and what he called potboiling to survive. His twin passions—for privacy and Oxford—commonly converged, as he notes: "I have deliberately buried myself in this little lost almost illiterate town, to keep out of the way so that news people wont notice and remember me" (*Letters*, 319). He consistently maintained that "What I have written is of course in the public domain and the public is welcome; what I ate and did and when and where is my own business" (*Letters*, 212). When in 1950 Faulkner was informed that he was to receive the American Academy's Howells Medal (awarded only every five years for distinguished American fiction), he declined to attend the ceremony because he was busy farming and there would be "too many people" (*Letters*, 302-303). Similarly, his initial response to having been awarded the Nobel Prize was that he could not accept in person, and that, in fact, "the award was made, not to me, but to my works.... I feel that what remains after the thirty years of work is not worth carrying from Mississippi to Sweden" (*Letters*, 309). Responding to various pressures, however, he not only attended in the end but delivered a "much reproduced speech [that] would be regarded by many in Stockholm as perhaps the most memorable ever given by a Laureate in literature."[8] And much as he spurned honors when he could, Faulkner infinitely preferred them to presumptuous journalists who, despite what he felt, believed that his life belonged to the American public: "Sweden gave me the Nobel Prize. France gave me the Legion d'Honneur. All my native land did for me was to invade my privacy over my protest and my plea. No wonder people in the rest of the world dont like us, since we seem to have neither taste nor courtesy, and know and believe in nothing but money and it doesn't much matter how you get it" (*Letters*, 354). He wrote a bitter essay on the subject called "On Privacy (The American Dream: What Happened to It?)."[9]

The pattern was established early on: only at the urging of Phil Stone, who underwrote the cost of *The Marble Faun*, did Faulkner supply the biographical sketch and publicity photographs requested by its publisher. Subsequent sketches were increasingly fanciful or deliberately misleading; responding to one such request in 1930, he wrote: "Sorry, I haven't got a picture. I dont intend to have one that I know of, either. About the biography. Dont tell the bastards anything. It cant matter to them. Tell them I was born of an alligator and a nigger slave at the Geneva peace conference two years ago. Or whatever you want to tell them" (*Letters*, 48). Faulkner held his position, ultimately, with fervor: "It is my ambition to be, as a private individual, abolished and voided from history, leaving it markless, no refuse save the printed books; I wish I had had enough sense to see ahead thirty years ago and, like some of the Elizabethans, not signed them. It is my aim, and every effort bent, that the sum and history of my life, which in the same sentence is my obit and epitaph too, shall be them both: He made the books and he died" (*Letters*, xiii). But his position was inherently untenable, his frustration inevitable; as Blotner comments, "he had signed the books, and fame had found him out."[10] He had sought success as a young writer, homage as well as money, but nonetheless scorned it when it arrived, especially since it resulted initially from a purely sensationalist reading of *Sanctuary*. As one commentator has noted: "For years Faulkner had fought for two things: recognition and privacy. Now he had the recognition, but no privacy at all."[11]

Such doubleness was a common feature of Faulkner's career. His love of the South and its devotion to its Lost Cause was juxtaposed with, but not qualified by, a strong sense of justice and humanity. Having had minimal formal education and living in isolation from the literary world, Faulkner cultivated the role of rural farmer, even to the extent of refusing an honorary Doctor of Letters degree from Tulane in 1952 because, he wrote ambiguously, it "would debase and nullify the whole aim of learning" (*Letters*, 329). Yet he was extraordinarily well read,[12] took pains to *flaunt* his "literariness" (in his titles, allusions, experimental styles, etc.), and ultimately acknowledged: "I learned to write from other writers" (*Letters*, 350). The complexities of his style and thought reveal an artist of uncompromising integrity, yet, desperate for money, he often wrote in his letters of his willingness to alter his work to make a sale, and he produced a large amount of what he considered hack writing. He was, simultaneously, the most ignored of America's great writers of his time and among its most widely read: throughout much of his career, his stories found mass-market favor in such periodicals as *The Saturday Evening Post* and *Collier's*, as well as more discriminating approval in journals like *Harper's*, *The American Mercury*, and *Scribner's*; and he was popular in Europe even when largely ignored in the U.S. A rural recluse, he spent a good deal of time working in Hollywood and New York, though for the money and not the glamor; deeply private, he increasingly responded in later life to invitations to serve as cultural ambassador abroad, to visit universities and meet with students, to speak out on public issues; profoundly dedicated to his family and home, he found satisfying love only beyond their confines. Robert Coughlan offers one of the best summaries of Faulkner's dualism: "He is thoughtful of others, and oblivious of others; he is kind, and he is cruel; he is courtly, and he is cold; he is a philosopher at large who has no integrated philosophy; he loves the South and feels revulsion for the South; he is a self-effacing but vain man who longed for recognition and rebuffed it when it came; a man of integrity

who has contributed to a false legend about himself. Of more
serious importance, he is a great writer and a bad writer."[13]
This last point refers to the extraordinary qualitative range of
Faulkner's writings.

The conflict between instinct and external pressures created
a pattern of failure and frustration, one central to Faulkner's
writing as well as to his life.[14] First, the art is a version, a
repetition, of the life, which was in many senses (like all lives)
a failure.[15] Then, each of the fourteen novels of the
Yoknapatawpha saga, collectively his greatest achievement, is
at once part of the vast chronicle into which they all fit and also
an independent recapitulation, a repetition with a difference,
of the whole—both what has gone before and what is yet to
come. Such a task, impossible of fulfillment, creates a restless
and urgent double rhythm in all of these books, as each of them
seeks to define a unique and self-contained version of
Yoknapatawpha County and yet also to represent the entire
saga and world.

Malcolm Cowley, in proposing to Faulkner the book that
became *The Portable Faulkner*, perceived the fiction of
Yoknapatawpha in similar terms: "Instead of trying to collect
the 'best of Faulkner' in 600 pages, I thought of selecting the
short and long stories, and passages from novels that are really
separate stories, that form part of your Mississippi series—so
that the reader will have a picture of Yocknapatawpha [*sic*]
county... from Indian times down to World War II" (*F-C*, 22).
And when the book was finished, Cowley underscored his
sense of its doubleness: "I am very pleased with the volume as
it now stands. Every story in it is (1) complete in itself, no
matter how long or short; and (2) contributes to the history of
Yoknapatawpha County, so that the volume as a whole is close
to being a novel in itself" (*F-C*, 62). It is, as Faulkner hoped it
would be, "a Golden Book of my apocryphal county" (*F-C*, 25).

To tell it once, as if once and for all, and then to tell it
again—that is Faulkner's reiterated purpose—to get it said in
some ideal, paradigmatic way: "I'm trying to say it all in one
sentence, between one Cap and one period. I'm still trying to

put it all, if possible, on one pinhead. I don't know how to do it. All I know to do is to keep on trying in a new way" (*F-C*, 14). And always, of course, falling short: "none of my work has met my own standards" (*Lion*, 244). Every finished book is necessarily inadequate, a failure; success is never an actuality, only a conceptual possibility for the *next* novel, the one still being written or conceived. "In my opinion," Faulkner has said, "my work has all failed, it ain't quite good enough, which is the only reason to write another one" (*F in U*, 143). Such a notion—of process as achievement, and of achievement as failure—is central to an understanding of Faulkner. It manifests itself over and over, in many different ways: in the writers he most admires (Melville, Tolstoy, Thomas Wolfe—because he rates them on what he calls "the gallantry of the failure, not on the success or the validity of the work" [*F in U*, 143]); in the way he answers the same question differently at different times ("I may answer or I may not, but even if I do, if the same question is asked tomorrow, the answer may be different" [*Lion*, 237]—as with his saying at one point that *The Unvanquished* is probably the best book with which to begin reading his work, and later that it is *Sartoris* [*F in U*, 2, 285]); in multiple manuscript variants (for example, the creation of the publishable *Sartoris* out of the rejected *Flags in the Dust*, or the rewriting of *Sanctuary* in the galley proof stage—at his own expense—"trying," as he put it, "to make out of it something which would not shame *The Sound and the Fury* and *As I Lay Dying* too much" [*ESPL*, 178]); in the proliferation of inadequate narrators in *As I Lay Dying* and *Absalom, Absalom!* who tumble over each other to tell their stories, saying, in effect, as Gavin Stevens says in *Requiem*, "Let me play too" or "I'm going to talk a while now"; in the way that the novels of the Snopes trilogy as well as *Sanctuary* and *Requiem* are not simply sequels—though they carry events forward in time—but also recreations, new ways of trying to get the story told by a Faulkner who had, as he put it, come to know "more about the human heart and its dilemma" between each retelling and who would, in any event, regard such discrepancies as "piddling."[16]

Perhaps the classic example, certainly the one closest to
Faulkner's heart, is that of *The Sound and the Fury*, his
favorite, the one toward which he felt "tenderest" (*Lion*, 245),
the one he considered his best work because "It was the best
failure. It was the one that I anguished the most over, that I
worked the hardest at, that even when I knew I couldn't bring
it off, I still worked at it. It's like the parent feels toward the
unfortunate child, maybe. . . . That was the most gallant, the
most magnificent failure" (*F in U*, 61). The book haunted
Faulkner, and he kept returning to it. He wrote the story of
Caddy Compson's muddy drawers from the perspectives of her
three brothers—but each of the perspectives seemed
inadequate to him, as did the composite. "And that failed,"
Faulkner has said, "and I tried myself—the fourth section—to
tell what happened, and I still failed" (*F in U*, 1). Sixteen years
later, Faulkner, who had offered to provide Cowley with "a
page or two of synopsis" for *The Portable Faulkner* (*F-C*, 31),
instead produced the Compson family genealogy, a fifth
version of the same story. At first Faulkner felt that he had
finally done the thing: "Here it is. I should have done this
when I wrote the book. Then the whole thing would have
fallen into pattern like a jigsaw puzzle when the magician's
wand touched it" (*F-C*, 36). Later, however, he saw the
genealogy as yet another failure, one that perhaps a *further*
version might correct: "I wrote it five separate times, trying to
tell the story, to rid myself of the dream which would continue
to anguish me until I did. . . . I couldn't leave it alone, and I
never could tell it right, though I tried hard and would like to
try again, though I'd probably fail again" (*Lion*, 244-45).

Faulkner says that he began *The Sound and the Fury* with
the image of Caddy's muddy drawers, viewed from below by
her brothers, as she climbs a tree to spy on the scene of their
grandmother's death. Then he sought to tell the story of that
image, that frozen moment, to dramatize how and why it
seemed to encapsulate and emblematize themes central to that
novel, and in fact to his work as a whole: loss of innocence,
specifically in terms of death and sexuality; the myth and

history of the past, specifically of the South; the circularity of
time due to the failure to escape the transitional moment; the
partial comprehension of reality on the part of those who bear
witness. Irving Howe has written that "*The Sound and the
Fury* does not launch an action through a smooth passage of
time; it reconstructs a history through a suspension—or
several suspensions—of time."[17] Faulkner has said that, for
the idiot Benjy, "time was not a continuation, it was an instant,
there was no yesterday and no tomorrow, it all is this moment,
it all is [now] to him" (*Lion*, 147). But the same holds true for
Faulkner himself: "There isn't any time. . . . There is only the
present moment, in which I include both the past and the
future, and that is eternity" (*Lion*, 70), or more succinctly,
"There is no such thing as *was*" (*Lion*, 255). But Benjy merely
encompasses the past without comprehending it; never
having truly experienced it, he can only serve to represent it as
incoherent, haphazard, purposeless. Faulkner, on the other
hand, comprehends it (at least in part) but without en-
compassing it, and then anguishes over his reiterated failure to
do so. "People," he has said, "learn only by error" (*Lion*,
244)—but not everyone does, not everyone is able to move
from initiation to experience. Many view the past, like "the
very old men [in "A Rose for Emily"]—some in their brushed
Confederate uniforms—[as] a huge meadow which no winter
every quite touches" (*CS*, 129).

Faulkner's doomed and damned characters all misread or
ignore the lessons of the past: seeking to ennoble and adhere
to a stultifying myth of a golden yesterday (Colonel Sartoris,
Ike McCaslin, Quentin Compson), or to rewrite it without
having first understood it (Sutpen, Joe Christmas), or merely
to repeat what has already failed (Gavin Stevens's love for
Eula, then Linda; Temple Drake's going off with Red, then
with Pete; Mink's murders of Houston and Flem); or, perhaps,
most heinously, to deny its very existence and stand, in
Coriolanus's words, "As though a man were author to himself"
(Flem Snopes, Jason Compson, Anse Bundren). At certain
moments, usually ones fraught with violence, some of them

seem actually to succeed: holding time at bay, "suspending" it, like the figures on Keats's Grecian urn that Faulkner is fond of citing,[18] while victim and executioner perform a slow dance of death. Such intricate pairings include Bon and Henry in *Absalom, Absalom!,* Joe Christmas and Percy Grimm in *Light in August,* the Bear and Boon in *Go Down, Moses,* Flem Snopes and his cousin Mink in *The Mansion,* the Negro and his Indian masters in "Red Leaves," and even Nancy and the governor in *Requiem for a Nun.* In these and other instances that might be cited the victims either run a circular path, a pattern suggestive of arrested motion, or they merely wait, immobile, set, already beyond mortality, time. As with Ratliff's representation of Eula's impregnation and Mink's return journey from Parchman to Jefferson, the focus shifts from action to narration, from events "out there" to an imaginative previsioning, from tale to teller. Incident becomes incidental, almost irrelevant, sometimes even absent: Bayard's narrative in *The Unvanquished* of his own *danse macabre* with Redmond not only forestalls but precludes—the very narrative itself implying and proclaiming his survival of death in order to make story of it, to transform into history its failure to happen.

It is only Faulkner's truly sane characters, however, who elude the confines of causality or manage to subsume it: Dilsey transcending time ("a cabinet clock ticked,... struck five times. 'Eight oclock,' Dilsey said" [*S&F,* 341-42]), Lena Grove, space ("My, my. A body does get around. Here we aint been coming from Alabama but two months, and now it's already Tennessee" [*LA,* 444]), and various narrators (Ratliff, Bayard Sartoris, Shreve, the furniture dealer at the end of *Light in August*) who, unburdened of facts and mythology, reenvision the past creatively yet empathetically, with a saving sense of humor or distance, and so can tell its story with some equanimity and even hope.

Faulkner's story, the one story he has to tell, is the *his*-story of the South into which he was born and which, in turn, has lived in his bones and words. Rather disingenuously he has written "that my material, the South, is not very important to me. I just happen to know it, and don't have time in one life to learn another one and write at the same time. Though the one I know is probably as good as another, life is a phenomenon but not a novelty, the same frantic steeplechase toward nothing everywhere and man stinks the same stink no matter where in time" (*F-C,* 14-15). But Faulkner's non-Yokapatawpha writings—the products of a genius's mind "running at only half-throttle"[19]—reveal highly crucial differences, for only writing of and out of the obsession with his desperately flawed inheritance truly matters for Faulkner and his readers. The South enraged and inspired him, and he returned the compliment. In prose admittedly difficult and obscure, "the involved formless 'style', endless sentences" (*F-C,* 14), yet precise and inevitable at its finest, he sought to express and create, "telling the same story over and over, which is myself and the world" (*F-C,* 14), always seeking beyond his known limits to tell it right *this* time, and always finding endlessly fascinating and different ways to fall short of his own standards. Such "failures" as Faulkner's, however, exist at the highest level of human achievement.

2

"I've Seed de First en de Last": *Sartoris/Flags in the Dust, The Reivers*

Faulkner's great achievement is his representation, in the extensive multivolume novel known as the Yoknapatawpha saga, of what he calls "my own little postage stamp of native soil." "I found out," he said in a 1955 interview, "that not only each book had to have a design, but the whole output or sum of an artist's work had to have a design." He adds that, with *Sartoris*, he discovered that his world "was worth writing about and that I would never live long enough to exhaust it." He also realized that his inherited material—the historical and mythical South—lent itself readily to the fiction-maker's skill, to his creation—or recreation—of "a cosmos of my own. I can move these people around like God" (*Lion*, 255). In the process of fleshing out the seemingly exhaustless recesses of that world of which he remains the self-proclaimed but unchallenged "sole owner and proprietor," Faulkner has produced something unique in American literature: a profound sense of historical processes and purposes. This chapter will consider the beginning and ending of Faulkner's Yoknapatawpha story, what Dilsey in *The Sound and the Fury* calls "de first en de last."

Sartoris/Flags in the Dust

Sartoris (1929), the first of Faulkner's saga, is a book he did not
write. What Faulkner wrote was *Flags in the Dust*, a work
posthumously reconstructed from partial and overlapping
typescripts and published in 1973, long after it had been
trimmed and reworked into *Sartoris* by Ben Wasson,
Faulkner's friend and literary agent, in response to a dozen
hostile publishers who felt, as Horace Liveright expressed it,
that *Flags* "lacked 'plot, dimension and projection.' He added,
'The story really doesn't get anywhere and has a thousand
loose ends.,'"[1] Faulkner's own view, on finishing *Flags*, was
that he had "written THE book, of which those other things
[his first two novels] were but foals. I believe it is the damdest
best book you'll look at this year, and any other publisher"
(*Letters*, 38). Critics have increasingly agreed with Faulkner's
judgment rather than with Liveright's, finding *Flags*, as
Douglas Day puts it, "far more complicated [than *Sartoris*] ...,
a more complete fictional document of a time and place in
history [and] a better introduction to the grand and complex
southern world that William Faulkner was to write about until
he died."[2] Consequently, the discussion that follows will
concentrate on *Flags* rather than on *Sartoris,* on the first that
became last to be published, on the failure that was finally
repeated and validated in print, on what was, for Faulkner,
"the germ of my apocrypha."[3]

Though not so single-mindedly focused on the Sartorises as
its sparer version (since it also explores at some length Horace
and Narcissa, Benbow brother and sister, and Byron, the first
of Faulkner's many Snopeses), *Flags in the Dust* also primarily
concerns this romantic, doomed family, community pillars and
harebrained adventurers. The novel's scope is extensive and its
tone one "of savage nostalgia," for its present characters (set in
1919) are far more obsessed with the Civil War than with the
one just concluded. Memory romanticizes the first Bayard
Sartoris, shot in the back by a cook with a derringer as he rides
into a Yankee commissary tent seeking to steal anchovies, and

his brother John, the "Cunnel," who, finding no solace in survival, successfully courts the death that war denied him. Three generations later, the same pattern recurs with little difference beyond a reversal of names: the present Bayard Sartoris returns from his war obsessed both with the memory of his twin brother's gallant and foolish death (flying up against overwhelming odds despite Bayard's attempt to stop him, thumbing his nose at Bayard as he steps parachuteless from his burning plane) and his need to find his own.[4] This he accomplishes after first marrying and impregnating Narcissa Benbow (compelled, by her hatred of him, toward his "fatality and doom") and then killing his uncle, old Bayard, with his manic, high-speed driving. Fleeing that fatality, Bayard manages to find an unsafe plane to test and kills himself in it simultaneously with the birth of his son, the next doomed Sartoris despite Narcissa's attempt to break the pattern by naming him Benbow instead of John. The novel's end is elegiac, evoking "ghosts of glamorous and old disastrous things. And if they were just glamorous enough, there would be a Sartoris in them, and then they were sure to be disastrous. . . . For there is death in the sound of it, and a glamorous fatality, like silver pennons down-rushing at sunset, or a dying fall of horns along the road to Roncevaux."

This evocation of *The Song of Roland* reveals it as the Sartoris Ur-Story, the paradigmatic tale of romantic failure and death against which theirs is to be measured. It is also the implicit source of the book's title, as we hear echoed in a much earlier reference to Aunt Jenny Du Pre, younger sister of the first John and Bayard, sole survivor of their generation, and the novel's chief storyteller: "her voice was proud and still as banners in the dust."

The book's major movement, then, is from death to death, its obsessive need, it seems, to retell the failures of the past in order to insure the repetition of "an old dead pattern." The novel, and thus the entire saga, begins in medias res, with the telling of its story and the story of its telling already ongoing, and the novelist hastening to keep pace as if fearful of falling ever further behind. This response to the rush of events, the valiant and vain compulsion to hold the world sufficiently still to come to terms with it, largely accounts for the breathless and gathering intensity of Faulkner's prose—here and elsewhere—always falling short of containing all it intends except in the odd, occasional moment when action is suspended or frozen, as if suddenly and forever impossible or unnecessary. Thus, the novel's penultimate scene occurs in the Sartoris graveyard where, all passion spent, Aunty Jenny comes to tell and toll her ghosts, "those fool pompous men lying there with their marble mottoes and things."

Flags begins by initiating a process common to Faulkner's fiction: that of telling the wrong story (it is different from the one outlined above) from the wrong point of view—as if, Faulkner seems to suggest, these things always work that way. Old man Falls ("goin' on ninety-fo' year old") is once again telling old Bayard (aged sixty-eight) not about the war just ended but about the Civil War, and not about an incident that he had himself experienced but one involving old Bayard and his father, the "Cunnel"—an incident not fully told until *The Unvanquished.*

> "How old was you then, Bayard?"
> "Fourteen," old Bayard answered.
> "Hey?"
> "Fourteen," Bayard shouted. "Do I have to tell you that every time you tell me this damn story?"

This exchange and the story it prefaces (of the "Cunnel's" outsmarting and escaping a Yankee patrol) dramatize not only memory's necessity but also its failure, and they represent a deflection from the present and immediate past into myth seemingly in order to ritualize a pattern that both validates and repudiates the present. For the latter attains whatever meaning it has only in relation to the past, and yet its immediacy denies it the patina of glamor and vitality with which storytelling glosses history. Thus the ghost of Colonel John Sartoris, dead at the height of his powers, haunts both this novel and his descendants, and assumes a life denied to Faulkner's old men: "Freed as he was of time, he was a far more definite presence in the room than the two of them cemented by deafness to a dead time and drawn thin by the slow attenuation of days. He seemed to stand above them, all around them, with his bearded, hawklike face and the bold glamor of his dream." Similarly haunted, the old black retainer Simon, himself soon to die violently like all the male Sartorises, encounters "that arrogant ghost which dominated the house and its occupants and the whole scene itself," for "it seemed to him that John Sartoris stood beside him with his bearded, hawklike face and an expression of haughty and fine contempt."

The representation of the living John Sartoris is quite otherwise, for he seemed to haunt his own life even as he does his successors; here he is on his last night, just before allowing himself to be killed by his former partner whom he has ruined: "It showed on his brow, the dark shadow of fatality and doom, that night when he sat beneath the candles in his dining room and turned a wine glass in his fingers while he talked to his son. . . . On his brow lay the shadow of his doom and a little weariness." Paralleling his ancestral counterpart, young Bayard, for all his restless energy, communes only with his ghosts, dedicates himself to self-destruction, and awakens shortly before his fatal plane crash already as dead as the brother who obsesses him: "He too was dead and this was hell, through which he moved forever and ever with an illusion of quickness, seeking his brother who in turn was somewhere seeking him, never the two to meet. He turned onto his back again; the shucks whispered beneath him with dry derision." Like many of Faulkner's characters, Bayard is most fully realized in storytelling—"recounting violence and speed and death"—but finds himself trapped in his own narrative rather than freed by it. The first words he utters—"I tried to keep him from going up there on that goddam little popgun"—become a fatal refrain, reiterated in language and then in action.

Aunt Jenny, though often sardonic and mocking of Sartoris men, more than anyone reiterates and romanticizes the Civil War events she never witnessed:

She had told the story many times since (at eighty she still told it, on occasions usually inopportune) and as she grew older the tale itself grew richer and richer . . . until what had been a hair-brained [*sic*] prank of two heedless and reckless boys wild with their own youth, was become a gallant and finely tragical focal-point to which the history of the race had been raised from out the old miasmic swamps of spiritual sloth by two angels valiantly and glamorously fallen and strayed, altering the course of human events and purging the souls of men.

Perhaps despite herself, her imagery becomes more paradigm than warning—ancient disaster now transmuted and seen as successfully "altering the course of human events"—and it sounds in Bayard's recounting of his own war experience: "he fell to talking of the war. Not of combat, but rather of a life peopled by young men like fallen angels, and of a meteoric violence like that of fallen angels, beyond heaven or hell and partaking of both: doomed immortality and immortal doom." Toward the end, Jenny herself (as if anticipating generations of Faulkner's readers) conflates the multiple, identically named Sartorises—the long dead, the recently and soon dead, those yet unborn. In the process, she relaxes her grip on time and myth, for "she no longer talked of her far off girlhood and of Jeb Stuart with his crimson sash and his garlanded bay and his mandolin, but always of a time no further back than Bayard's and John's childhood, as though her life were closing, not into the future, but out of the past, like a spool being rewound." Yet clinging with what seems an equal mixture of fatalism and pride to the Sartoris pattern of glamor and doom, she mocks Narcissa's rebellious naming of her child: " 'And do you think that'll do any good?' Miss Jenny demanded. 'Do you think you can change one of 'em with a name?' " But Narcissa, "as though she were not listening," fails to react: "she smiled at Miss Jenny quietly, a little dreamily, with serene fond detachment."

The novel ends on this note of stalemate, one that makes manifest what has been implicit throughout: that action's failure to do other than repeat old patterns demonstrates that it is not storytelling's antithesis; silence is. Like Narcissa at the end, old Bayard had survived ("I am the first Sartoris there is any record of, who saw sixty years") by limiting words spoken and heard, for while Jenny claims telling as her prerogative Bayard uses "the walled serene tower of his deafness" as an instrument of control—and instead of recounting mythic tales carefully inscribes their mundane end like markings on a tombstone. In the old parlor with its "atmosphere of solemn and macabre fustiness," he enters into silent communion with "dead Sartorises [who] gather and speak among themselves of glamorous and old disastrous days"; but he visits it not merely to experience "Time rolled back again" or to finger the now useless collection of objects it contains, but to perform a ritual "commemorating the violent finis to some phase of his family's history" in the ancient Sartoris Bible. He has two to record this time: the deaths of his grandson John in the war and of young Bayard's wife and son in childbirth. Being practical he had, in fact, waited until he could include young Bayard as well, "but the other grandson still possessed quickness and all the incalculable portent of his heritage. So he had forborne for the time being, expecting to kill two birds with one stone, as it were." Ironically, his own death is most imminent, with young Bayard's to follow shortly thereafter—and no one, either living or dead, appears to record or receive them.

Old Bayard's gesture, a would-be antidote to illusion, is mocked in the making, for even before time reduces it to illegibility, it has erased all who might have sought meaning there. Similarly futile are Horace Benbow's glass-blowing attempts to freeze time, or at least to preserve isolatable moments from its ravages. Horace's art is as grotesque and ineffectual as Bayard's pragmatism: "Sheerly and tragically beautiful. Like preserved flows. . . . Macabre and inviolate; purged and purified as bronze, yet fragile as soap bubbles.

Sound of pipes crystallized." This disturbing echo of Faulkner's favorite poem, Keats's "Ode on a Grecian Urn,"

> Heard melodies are sweet, but those unheard
> Are sweeter; therefore, ye soft pipes, play on;
> Not to the sensual ear, but, more endeared,
> Pipe to the spirit ditties of no tone,

suggests not a transcendence of human action, but Horace's unhealthy attempt to escape it, to refine into art and silence his revulsion from the war that he, like young Bayard, has survived, and his subsequent failure to cope with people. A second description of Horace's art is even more revealing: he "produced one almost perfect vase of clear amber, larger, more richly and chastely serene and which he kept always on his night table and called by his sister's name . . . as Thou still unravished bride of quietude." He soon becomes placid, purposeless, unable to act self-protectively in response either to spoiled white Southern womanhood in the person of Belle Mitchell or to her more overtly predatory sister, Joan. No wonder Horace, having been chewed up and spat out by Joan, is reduced to degrading servitude by Belle: toting home stinking, melting shrimp for her while the phrase "Thou wast happier" sounds in his head—until he flees in desperation from his stultifying marriage at the opening of *Sanctuary*.

The novel's last words, a final obeisance to Keats, suggest quiescence and acquiescence: "beyond the window evening was a windless lilac dream, foster-dam of quietude and peace." But the pattern of action and narration represented in *Flags*— violent deaths, appalling sex and worse marriages, self-indulgent garrulity—suggests that such a moment is barely a pause in the world's horrendous affairs. Our worst suspicions are indeed confirmed if we follow Horace into the sordid world of *Sanctuary* or read "There Was a Queen," a short story in which Narcissa sleeps with a Federal agent in exchange for obscene letters written to her by Byron Snopes, an act whose telling kills Aunt Jenny.

In the end, the main problem with *Flags* is not its amorphous structure or multiplicity of plots—Faulkner was

right that its excesses make it more interesting than *Sartoris,*
not less—but its incertitude of tone and point of view. Those
characters who provoke our sympathy—old Bayard, Aunt
Jenny, Horace, Narcissa—also alienate it by their ineffectual,
self-defeating behavior, while the entire novel (not just some
individuals within it) seems to yearn for lost glory. But as is
also demonstrated, no golden age *ever* existed—and only time
and distorting memory allow anyone to think otherwise.
When Aunt Jenny first tells her Civil War story, it is not so
much about the past as about past memories of an even more
distant past:

Stuart's military family sat in scented darkness beneath a new moon,
talking of ladies and dead pleasures and thinking of home. . . . They
sat in the poignance of spring and youth's immemorial sadness,
forgetting travail and glory, remembering instead other Virginian
evenings . . . until they had talked themselves into a state of savage
nostalgia and words grew shorter and shorter and less and less
frequent.

"Dead pleasures . . . and youth's immemorial sadness, . . .
forgetting travail and glory . . . [in] a state of savage
nostalgia"—memory remembers memory remembering, and
makes of it a weapon with which not only to abuse the present
but also to deny it any possible meaning or value. And what is
true of the present is equally true of the past:

Old Bayard shook the ash from his cigar. "Will," he said, "what the
devil were you folks fighting about, anyhow?"
"Bayard," old man Falls answered, "damned ef I ever did know."

No wonder, then, that all human action in the novel—as well
as its various alternatives: storytelling, art, passivity, silence—
is futile; not only has it been tried and found wanting, but it is
defined as invalid—at best, as the repetition of failure—from
the outset. In his first Yoknapatawpha novel Faulkner had set
himself a problem with which he was to wrestle for the rest of
his life.

The Reivers: A Reminiscence

The Reivers: A Reminiscence (1962), Faulkner's last novel, is his pleasantest—a nostalgic retrospective in which, all passion and illusion largely spent, all the time in the world exists to indulge nostalgically in memory and storytelling about that most enduring of themes: the simultaneous discovery and loss of innocence. The book begins, as James Carothers has noted, with "the shortest frame ever provided for a frame-tale in American literature, 'GRANDFATHER SAID.' "[5] Everything else in the novel represents the account, presumably written, by Lucius Priest III of what his grandfather, Lucius Priest II, told him in 1961 about events in 1905 when, as a boy of eleven, he experienced an initiatory adventure whose lesson, finally enunciated by *his* grandfather, Lucius Quintus Carothers Priest, helped to shape the man and storyteller he subsequently became.

Lucius, the only Faulkner protagonist privileged to narrate his entire novel (after the first two words), begins with, "This is the kind of a man Boon Hogganbeck was," and then proceeds to tell "how Boon Hogganbeck [the hero of the bear hunt in *Go Down, Moses*] got married in 1905. He and an eleven-year-old McCaslin and a Negro (McCaslin) groom stole an automobile and swapped it for a race horse"[6]—and then won it back in a series of extraordinary horse races so that they could return home.

The novel's main action begins when Lucius's grandfather, known as "Boss" Priest, buys Jefferson's first car, despite himself, because Colonel Sartoris, "president of the newer, the mushroom Merchants and Farmers Bank," had sponsored "a city ordinance against the operation of any mechanically propelled vehicle inside the corporate limits. So, as president of the older, the senior bank in Yoknapatawpha County, my grandfather was forced to buy one or else be dictated to by the president of the junior one." And immediately Boon Hogganbeck—who "was tough, faithful, brave and completely unreliable . . . and had the mentality of a child"—fell helplessly in love with it. At the first opportunity (with Lucius II's parents and grandparents away for the funeral of his maternal grandfather), Boon "seduces" Lucius into heading for Memphis and its tawdry excitement with him and, it turns out, the stowaway groom, Ned McCaslin.

The narrative, generational, and familial confusion of the opening—all those Luciuses, Priests, and McCaslins, grandfathers and grandsons, temporal shifts—seems gratuitous at first; but it causes no difficulty after the first half-dozen pages (by which time the structure of the novel— retrospective chronological narrative plus occasional contemporary commentary—becomes perfectly clear), is easier in the reading than in the retelling,[7] and in fact serves a positive function. What happens is that, for all the novel's focus on immediacy of action—a boy caught up in the discovery of his own nature and the world's—a pattern emerges that dramatizes Faulkner's assertion, in the Nobel Prize speech, "that man will not merely endure: he will prevail." Where Sartorises and Sutpens, Compsons and Snopeses, seem hell-bent on destruction and damnation throughout Faulkner's fiction, McCaslins and Priests and Edmondses generally demonstrate not only coping and surviving mechanisms, but also a facility for communicating, if not from one generation to the next then to the next but one, such wisdom as age manages to attain.

Such luxury as this process represents is partly a function of the temporal setting of *The Reivers;* whereas "the saga of the automobile's intrusion on a horseflesh economy [parallels] the story of Lucius's loss of 'innocence,' "[8] it is also true that this intrusion, around the turn of the century, initially inspired a sense of freedom and adventure. And that freedom was as yet uncontaminated by the connotations of speed and death that became associated with automobiles after World War I—largely because of men like Bayard Sartoris who responded badly to survival. Thus, Boon found in the car "his soul's lily maid, the virgin's love of his rough and innocent heart," a notion that assumes a double meaning when the car becomes, ultimately, Boon's vehicle for attaining love with a good woman, marriage, and a child. That kind of language and outcome, here associated with the automobile, seem valid and possible because of the particular temporal layers Faulkner represents in this novel, and nowhere else. Having begun exactly one hundred years before the novel's narrative present, the Civil War, with its false Sartoris pride and its hollow courtesy, "an anachronism like anchovies" (*Flags*, 18), has at last faded into the distant past. In place of restless and doomed Sartorises despairing of modern banality in the early twentieth century and desperately evoking—or projecting—a romanticized grandeur they never knew, *The Reivers* offers a leisurely midcentury recollection of the relatively simple and peaceful time at the very beginning of the technological era. Neither burdened by the past nor obsessed with it, *The Reivers* happily both welcomes such beneficent legacy as it bestows and creates its world anew.

From its conception, twenty years before its writing, Faulkner thought of *The Reivers* as his "Huck Finn novel" (*Letters*, 123, 135). Like his predecessor, Lucius undertakes a journey that proves as much psychological and moral as physical, and during it he encounters and overcomes various difficulties, assimilates much about the nature of the world and its creatures (including himself), yet manages both to sustain and impart his own sense of values: like Chaucer's moral clerk, "gladly wolde he lerne, and gladly teche." Just as Huck—deeming it evil to violate society's mores and laws—nonetheless determines to go to hell rather than betray his friend, the runaway Jim, to his owners, so Lucius also persists in the action he has helped to initiate: "it was too late now; I had already chosen, elected; if I had sold my soul to Satan for a mess of pottage, at least I would damn well collect the pottage and eat it too." But this echo of Huck occurs early on, when Lucius, bent solely on pleasure, grandiosely insists he has made a Faustian compact. The pattern that subsequently emerges, however, more profoundly repeats Huck's loyalty—regardless of cost to himself—to his own moral code and to its appropriate beneficiaries. Thus, for all his deviation from what he calls Virtue, Lucius refuses proffered alcohol ("I'm not old enough yet"), scrupulously keeps his word after discovering that lying is just too much trouble, "makes his manners" to all adults he meets, and above all adheres to his fellow picaros despite knowing that only they would suffer his family's wrath for their joint actions: "I was safe, immune; I was not only just a child, I was kin to them." Despite his reiterated "remember, I was just eleven," Lucius never denies that he, the expedition's true leader, could have called it off at any time and that only he can provide the means of their returning home.

Despite their similarities, *The Reivers* differs from *Huckleberry Finn* in two important ways.[9] First, the fact and tone of its retrospective narrative—one of mild self-deprecation—offer reassurance, from the first, about the successful completion of the journey and its lack of dire consequences. Of all the Yoknapatawpha novels, only in *The Reivers* is life neither lost nor seriously threatened. Second, where Huck's journey culminates in his decision "to light out for the Territory ahead of the rest, because Aunt Sally she's going to adopt me and sivilize me, and I can't stand it," Lucius's takes him from his social milieu in order that he might return and, in Eliot's phrase, "know the place for the first time." He learns not how to escape but how to belong, and not by compromising but through proper self-knowledge and valuation. He becomes that seeming anachronism that his grandfather invokes and personifies: a gentleman.[10]

Faulkner builds that end into the rhythm and structure of the book from the beginning—by presenting the tale as pleasant reminiscence, by creating a book about beginnings (the book even ends with a birth) that opens fifty-six years after the end of its narrated time, and by endowing his protagonist from the first with much of the knowledge and experience he seeks. Even as he describes Boon's "seducing" him to the journey to Memphis, Lucius emphasizes his own lack of innocence and ignorance, for "There is no crime which a boy of eleven had not envisaged long ago." His imagery is often that of victim, helpless before Boon's superior prowess at manipulation, but the reality is something else, or something additional:

I know better now of course, and I even knew better then: that Boon's fall and mine were not only instantaneous but simultaneous too.... But that's what I would have liked to believe: that Boon simply licked me. Anyway, that's what I told myself at the time: that, secure behind that inviolable and inescapable rectitude concomitant with the name I bore, patterned on the knightly shapes of my male ancestors as bequeathed—nay, compelled—to me by my father's word-of-mouth, ... I had been merely testing Boon; not trying my own virtue but simply testing Boon's capacity to undermine it.

Almost in the same breath, Lucius can refer to their being "mutual in crime, confederate of course but not coeval yet because of my innocence," to the early stages during which "I had matured terrifyingly," and to his *greater* responsibility: "I was as bent as Boon, ... even more culpable. Because ... I was smarter than Boon. I realised, felt suddenly that same exultant fever-flash which Faustus himself must have experienced: that of we two doomed and irrevocable, I was the leader, I was the boss, the master." Thus, to Boon's silent appeal to call the trip off before it is too late, Lucius says he responded without "virtue and pity," in fact with mockery, having "progressed in evil" so fast that he was already lying like an adult (for profit) rather than like a child (for pleasure).

Lucius's dedication of himself to what he calls "Non-virtue" assumes this double rhythm throughout. Sensing its implications and dangers, feeling constantly in over his head, "anguished with homesickness," he nonetheless commits himself to the next step and then the next, plunging into ever deeper waters almost despite himself and even while condemning his own actions. Somehow he always triumphs more or less on his own terms, and then wonders whether he might *now* be allowed some respite. Yet again, each new encounter seems a repetition, the process of education working much like memory. When, for example, Lucius first enters Miss Reba's brothel (Boon's goal in Memphis), it seems almost a return for him since he senses "a smell I had been waiting all my life to smell," as if he, like Boon, were an habitue. Soon after, he has no difficulty recognizing what he calls "other boarding houses (I was experienced now; I was a sophisticate—not a connoisseur of course but at least cognizant; I recognised a place similar to Miss Reba's when I saw one)." He adds, with self-mocking pride, "I had been in Memphis . . . less than six hours, without my mother or father either to instruct me; I was doing pretty well."

Having alternately asserted and denied all the child's defenses against accepting responsibility for his actions— innocence, powerlessness, "the whole thing no more than a dream from which I could wake tomorrow, perhaps now, the next moment, and be safe, saved"—Lucius longs to erase the action itself, to wipe it not only from the present but from the past as well: "not just to retrace but to retract, obliterate . . . [return] to Jefferson, in reverse if necessary, travelling backward to unwind, ravel back into No-being, Never-being . . . so that [all that had happened] had never been." But it is, only the sixty-six-year-old Lucius who can return, through narrating, and his repetition is an affirmation, not a retraction; the young Lucius can only go forward: "It was too late. Maybe yesterday, while I was still a child, but not now. I knew too much, had seen too much. I was a child no longer now; innocence and childhood were forever lost, forever gone from me." And yet, of course, they continue to exist in the recapturing process of his and Faulkner's telling.

For Faulkner, too, *The Reivers* is full of returns, reflections, reenvisioning. It exhibits "the full spectrum of Faulkner's social world . . . the full range of the classes and kinds of people who live in his famous county."[11] More than any other of his novels, it echoes and transforms the material of earlier fiction: the obsession with the automobile and the paean to the virtue and intelligence of mules in *Flags;* the boy's initiation into manhood (*The Unvanquished,* "The Bear," *Intruder in the*

Dust); the momentous journey (*As I Lay Dying*); the surrounding wilderness that had seen "old Thomas Sutpen's vast kingly dream" destroy itself and Sutpen too (in *Absalom, Absalom!* and "Wash"), then served as site of the annual hunt before being sold off for timber (*Go Down, Moses*), though "Even in 1905 there was still vestigial wilderness"; a series of complex wagers and finagling (*The Hamlet*, "Was"); the dignified black patriarch who, lacking power, nonetheless survives on his own and not the white man's terms ("The Fire and the Hearth," *Intruder in the Dust*); the invasion of Jefferson by Flem Snopes and "his tribe" and his eventual murder "by the mad kinsman who perhaps didn't believe his cousin had actually sent him to the penitentiary but at least could have kept him out or anyway tried to" (Snopes trilogy); the heroine, here the reformed prostitute, whose serenity transcends the anxious busyness of the men who surround her (*Light in August*),[12] and so on.

Of Faulkner's earlier books, *Go Down, Moses* most directly anticipates *The Reivers*, partly because of historical reasons: Faulkner first outlined the plot of *The Reivers* in a letter of May 1940, but *Go Down, Moses* (1942) was the book he produced instead. There are, not coincidentally, both numerous echoes and parallels as well as some telling differences between the two. Just as the wilderness in *The Reivers* is a slightly fabulous place associated increasingly with the past, so Memphis in the earlier book is a distant contrast to the world of the woods. The Boon who hunted and killed bears now pursues whores—and winds up captured by one. Ike McCaslin, Lucius's elderly cousin and a minor character in *The Reivers*, is the young protagonist of *Go Down, Moses* undergoing education and initiation in the woods, as Lucius does in the whorehouses and racetracks of Memphis and its environs. Through adherence to personal codes of morality and behavior, both young men seek, by questionable means, to earn the rights and name due to manhood.

As discussed below (see pp.72-77), the Ike of *Go Down, Moses* inherits two claims to the woods: that of the huntsman

who meets it successfully on its own terms and that of legal
ownership. Because the legacy comes to him via what he views
as a curse—resulting from the ownership and rape of land and
people that he associates with his grandfather, Lucius Quintus
Carothers McCaslin—Ike repudiates it. Only in this way, he
believes, can the white descendants of old McCaslin free
themselves of original sin—and yet Ike's own subsequent
failures cast grave doubts on the wisdom and efficacy of his
choice.

The progenitor's presence persists in *The Reivers*, largely
through naming, but it is no longer threatening; it becomes, in
fact, a source of family pride. Lucius's own kindly
grandfather—orphaned by the Civil War—originally "came
to Mississippi hunting for the de-scendants of a distant
kinsman named McCaslin—he and the kinsman even had the
same baptismal names: Lucius Quintus Carothers—and found
one in the person of a great-granddaughter named Sarah
Edmonds and in 1869 married her." Ned—who always gives
his name as "Ned William McCaslin Jefferson Missippi"—
claims direct and immediate descent, "that his mother had
been the natural daughter of old Lucius Quintus Carothers
himself and a Negro slave; never did Ned let any of us forget
that he, along with Cousin Isaac, was an actual grandson to old
time-honored Lancaster where we moiling Edmondses and
Priests, even though three of us—you, me and my
grandfather—were named for him, were mere diminishing
connections and hangers-on."

Both grandfathers and the name Lucius—in fact, naming
generally—assume radically different connotations
throughout *The Reivers* from what they did in the earlier
book. After determining to reform because of Lucius's
chivalric defense of her, Corrie feels constrained to tell him
her "old-timey countrified name," Everbe Corinthia, of which
she is ashamed. She does not know, because he has kept her
secret, that he both already knows and accepts it.

"You mean, it's all right? You say it." I said it. She listened. Then
she kept on listening, exactly as you wait for an echo. "Yes," she said.
"That's what it can be now."

Offering him her name, she can receive it back as hers because
he has lovingly treasured and proffered it.

The relationship between the prostitute and the reluctant
adventurer proves healing not only for her but also for him,
for in the end the young gallant receives three marvelous
accolades. First, Boon—frustrated by Corrie's ill-timed
reformation ("Why the hell has she got to pick out me to
reform on? God damn it, she's a whore, cant she understand
that?")—proclaims his marriage to her: "If you can go bare-
handed against a knife defending her, why the hell cant I
marry her? Aint I as good as you are, even if I aint eleven years
old?" Second, his grandfather acknowledges his maturation by
refusing him the punishment that is the child's refuge and
release; he tells Lucius that "A gentleman accepts the
responsibility of his actions and bears the burden of their
consequences." And, third, Corrie repays Lucius's gift of her
name by bestowing *his* upon her and Boon's newborn son.
This final benign evocation of the evil patriarch of McCaslins
and Priests serves at last to transform and exorcise both the
patriarch and the malevolence long attached to his name, and
to proclaim the latter's new talismanic qualities that Lucius
has earned for it.

The final beginning to which Faulkner returns in *The
Reivers* is his own, for the book is as much his reminiscence—
of a happy and relatively untroubled youth—as it is Lucius's.
Like Lucius, who is almost his exact contemporary, Faulkner
was the oldest of four brothers; both fathers (Faulkner's
named Murry, Lucius's named Maury) ran livery stables,
where their eldest sons were put to work, and played minor
roles in their sons' lives. The main familial relationships in the
novel are those between grandfathers and grandsons;
Faulkner, in fact, dedicated the book to his grandchildren. Like
Lucius, Faulkner felt great homesickness when away from his
parents during his early years, was fascinated by the wonder
and lure of Memphis, and had numerous "run-ins with
authority [that] seemed to fall into two classes, temperamental
and technological"[13]—although Faulkner was drawn to planes

rather than to cars. Faulkner always used the past—his own, his family's, the South's—creatively, as grist for written and oral storytelling. "I don't have much patience with facts," he said on one occasion, "and any writer is a congenital liar to begin with or he wouldn't take up writing. And so I couldn't tell the truth about history. That's why I'll never write a[n] [auto]biography. I couldn't tell the truth about Faulkner, I'm sure."[14] Though the events and stories of his youth permeate all his fiction, it is in his last novel that Faulkner comes closest to telling that truth—or at least one version of it.

3

"Dark Houses": *The Sound and the Fury, Absalom, Absalom!*

Read together, *The Sound and the Fury* (1929) and *Absalom, Absalom!* (1936) tell, among others, the story of the Compson family, one of Yoknapatawpha's oldest and, by 1910 (the year of Quentin Compson's suicide), most fallen from former prominence. The collapse of the Compsons, like that of the Sartorises in *Flags in the Dust*, is depicted as the final phase in a slow, entropic degeneration, the last in a succession of failures in a family haunted by its own history. Faulkner speaks of Quentin, always on the verge of extinction, as failure's heir:

> The action as portrayed by Quentin was transmitted to him through his father. There was a basic failure before that. The grandfather had been a failed brigadier twice in the Civil War. . . . Something had happened somewhere between the first Compson and Quentin. The first Compson was a bold ruthless man who came into Mississippi as a free forester to grasp where and when he could and wanted to, and established what should have been a princely line, and that princely line decayed. (*F in U*, 3)

Appropriately, Faulkner's working title for "my dark story of madness and hatred,"[1] that became the novel of the Compson "decaying house," was "Twilight"; and the original title for the parallel story of Sutpen family disaster, *Absalom, Absalom!*, was "A Dark House." Hence the title and central motif of this chapter.

Each book shadows the other: both have four main narrators (Quentin doing double duty) who elucidate a crucial, absent character; both tell of the founding and ruin of powerful houses, though *The Sound and the Fury* focuses on the latter action and appends the former in a coda, while *Absalom, Absalom!* focuses retrospectively on the founding and treats the ruin as a frame, a place to begin and end. Both start in the disastrous fallen present and demand understanding of its causes; both concern failed parents whose children, out of desperate love and hatred, rise up to destroy each other and themselves. Faulkner also establishes "intricate relations" between these two books with parallel themes of incest, a brother's obsession with what he defines as his sister's honor, suicide/fratricide as a means of defending that honor from its familial threat, and the air of frustration, fatalism, and doom that hangs over everything. Thus, for Quentin, "*Absalom* is . . . both elaborative and corroborative: an analogue to the story he lives, it extends, perhaps delays, and certainly mirrors the murder and incest of which he dreams and the suicide that he commits in *The Sound and the Fury.*"[2]

The second of these novels, its present the year (1909-10) that culminates in Quentin's suicide in the first, might be called a "prequel" to the first: a later work about earlier events in the lives of major characters in the first, and also a reconceiving of those events in terms of a second family. Subsequently, when Faulkner in 1945 wrote for *The Portable Faulkner* the Compson genealogy that has ever since been included as part of *The Sound and the Fury,* he told of one Jason Lycurgus Compson who imposed a plantation upon the wilderness using the same French architect as does Thomas Sutpen in *Absalom, Absalom!* and also established a line that ends in degeneracy and self-annihilation. Still later, Faulkner returned again briefly to Compsons in *The Mansion* (1957), the third book of the Snopes trilogy, to add a final twist and echo: back from the asylum to which his brother Jason had committed him, the idiot Benjy, duplicating the end of the Sutpens, "not only burned himself up but completely destroyed the house too" (*M*, 322).

That he kept returning to earlier material—Compsons, Sartorises, Sutpens, and Snopeses all make cameo appearances in Yoknapatawpha novels not primarily concerned with them—accords with Faulkner's ongoing relationship to the world that he felt created him as he created it. That versions contradict each other—for example, *The Sound and the Fury*'s Appendix says that Jason, scorning inheritance that lacked cash value, had chopped "up the vast oncesplendid rooms into what he called apartments and [sold] the whole thing to a countryman who opened a boardinghouse in it"—partakes of the same explanation. No view is final, no fact stable, no resolution or book complete: "the characters themselves are walking out of that book still in motion, still talking, and still acting" (*F in U*, 198).

None of this is meant to argue that these two novels need be read as a unit, for each—as their separate treatments below should suggest—is among Faulkner's noblest, fullest, most self-contained. Yet they do enrich and expand each other, representing in radically different format failures that seemed wholly perceived and explored by the other. In the uniqueness and interconnectedness of these two extraordinary books— perhaps his most perfect—Faulkner fuses process and product, the dynamic and statis, and reerects, through narrative, edifices already long fallen in the lives of his characters and the South.

The Sound and the Fury

The Sound and the Fury begins in liberating failure, for the multiple rejections of *Flags in the Dust* convinced Faulkner that it would never be published. Instead of abandoning writing, however, he felt suddenly free to write solely for

himself rather than for readers in whom he had ceased to
believe. He could therefore be as personal and experimental as
he wished. *The Sound and the Fury* "accordingly represented a
move back toward Faulkner's childhood and the family
configuration of his earliest years—a move into the past and
into the interior. At the same time, through the fictional
techniques and strategies that Faulkner used to discover,
displace, and transfigure the memories he found waiting for
him, his novel represented an astonishing breakthrough. A
moving story of four children and their inadequate parents,
The Sound and the Fury is thematically regressive, stylistically
and formally innovative."[3] In the most interesting and
revealing comment he ever made on any of his novels, an
introduction to a projected and then abandoned edition of *The
Sound and the Fury* in 1933, Faulkner says:

> This is the only one of the seven novels which I wrote without any
> accompanying feeling of drive or effort, or any following feeling of
> exhaustion or relief or distaste. When I began it I had no plan at all. I
> wasn't even writing a book. I was thinking of books, publication, only
> in the reverse, in saying to myself, I wont have to worry about
> publishers liking it or not liking this at all ... One day I seemed to shut
> a door between me and all publishers' addresses and book lists. I said
> to myself, Now I can write. Now I can make myself a vase like that
> which the old Roman kept at his bedside and wore the rim slowly
> away with kissing it. So I who had never had a sister and was fated to
> lose my daughter in infancy, set out to make myself a beautiful and
> tragic little girl.[4]

Though Faulkner is often unreliable on himself and his
fiction, the tone and feelings expressed here are consistent
both with remarks about *The Sound and the Fury* he made
throughout his life (only with reference to the writing of this
book did he use sexually charged words like "ecstasy" and
"rapture") and with his subsequent actions: repeated
returnings to the book (and material) "that caused me the
most anguish" and that he tried hardest to "tell . . . right."
After writing it, he called it "the damndest book I ever read. I
dont believe anyone will publish it for ten years."[5] He was

both wrong about that and a bit regretful, for alone of all his books he seemed always to want to be writing this one, never to have it be finished.

The Sound and the Fury is the opposite of *The Reivers:* its story—that of the fragmenting and self-destructive Compson family (parents, three sons, a daughter, and then the daughter's daughter)—is simple but its telling is complex. Two sets of disasters intersect as inadequately equipped children come of age within what the Appendix calls "the rotting family in the rotting house." This double process is emblematized by the death of the maternal grandmother and the famous "muddy drawers" episode or image: Caddy, having splashed in the stream with Quentin, climbs a tree to peer into the death room, from which they have been kept, while her brothers remain timidly below, even further removed from comprehension. From this frozen moment, the novel centers on the interaction of events and perception, the encroaching world and the various inadequate responses to it on the part of children who "have grown up deprived of love in a home poisoned by a cold, hypochondriacal mother and a weak, nihilistic, alcoholic father" (Blotner, 573).

Although Faulkner said of the novel that "It's the tragedy of two lost women: Caddy and her daughter" (*Lion*, 222), no event or series of events has paramount significance or even independent existence. In his pioneering essay on time in *The Sound and the Fury*, Jean-Paul Sartre wonders about the story's central complication—"Is it the castration of Benjy or Caddy's wretched amorous adventure or Quentin's suicide or Jason's hatred of his niece? As soon as we begin to look at any episode, it opens up to reveal behind it other episodes, all the other episodes. Nothing happens; the story does not unfold; we discover it under each word, like an obscene and obstructing presence."[6] Benjy's castration and Caddy's lovemaking are part of the novel's pattern of failure repeating failure: events are both terrible in themselves and also negative presences, gaining existence only in the reactions they provoke. Quentin's suicide, too, is always about to happen—and then long past. The tale exists only in the telling.

Each of the novel's four narrative sections represents a single point of view: each of the first three belongs to one of the sons (Benjy, Quentin, Jason, respectively), while in the fourth, Faulkner says, "I tried to gather the pieces together and fill in the gaps by making myself the spokesman" (*Lion,* 245). The structural complexity of the novel results in part from the several ways its four sections may be linked and separated. As ordered, the sections comprise a sequence from the intensely closed and private to the open, shared, and public; 1, 2, and 3 belong to the differently obsessed Compson brothers, while 4 is broadly humane; 1 and 4, though strikingly different, are, nonetheless, objective recountings that frame the intensely subjective 2 and 3; 1, 3, and 4 form a skewed temporal sequence (April 7, 6, and 8, 1928), while 2 occurs much earlier, on the day of Quentin's suicide: June 2, 1910. Generally avoiding the convoluted and elaborate syntax that makes meaning elusive in *Absalom, Absalom!, The Sound and the Fury* offers as its major challenge the associational and analogical workings of several minds. The most notable are that of the idiot Benjy, for whom "time was not a continuation, it was an instant, there was no yesterday and no tomorrow, it all is this moment.... He doesn't know whether he dreamed it, or saw it" (*Nagano,* 106; Faulkner shuffles more than a dozen events, occurring from 1898 to 1928, through Benjy's mind and narration), and that of Quentin, "an educated half-madman [who] dispensed with grammar" (*F in U,* 95) in a stream of consciousness very much like the abstruse Stephen Dedalus in the "Proteus" chapter of Joyce's *Ulysses.*[7] Jason's and Dilsey's sections, though technically straightforward, emotionally and morally challenge both the novel's other perspectives and its readers.

Although Faulkner considered various ways to order its four sections, *The Sound and the Fury* begins with Benjy because he matters most—not in himself (since he lacks a self) but as a litmus test or "a mirror of moral conscience, in which the various members of the family can see their own actions reflected and implicitly evaluated."[8] His role is so central and primary that, as James Meriwether emphasizes, to print the geneology as an introduction or first chapter, as, for example, the 1946 Signet paperback edition did, is to spoil "the effect of the novel's original beginning with Benjy's monologue. . . . Unwary readers found themselves presented with what appears to be a five-part novel, the first part of which relieves them of the burdens which the second part was originally designed to impose upon them in the way of careful and creative reading."[9] Those burdens are both moral and psychic, for, like all the characters upon whom Benjy impinges, we too are meant to respond to his unmediated, helpless presence. His unique condition—both perpetual innocence ("in the sense that God had stricken him . . . mindless at birth, there was nothing he could ever do about it" [*Nagano*, 104] and a curious objectivity (he records the world around him without comment or filter, and much of what his account reveals is validated by verbatim repetition in subsequent sections)— makes of him a kind of control in the psychodrama of character revelations and interactions. He provokes Caddy's tenderness and vain promises not to grow up ("I wont anymore, ever. Beny. Benjy."); Jason's venom and shame (like Darl's siblings in *As I Lay Dying,* Jason finally succeeds in sending Benjy to the asylum in Jackson); his mother's false solicitude that is really self-pity; Dilsey's love and nurture; the hatred and fear of Caddy's daughter, Quentin II; the adolescent callousness of his black attendants—all responses that define only those who make them. Quentin alone of the novel's significant characters seems essentially indifferent to Benjy and undefined by him, perhaps because Caddy serves this function for Quentin. Roskus, Dilsey's husband, calls Benjy "a sign" of Compson bad luck, but he is, rather, a blank slate on which those around him trace their own versions of that luck. Versh is no more right nor wrong than his father when he says to Benjy, "You's born lucky and dont know it." Though his crying registers changes in those around him, especially in

Caddy, Benjy remains undefined by time and contingency.

The difficulties in following Benjy's monologue are lessened with rereading, with increased awareness of Faulkner's devices for signaling temporal shifts: the sequence of Benjy's black attendants (Versh, then T. P., and now Luster), typographical alteration between roman and italic (Faulkner had originally wanted different-colored print, but by the time it might have been feasible he felt it was unnecessary), key words and repeated phrases associated with specific occurrences, references to Benjy's age, and so on. Readers are also required to adjust to certain oddities about Benjy and his style. For one thing, his lack of rational faculties is compensated for by the hyperawareness of his other senses, especially hearing and smell. "I could hear the fire and the roof," he says; *"I could hear it getting night. . . . my hands could see the slipper."* In Benjy's central refrain, Caddy "smelled like trees," and he registers other odors with pain and outrage: not only her first wearing perfume but her kissing a boy and her loss of virginity as well. Benjy can smell death as well as sex, though he can name or understand neither of them. He externalizes changes of perception: "Then the barn wasn't there and we had to wait until it came back"; "The room went away . . . and the room came back." His basic form of punctuation is the period, with the merest sprinkling of commas, since everything in his world—including questions—exists as simple declaratives. Benjy's version, at first glance merely confusing, in fact represents a powerful insight into the relationship of all things. As Roskus says of Benjy, "He know a lot more than folks thinks"—though he knows it differently.

On the other hand, Quentin might be said to know less "than folks thinks," except that he fools no one. Caddy, knowing he is sexually innocent, pities his boast of expertise. Trying to run Caddy's lover, Dalton Ames, out of town, Quentin fails to obtain even the satisfaction of being beaten up: he faints, though in order to minimize Quentin's embarrassment Ames says he hit him. Herbert Head, the "blackguard" Caddy marries in order to legitimize her unborn child, dismisses Quentin's impotent threat to tell Caddy what he knows about him. Where events for Benjy are literal, external, spatial, and simultaneous, Quentin's section is all imaginative projection and process: subjective, temporal, and largely a series of internal dialogues—between himself and, alternately, Caddy and Mr. Compson; between inner and outer realities, stasis and flux, purity and filth, death and life. For Benjy, the past recurs when triggered by something in the present—a word, a place, a sense impression—except that past and present are coexistent for him: "His memory has no memories. He cannot remember; he cannot forget."[10] Quentin's memory also works oddly, though in opposite fashion: either creatively or forward, "Quentin thinks of his last day in the past, like someone who is remembering."[11] While recalling Jason as a child, rotund and clumsy, running and falling "like a trussed fowl," Quentin sees his roommate Shreve seeming to repeat the past by "coming up the walk, shambling, fatly earnest, his glasses glinting beneath the running leaves like little pools." When Shreve, seeing Quentin dressed up, asks, "Is it a wedding or a wake?" he unknowingly verbalizes Quentin's two obsessions: the memory of Caddy's wedding and his impending suicide, itself seeming already past. In one more instance of the same curious technique, Faulkner has Quentin feel Caddy's blood pulse rapidly when he says, "Dalton Ames," then recalls him to the present where he finds Shreve nursing him much as Caddy had after the first fight he initiated when he said, "Did you ever have a sister? did you?" In both instances, Quentin succeeds only in embarrassing himself—though in the second one (as if his blood flowed from recalling Caddy's) he has been badly beaten.[12]

Actions in section 1 are always implicit, tacit, because Benjy records and recounts his reactions to them without interpretation; in II, action is suspect because envisaged by Quentin, for whom nothing exists except a priori assertion— like his insistence on a family curse. Quentin's most powerful memories, in fact, are negative ones—experiences that never were, or that happened to others, or that might yet be—

committing incest with Caddy, shooting Herbert, the
confessional conversations with his father,[13] castration,
drowning, Judgment Day, Caddy and himself alone in hell
"walled by the clean flame." Overhearing a group of boys
boasting of how they will spend prize money for catching a big
fish that they have not yet won, Quentin might well be
defining the workings of his own multifarious imagination:
"They all talked at once, their voices insistent and
contradictory and impatient, making of unreality a possibility,
then a probability, then an incontrovertible fact, as people will
when their desires become words." Desperate to affirm purity
he finds lacking in a world of filth and decay (a world that
offers him only Faulkner's originating image of sexuality and
death associated with Caddy's "muddy drawers"), Quentin
seeks to impose it on the unwilling and inappropriate Caddy.
But, as he hears his father saying, "it's because you are a virgin:
dont you see? Women are never virgins. Purity is a negative
state and therefore contrary to nature. It's nature is hurting
you not Caddy and I said That's just words and he said So is
virginity." Even worse than the loss is the fear of eventual
indifference to the loss: "you cannot bear to think that
someday it will no longer hurt you like this ... [that] even she
was not quite worth despair." Having failed to keep Caddy
intact, Quentin contemplates with horror the possibility that
he might come to share his father's cynical view that "people
cannot do anything ... very dreadful at all they cannot even
remember tomorrow what seemed dreadful today."

What Quentin longs for above all is time's surcease ("to
isolate [Caddy] out of the loud world"), something like Benjy's
atemporality. Using Benjy as frame, the novel opens and
closes with spatial imagery: first, "*Through* the fence, *between*
the curling flower spaces," and then, after Benjy's shocked
bellowing summons Jason who forces Luster to drive the right
way around the town square, "cornice and façade flowed
smoothly once more *from left to right;* post and tree, window
and doorway, and signboard, *each in its ordered place*" (my
emphasis). But Quentin, also desperate for fixity, for certitude,

can find no release in or from process, only repetition of what
has already failed: "Again. Sadder than was. Again. Saddest
[word] of all. Again."

Two key speeches from *Macbeth* are suggested by this
conflict: first, the famous one from which Faulkner took his
title—with its sequence of unstoppable time, "Tomorrow and
tomorrow and tomorrow," repeated by the clock tower in
Harvard Square that sounds Quentin's foreshortened last
quarter hours for all his attacks on time. Second, an earlier
speech, which occurs before Macbeth has done the "bloody
business" that time can never reverse or even contain, is also
echoed:

> If it were done when 'tis done, then 'twere well
> It were done quickly: if the assassination
> Could trammel up the consequence, and catch
> With his surcease success; that but this blow
> Might be the be-all and the end-all here,
> But here upon this bank and shoal of time,
> We'ld jump the life to come. (I, vii, 1-7)

Failed idealists, both Quentin and Macbeth dream of
committing the Faustian deed, one so momentous that it will
rupture causality, alter the very fundament on which the world
is predicated, create only intended consequences, and be
absolutely unrepeatable. Thus, Quentin thinks: "Because if it
were just to hell; if that were all of it. Finished. If things just
finished themselves. Nobody else there but her and me. If we
could just have done something so dreadful that they would
have fled hell except us." Out of inertia and boredom, Macbeth
can only escalate horror:

> I am in blood
> Stepp'd in so far that, should I wade no more,
> Returning were as *tedious* as go o'er
>   (III, iv, 136-38; my emphasis)

Quentin, Macbeth's antithesis in terms of action, becomes victim not of deeds performed that have escaped his control, but of those performed only in imagination and memory. Quentin, then, longs neither to commit incest with Caddy nor to kill her but to have done so—in fact, never to *do* anything but somehow to have *done* everything.

The crucial exchange between Quentin and Caddy—he desperate to stop time so they need not grow up, continue to the next weary stage; she knowing it is already too late, is always already too late—occurs after her loss of virginity. He feels "her heart thudding"; then, as he holds her throat, "her blood pounded against my hand." Yet, though she is unresisting, he cannot use the knife he holds there, can only remind her of the "muddy drawers" episode he fears will be forgotten—and so finds himself helpless to hold anything back from time, an irony underscored by Caddy's then asking him what time it is.

Quentin's section, his long, slow dying, climaxes in his drowning that occurs in the blank space between his section and Jason's. In contrast to Benjy's spatial focus, it begins on the temporal note that pervades it: "When the shadow of the sash appeared on the curtains it was between seven and eight oclock and then I was in time again, hearing the watch." In his final paragraph—beginning "The last note sounded. At last it stopped"—we hear an echo, after all his searching for permanence, of *another* Shakespearean challenger of order on the verge of death, the Hotspur of *I Henry IV*. Unable, in the end, to make time do his bidding any more than Macbeth or Quentin could, Hotspur signals his end as if it were universal:

Thought's the slave of life, and life time's fool;
And time that takes survey of all the world,
Must have a stop. (V, iv, 81-83)

The ultimate Faustian gesture is reduced from cosmos-shaking defiance to the oldest failure of all: self-destruction, and the self-delusion that accompanies it.

Faulkner has said that Quentin, "about half way between madness and sanity" (*F in U*, 94-95), is a mean between the

idiot Benjy and Jason, "The first sane Compson since before
Culloden and (a childless bachelor) hence the last" (Appendix,
420). Jason also represents "complete evil. He's the most
vicious character in my opinion I ever thought of" (*Nagano*,
104). Certainly Jason embodies a rich complex of negative
qualities: he is a liar, thief, and hypocrite, avaricious, brutish,
and so mean-spirited that he burns free carnival tickets rather
than give them to Luster. He gets along with no one, seeing
himself as the victim of multiple conspiracies when something
like the opposite is closer to the truth. He hates and resents
Jews and blacks—and apparently everyone else: no one else
works, everyone is out to take advantage of him, even the
town pigeons, which he thinks should be poisoned. His
proper sphere is that of commerce—the store in which he
resentfully works, the stock market in which he speculates—
rather than the house he nominally controls but in which his
mother and Dilsey limit his freedom to tyrannize. He is
doubly an embezzler—using his mother's money for his
business ventures, stealing while pretending to destroy out of
principle the checks Caddy sends Quentin II—and doubly a
loser: his stocks go down, and Quentin II, when she elopes,
steals his tin box, his cache of her money and his hoarded over
fifteen years.

For all his manipulating of others, Jason is a sadomasochist
and his own best target, taking perverse pleasure in that "he
could almost smell ... the impending disaster" as he fruitlessly
chases his niece:

He looked at the sky, thinking about rain, about the slick clay road,
himself stalled somewhere miles from town. He thought about it
with a sort of triumph, of the fact that he was going to miss dinner,
that by starting now and so serving his compulsion of haste, he would
be at the greatest possible distance from both towns when noon
came. It seemed to him that, in this, circumstance was giving him a
break.

His paranoia and revenge, like his narration, are self-
reflexive—denying his assertions of control, allowing them
no greater success than those of his brothers.

His narrative, which is as brutally present and immediate as
he is, becomes less a recounting than a series of attacks—
mocking, undermining, complaining—on everyone and
everything. He lavishes on his telling, as on his world, only the
hatred and bitterness he finds marshaled against him because
he projects them—and against which the only possible
defense is a good offense. Yet he retains and nurtures lifelong
grievances, as if jealously demanding a share in his siblings'
doom: "it seemed to him that the fact that the way was
clearing was another cunning stroke on the part of the foe, the
fresh battle toward which he was carrying ancient wounds."
He is, in fact, as determined by the past as are his brothers,
especially the past that failed to happen: not being his father's
favorite (and having to bear his mother's oppressive love), not
going to Harvard, not getting the bank job promised him by
Caddy's husband. But the theft of his hoard is his most
debilitating and ironically appropriate loss: "to have been
robbed of that which was to have compensated him for the
lost job, which he had acquired through so much effort and
risk, by the very symbol of the lost job itself, and worst of all,
by a bitch of a girl"—by "Caddy's debased copy."[14]

Though intent on what seems to him realistic and practical,
Jason shares his brothers' obsession with Caddy: she got
pregnant, she got out, she lost the husband (presumably
because she was pregnant) who had seemed Jason's
benefactor, she left him with charges he loathes. For all his
differences from them, Jason bears marked resemblance to his
brothers' absolutism, especially where Caddy is concerned.
Though haunted by images of half or reflected life—shadows,
mirrors, twilight—both Benjy and Quentin view the world in
terms of binary oppositions:[15] Caddy, virgin or not, present or
absent; things perfect or terrible; they totally content or
desperate. Willing to drag "Omnipotence down from His
throne, if necessary," Jason sees himself locked in a battle of
mighty opposites: "He could see the opposed forces of his
destiny and his will drawing swiftly together now, toward a
junction that would be irrevocable; he became cunning. I cant

make a blunder, he told himself. There would be just one right thing, without alternatives: he must do that." His chief antagonist, however, is nothing so grandiose as this suggests, but merely his seventeen-year-old niece, whom he labels definitively at the beginning and end of his section: "Once a bitch always a bitch, what I say." Thus, his reiterated, "If it's in the blood, you cant do anything with her." He goes even further, seeing the family' s degeneration (though not his own) as directly proportional to past glory: "Blood, I says, governors and generals. It's a damn good thing we never had any kings and presidents; we'd all be down there at Jackson chasing butterflies." As his language reveals, Jason is very much his parents' child: a self-pitying whiner like his mother, a fatalist like his father: "Sometimes I think what's the use of anything. With the precedent I've been set I must be crazy to keep on." Even self-knowledge and self-mockery fail to redeem Jason.

The one person Jason fears and respects is Dilsey, for they inhabit opposite ends of the human and moral spectrum. Rather than trying to dominate a recalcitrant world, she accommodates herself to it without loss of self or values; yet as cook and nursemaid, she alone holds the House of Compson together—even as she and it shrink over time—and thereby sets limits to Jason's fatalism and tyranny. Faulkner called Dilsey "one of my own favorite characters because she is brave, courageous, generous, gentle and honest" (*Lion*, 244-45). The novel's sole nurturing force, she raises both the Compson children and her own, though without illusion or false expectation. She says to Luster: "You got jes es much Compson devilment in you as any of em." She moves at her own pace—"with a sort of painful and terrific slowness"—in a dynamic of mutual respect with clocks and calendars, those inadequate measures of time. Giving Quentin the family watch, "the mausoleum of all hope and desire," Mr. Compson had vainly warned him: "not that you may remember time, but that you might forget it now and then for a moment and not spend all your breath trying to conquer it." But that is exactly what Quentin does, trying to kill time (in both senses: smashing his watch, stalling his death) before he kills himself. Equally extreme are Benjy, totally lacking a temporal sense, and Jason, for whom time is literally money, the dominance of things. But Dilsey, who says "Eight oclock" when she hears the clock strike five, perfectly embodies Mr. Compson's wisdom. She balances the petty pace measured by clocks, the calendar's longer view (her day is Easter Sunday), and the millenial vision of the preacher's sermon that she expresses as if it were mere fact: "Ive seed de first en de last. . . . I seed de beginin, and now I sees de endin." Though in her case everything and everyone *do* conspire to make her life as worrisome as possible, she remains unself-pitying and whole, one of Faulkner's truly sane characters.

Faulkner concludes with her section because, to the extent possible, she holds the book as well as its families together. Lacking self-consciousness though not self-awareness, Dilsey is neither her section's narrator nor even its sole focus (much of 4 follows Jason's fruitless chase after Quentin and the money); yet she pervades it, remaining a harmonizing spirit in a sundering house. Thus, the novel's final line— "each in its ordered place"—expresses not only Benjy's need but something of Dilsey's achievement. And when Faulkner came to write the genealogy, which is now effectively the novel's fifth section, he ended it too with Dilsey, and blacks generally, in concord with time. The last two words are "They endured"—a theme he was to elaborate not only in later fiction but also in the credo affirmed in his Nobel Prize speech. The challenge that Dilsey poses is that of goodness in an evil world, a challenge that Faulkner thought he failed to meet himself: "She's much more brave and honest and generous than me" (*Lion*, 245).

Yet Faulkner also saw Dilsey (along with Thomas Sutpen and Joe Christmas) as one of his most tragic characters (*F in U*, 119). For all her efforts, Dilsey ultimately offers no stay against time's ravages, and in fact no one ever listens to or is aided by her. The description of her early in section 4 emphasizes her losses:

The gown fell gauntly from her shoulders, across her fallen breasts, then tightened upon her paunch and fell again.... She had been a big woman once but now her skeleton rose, draped loosely in unpadded skin that tightened again upon a paunch almost dropsical, as though muscle and tissue had been courage or fortitude which the days or the years had consumed until only the indomitable skeleton was left rising like a ruin or a landmark above the somnolent and impervious guts, and above that the collapsed face that gave the impression of the bones themselves being outside the flesh.

Although she sings whenever she is allowed a moment's respite, her song is not joyous but a keening, a lament, "something without particular tune or words, repetitive, mournful and plaintive, austere"; and after she hears the impassioned sermon about salvation, "Two tears slid down her fallen cheeks, in and out of the myriad coruscations of immolation and abnegation and time." And in the Appendix, finally beyond time, the novel proper, and the rotting Compson House, she refuses to be drawn back—by "the mousesized mousecolored spinster" librarian eager to save the "cold serene and damned" Caddy—into failures that she could sometimes forestall but never prevent either by action or, superstitiously, by refusing to name them: "Never you mind."

Naming and renaming are, in fact, central to the novel's double rhythm of failure. Commenting on one of Benjy's key memories, Roskus says he first saw the Compson bad luck not when Benjy was born or even named—he was originally named Maury, for Mrs. Compson's parasitical brother—but when he is renamed Benjamin for the son of Israel sold into bondage by his brothers.[16] Sounding like Aunt Jenny at the end of *Flags* when she mocks Narcissa for naming her son Benbow rather than John in hopes that he will escape Sartoris doom, Dilsey agrees with Roskus's assessment: *"How come it is, Dilsey said. He aint wore out the name he was born with yet, is he.... Name aint going to help him. Hurt him, neither. Folks dont have no luck, changing names."* In a sense, however, Benjy immediately undergoes a second renaming, for while Mrs. Compson, perhaps the vulgarest character

Faulkner ever created, insists that "Nicknames are vulgar," no one but her ever calls him Benjamin.

The pattern that Benjy's name change seeks to break, though out of shame at his being retarded rather than understanding, is incestuous, an imposed familial handicap: everyone is called for someone else. The Faustian Quentin is named for "the last Compson who would not fail at everything he touched save longevity or suicide" (Appendix, 408). He gives his name to Caddy's illegitimate daughter, "nameless at birth and already doomed to be unwed from the instant the dividing egg determined its sex" (Appendix, 424), because Caddy "two months pregnant with another man's child which regardless of what its sex would be she had already named Quentin after the brother whom they both (she and the brother) knew was already the same as dead, when she married" (Appendix, 412-13). Consequently, according to Mrs. Compson, "she has inherited all of [Caddy's] headstrong traits. Quentin's too. I thought at the time, with the heritage she would already have, to give her that name, too. Sometimes I think she is the judgment of Caddy and Quentin upon me." And what Jason most resents about her is that she had "no more respect for what I try to do for her than to make her name and my name and my Mother's name a byword in the town."

Jason is named for his father (as Caddy desperately reminds him when she begs him to take care of Quentin II), his flamboyant ancestors, and, like the renamed Benjy, a figure out of mythology. Naming's failure could not be more ironic. Caddy, in this, as in most other ways, is a special case: her name is, simultaneously, uniquely her own, totally effaced (it is forbidden to be spoken in her family home after she deposits her illegitimate child there), and pervasive—not only in everyone's memory but also in the continuous cry of "caddie" emanating from the former Compson pasture that is now a golf course.[17]

Caddy partakes of the same multiple roles in the novel as her name:

She exists only in the minds and memories of her brothers. We can find out what she represents for Benjy, Quentin, and Jason; we never discover what she actually is. Hence her many and contradictory faces: she is in turn sister and mother, virgin and whore, angel and demon; she at once embodies fecundity and foulness, the nostalgia for inocence and the call to corruption, the promise of life and the vertigo of death.[18]

Faulkner began with an image of her in mind and made a novel of a short story because he fell in love with her: "perhaps the only thing in literature which would ever move me very much."[19] He made her central to memory and action—"both the tragic victim of her family and the unwitting agent of its doom"[20]—but gave her no section of her own. She exists only as others respond to her, only as recollection: for Benjy, a consoling slipper or a cry of what sounds like her name; for Quentin, the imperfect object of all desire, the failure of all his quixotic idealism; for Jason, "a woman that cant name the father of her own child," a bitch who has left him a bitch to rear; for herself, as Faulkner puts it in the Appendix, "Doomed and knew it, accepted the doom without either seeking or fleeing it." For Faulkner, she combines, as André Bleikasten indicates, two keys to this book and to his world: "In his introduction to the novel, he refers to absence ('I, who had never had a sister') as well as to mourning ('. . . fated to lose my daughter in infancy'), equating in retrospect the imaginary *lack* with an actual *loss*."[21] Caddy's absence in her novel, then, provokes not only her brothers to create her, but Faulkner—whose sister she *first* failed to be—to represent her as the richest image and fulfillment of the creative act itself. Consequently, *The Sound and the Fury*—the remarkable rendering of a House and a people teetering simultaneously on the edge of destruction and, to paraphrase Yeats, on the eternity of artifice—remains what Faulkner called it: his "most splendid failure" (*F in U*, 77).

Absalom, Absalom!

Absalom, Absalom! is both Faulkner's most complex narrative and his most convoluted narrative about narration.[22] Like
Flags in the Dust and *The Sound and the Fury*, it begins in a
present (1909) that is both atrophied and dominated by a dead
past, and it circles continually back to that past because the
present, its dark shadow, offers no alternative action, no
possibility of going forward in time—except to death. Yet
even the anticipated deaths are past since one of the narrators,
Rosa Coldfield, insists that she died forty-three years ago and
two others, Quentin Compson and his father, died in *The
Sound and the Fury*. In the process of circling back in order to
begin, *Absalom, Absalom!* reveals what it becomes—not only
the tale it ostensibly seeks to tell, but its failure to tell that tale,
the failure of all tale-telling as elusive raw material coheres
only momentarily out of *"the maelstrom of unbearable reality."* So, from "the long still hot weary dead September afternoon" and the "dim hot airless room with the blinds all closed
and fastened for forty-three summers," the novel initiates its
repeated return to mourning's source, "old ghost-times"
whose continuity is vivified rather than exorcised by narrative.

Miss Rosa, the novel's first, oldest, and most obsessive
storyteller, appears "in the eternal black which she had worn
for forty-three years now, whether for sister, father, or not-
husband none knew." She is, it eventually becomes clear, in
mourning for her own death, which she dates precisely: "my
life was destined to end on an afternoon in April forty-three
years ago, since anyone who even had as little to call living as I
had had up to that time would not call what I have had since
living." Her posthumous existence began when, though she
had watched Thomas Sutpen, her brother-in-law, destroy his
family and had "demonized" him even before she first saw him
as a child, Rosa had nonetheless agreed to marry him—and
then recoiled in horror from his proposal "that they breed
together for test and sample and if it was a boy they would
marry." She has spent the nearly half century since in "impo-

tent and static rage," unalive except in evoking the "fiend blackguard devil" who, though long dead, remains more vital than she: "as though in inverse ratio to the vanishing voice, the invoked ghost of the man whom she could neither forgive nor revenge herself upon began to assume a quality almost of solidity, permanence."

Sutpen, the figure against which first Rosa and then all others react, is the heroic yet oddly negative progenitor of action, family, plantation, self, and doom. A complex cast of narrators—Rosa, Mr. Compson, Quentin, his Harvard roommate Shreve, plus a free-floating anonymous voice and, indirectly, Quentin's grandfather (General Compson) and Sutpen himself—all compete not so much to represent Sutpen as to justify their reactions to him. In the process his life, like everything else in the book, is not so much told as withheld, suspended, deflected, denied. Versions vie, through a kind of backward and negative accretion, to wrap him in their own imaginings with little regard for fit or contradiction.[23] Eventually a composite emerges of a rootless phantom without a past, "completely the slave of his secret and furious impatience" who, seemingly bent equally on self-creation and self-destruction, bursts upon Jefferson, imposes his Faustian will and shadowy presence, and then allows all he has built to be destroyed rather than acknowledge his firstborn. Rosa, herself repeatedly described as having lacked a childhood, focuses her account on two key moments: first (and before she is born), Sutpen's sudden appearance in Yoknapatawpha in 1833 having "had no past at all or did not dare reveal it" but possessing twenty wild slaves and a manacled French architect, and, second, his outrageous proposal to her (in 1866) that signals her death.

Upon his arrival, Sutpen—a demonic creator—attacks the "tranquil and astonished earth [in order to] drag house and formal gardens violently out of the soundless Nothing and clap them down . . . , creating the Sutpen's Hundred, the *Be Sutpen's Hundred* like the olden time *Be Light*." And between Rosa's two key moments, Sutpen—acting always "with the same cold and ruthless determination," qualities the anonymous narrator ascribes to Rosa—has a mulatto daughter named Clytemnestra, marries Rosa's sister Ellen (Rosa still not yet born), sires an acknowledged son (Henry) and daughter (Judith), forbids the marriage of Judith to Charles Bon (Henry's best friend from college), fights in the Civil War during which Ellen dies, and returns home shortly after Henry kills Bon at the gates of Sutpen's Hundred in order to prevent the marriage.

Halfway through the novel—as Sutpen's absolute yet passive antagonism toward Bon compounds mystery and disaster-the narrative again goes backward in order to go forward. We learn that Rosa's notion that Sutpen "had been created out of thin air" is truer than she knows. For Sutpen, as he tells General Compson, was shocked into consciousness and self-creation when, as an impoverished boy of fourteen standing at the front door of a mansion to deliver a message, he was told by a black servant to go around to the back before he could even say why he was there. Instead of obeying, however, Sutpen goes off to a cave to ponder the rebuff, decides that he was at that door not to deliver a message but only in order to be turned away, knows that "he would have to do something about it in order to live with himself for the rest of his life and he could not decide what it was because of that innocence which he had just discovered he had," and then redreams himself as rich, powerful, and patriarchal in order to forestall and erase that moment of utter victimization. He resolves not to remake the world so that such occurrences cease, can never be, but to get that "boy-symbol" inside that house, in fact to own it in order to determine who else may enter.

But when Bon appears, Sutpen is helpless to prevent *his* entry—though for Sutpen he represents the once and future failure of his design. After thinking things through, Sutpen had run away to Haiti—not quite believing in its existence—because he had heard that fortunes could be made there by those possessing what he called courage and shrewdness, though he meant unscrupulousness. There he had acquired wealth, a wife, and a son—and then abandoned this family too when he discovered his wife to be a mulatto: "I found that she was not and could never be, through no fault of her own, adjunctive or incremental to the design which I had in mind, so I provided for her and put her aside." Thus, Sutpen's arrival in Jefferson as well as his subsequent marriage and family repeat an earlier failure—he calls the first marriage a mistake "that he entered in good faith"—that now returns to haunt him in the person of Bon, his first son. And Sutpen is appalled, immobilized, desperate not to act until he can correctly name his antagonist—irony, fate, coincidence, retribution—and so "saying nothing yet . . . just waiting, . . . waiting for what nobody knows, perhaps . . . for the crisis to come to him—this man of whom it was said that he not only went out to meet his troubles, he sometimes went out and manufactured them." Seeing Bon as "he stood there at his own door, just as he had imagined, planned, designed, and sure enough and after fifty years the forlorn nameless and homeless lost child came to knock at it . . . , he must have felt and heard the design—house, position, posterity and all—come down like it had been built out of smoke." Sutpen's choice is stark, simple: Repeat the old mistake or make a new one. "I was faced," he says,

with condoning a fact which had been foisted upon me without my knowledge during the process of building toward my design, which meant the absolute and irrevocable negation of the design; or in holding to my original plan for the design in pursuit of which I had incurred this negation. I chose. . . . Yet I am now faced with a second necessity to choose, the curious factor of which is . . . that either choice which I might make, either course which I might choose, leads to the same result: either I destroy my design with my own hand . . . or do nothing, let matters take the course which I know they will take and see my design complete itself quite normally and naturally and successfully to the public eye, yet to my own in such fashion as to be a mockery and a betrayal of that little boy who approached that door fifty years ago and was turned away, for whose vindication the whole plan was conceived and carried forward to the moment of this choice.

The novel's last narrator to speak, Sutpen is driven to storytelling, "that patient amazed recapitulation, not [with] any hope of ever understanding it, but trying to explain to circumstance, to fate itself, the logical steps by which he had arrived at a result absolutely and forever incredible, repeating." Since understanding is not story's end but already precluded, story can achieve or mean no more than action—or inaction, since "for a time he did nothing and so perhaps helped to bring about the very situation which he dreaded." Similarly, Sutpen's simple, "innocent" notion of unfairness asks the key question in exactly the wrong way, with the right answer denied in advance: "You see, I had a design in my mind. Whether it was a good or a bad design is beside the point; the question is, Where did I make the mistake in it, what did I do or misdo in it, whom or what injure by it to the extent which this would indicate." To deem "beside the point" what is central, to define morality in strictly aesthetic terms or "like the ingredients of pie or cake," to treat people as counters or abstractions, to impose a totally self-centered vision on a recalcitrant world—all of this is to assert failure as implicit, inevitable, and just.

Sutpen is doomed before he begins, "that design to which he had dedicated himself [having died] still-born." In a sense, he spends his life merely repeating the motions of inherited failure, for "his desire to make himself a king and found a line of princes" is inspired in part by his sudden sense of his forbears as people "who have lived 'without hope or purpose,' performing labor that was 'brutish and stupidly out of proportion to its reward.' "[24] With hope and purpose, therefore, Sutpen had sought to will himself a dynasty's patriarch, but his very different labor is also "brutish and stupidly out of proportion to its reward," and so causes him to occupy a place he meant to escape in the chain of generational failure. Not only Faulkner's children but his parents and grandparents too are haunted by inadequate ancestors, and their tragedy entails their ratifying rather than breaking the inherited pattern. Even as parents assume that their heirs will escape *their* past by conforming to imposed schemes, they self-defeatingly burden their progeny with new modes of destruction. Thus Sutpen, seeking to displace or deny his dehumanizing rebuff, can only ratify and repeat it by negating everyone close to him: the family he deserts without a word or backward glance, the wife and child he puts aside as tainted, a mistake, the second wife he drives into madness, the son he denies even at his door, the other son he uses to murder the first, the daughter he renders "already the same as a widow without ever having been a bride," the would-be third wife he reduces to "lonely thwarted old female flesh embattled for forty-three years in the old insult," the grandchild of Wash Jones, his old drinking companion, whom he seduces and scorns when the baby is a girl, and finally Wash, "poor white trash" who had also never been admitted to his front door, whom Sutpen goads into killing him out of what seems despair of beginning—and failing—yet again.

Though all the versions of Sutpen differ from each other, none of them shares—as he repeatedly, innocently, seems to assume they do—his amoral self-projection, his denial of morality's relevance. General Compson, the closest thing to a friend and confidant Sutpen had, is outraged that his vocabulary lacks words like "conscience" and "morality"; and he says to Sutpen, *"Given the occasion and the need, this man can and will do anything."* Others oppose Sutpen more overtly: his discarded first wife sends Bon to threaten his complacency; the unacknowledged Bon provokes Henry to destroy them both; the indignant Wash Jones murders Sutpen, and then his granddaughter and the child; and Rosa, frozen within "the old insult, the old unforgiving outraged and betrayed by the final and complete affront which was Sutpen's death,'" gains a kind of revenge through rendering—in a manner "cold, implacable, and even ruthless" that matches Sutpen's—a story of gothic horror with Sutpen cast not as the Horatio Alger hero his dream intends but as the ogre who haunts the mind's and houses' dark corners in childhood nightmares.

Rosa's narrating to Quentin seems motivated by contradictory impulses. Quentin thinks she wants her story widely

disseminated, *"so that people whom she will never see and
whose names she will never hear and who have never heard
her name nor seen her face will read it and know at least why
God let us lose the War: that only through the blood of our
men and the tears of our women could He stay this demon and
efface his name and lineage from the earth,"* but he then
realizes that she, "the town's and the county's poetess laureate," could do that herself. Mr. Compson suggests that her
telling Quentin, the grandson of Sutpen's "friend," is a way of
keeping it in the family, the skeletons in the closet—a way of
not telling it. But sheer affinity—one obsessed ghostly survivor of a dark and divided house recounting her losses to that of
another—surely accounts for much; further, Quentin's heritage of ancient glory and failure is itself Rosa's fabulous story:
"Quentin had grown up with that; the mere names were
interchangeable and almost myriad. His childhood was full of
them; his very body was an empty hall echoing with sonorous
defeated names; he was not a being, an entity, he was a
commonwealth. He was a barracks filled with stubborn back-
looking ghosts." But more than that: Quentin is not only
recipient and heir of Rosa's and the South's dead past, he is
himself, fifty years too late, more her contemporary than his
own, both the ghostly voice that speaks in the dead present and
the myriad unalive of whom it speaks.

He would seem to listen to two separate Quentins now—the
Quentin Compson preparing for Harvard in the South, the deep
South dead since 1865 and peopled with garrulous outraged baffled
ghosts, listening, having to listen, to one of the ghosts which had
refused to lie still even longer than most had, telling him about old
ghost-times; and the Quentin Compson who was still too young to
deserve yet to be a ghost, but nevertheless having to be one for all
that, since he was born and bred in the deep South the same as she
was—the two separate Quentins now talking to one another in the
long silence of notpeople, in notlanguage.[25]

Thus, Rosa's story—like all the others in the novel—is both a
repetition and an irrelevance, as Quentin emphasizes when,

much later, Shreve picks up the narrative thread: *"Am I going to have to have to hear it all again* he thought *I am going to have to hear it all over again I am already hearing it all over again I am listening to it all over again I shall have to never listen to anything else but this again forever."* Just as Quentin "had been born in and still breathed the same air in which the church bells has rung on that Sunday morning in 1833" when Sutpen first appeared, so he hears what he has always heard: the fable of the archetypal dark and divided house—that of the U.S. during its fratricidal War—and the South's subsequent enduring desolation.[26] Even more perverse than Quentin's sense of displacement, Mr. Compson suggests that Rosa sees him, because of his grandfather's relationship with Sutpen, as both antecedent to her and conniving in her doom: "Maybe she considers you partly responsible through heredity for what happened to her and her family through him." Those who inherit Southern devastation, it seems, have also invented it—"author and victim too," Mr. Compson calls them—as Shreve's mocking attitude toward those who live there and Quentin's almost maniacal insistence that he does not hate it confirm: " 'I dont hate it,' Quentin said, quickly, at once, immediately; 'I dont hate it,' he said. *I dont hate it* he thought, panting . . . *I dont. I dont! I dont hate it! I dont hate it."* [27]

The Southern leaders during the War—"with the shapes of men but with the names and statures of heroes"—are wholly romanticized, and by no one more than Rosa who, already obsessed with telling that story at war's beginning, wrote "a thousand or more . . . odes to Southern soldiers," "a schoolgirl's poetry about the also-dead." Like Miss Jenny in *Flags,* Rosa created mythical figures to fulfill her own image and need, and so felt doubly betrayed by the failure of both men and image. She was, if anything, inspired rather than deterred by the action of her anti-heroic father—"a man of uncompromising moral strength"—who, refusing to countenance the war, nailed "himself in his attic and starve[d] to death rather than look upon his native land in the throes of repelling an invading army." Rosa, who "without knowing it" hated her father from birth because it had caused her mother's death, learns the hard way that she is truly her father's daughter. Late in the novel, Coldfield's motivation is revealed as hatred of the South, and presumably himself, for abetting Sutpen's success, "for having erected its economic edifice not on the rock of stern morality but on the shifting sands of opportunism and moral brigandage" (260)—a view of Sutpen that Rosa, we see early on, has relearned too late: "Oh, he was brave. I have never gainsaid that. But that our cause, our very life and future hopes and past pride, should have been thrown into the balance with men like that to buttress it—men with valor and strength but without pity or honor. Is it any wonder that Heaven saw fit to let us lose?" (20). Rosa speculates rhetorically on the "fatality and curse" on her family and the South that they should be so singled out: "I used to wonder what our father or his father could have done before he married our mother that Ellen and I would have to expiate and neither of us alone be sufficient; what crime committed that would leave our family cursed to be instruments not only for that man's destruction, but for our own." History as a malevolent pattern, Southern history, for example, requires that not only the sins but also the morality of the fathers be visited upon the child, *"and so,"* Rosa ultimately maintains, *"these forty-three years of impotent and unbearable outrage were the revenge on her of some sophistricated and ironic sterile nature for having hated that which gave her life."*[28]

Sutpen, who as Colonel became one of Rosa's heroes as well as her ogre, enacts his own version of the Southern Lost Cause, for both are founded and fought on the same evil base. It is ironically appropriate that the two intertwine, become as if one story. Having been told by Sutpen that Bon is his brother and therefore must not marry Judith and by Bon that the merest acknowledgment from Sutpen would free him to leave Judith in peace, Henry uses the War—itself a macrocosm of fratricidal self-destruction—as what Mr. Compson calls an extravagant hiatus in Stupen doom, an extraordinarily wasteful means of postponing his murder of Bon. Framed by Bon's appearance and reappearance at Sutpen's Hundred, the War exists as if merely to suspend Sutpen action and doom, to render ti discontinuous, fragmented, meaningless.

Bon and Henry—the former unacknowledged by Sutpen, the latter, mirroring that lack, having "formally abjured his father and renounced his birthright"—depart Sutpen's Hundred on the eve of war and spend the next four years in suspension: "probation... durance... armistice" and the vain hope "that the War would settle the matter, leave free one of the two irreconcilables, since it would not be the first time that youth has taken catastrophe as a direct act of Providence for the sole purpose of solving a personal problem which youth itself could not solve." Yet when it tries to do so, one of them rescues the other (it seems not to matter who rescued whom, and it is told both ways [124, 344-45]). The long Southern retreat, when it comes, seems purposeful to Bon, designed to bring "him within reach of his father, to give his father one more chance" to acknowledge his existence. But instead there occurs a second confrontation between Sutpen and Henry— the latter, having spent the war reconciling himself to incest, at last willing to allow Bon to act. But now Sutpen tells him that Bon is part Negro, and Henry, having run out of war and delay, is constrained to face Bon's desperate last challenge: *"So it's the miscegenation, not the incest, which you cant bear. . . . He did not have to do this, Henry. He didn't need to tell you I am a nigger to stop me. He could have stopped me without that, Henry . . . . No I'm not [your brother]. I'm the nigger that's going to sleep with your sister. Unless you stop me, Henry."* And so they return to Sutpen's Hundred at war's end—loss begetting loss—so that Henry can play archetypal defender of white Southern womanhood (though the War, we are told, has turned all the women into ghosts) who fears, above all, "that there was a nigger in the woodpile somewhere": killing Bon at the gates rather than allow him to enter, to penetrate to where Judith awaits her brother/groom. Sutpen's white heir, barring his mansion to the black intruder, thus fulfills Sutpen's dream of repeating and reversing the

terms of his own rejection—but the cost, as the novel's retro-
spection emphasizes from first to last, is dream's destruction,
not only because it is inherently evil, a failure from its incep-
tion, but also because the book begins with, and never loses
sight of, not the dream but its heinous implications and
consequences.

Behind the historical dark, divided house that contains those
of *Absalom*'s several families lies yet another: the mythical one
evoked by Faulkner's title. The Biblical King David and his
offspring also enact a pattern of incest and fratricide, generational conflict and betrayal, dynastic self-destruction. David's
reiterated naming of the son who was killed (against David's
orders) while rebelling ungratefully against his benign rule—
"O my son Absalom! my son, my son Absalom! would God I
had died for thee, O Absalom, my son, my son!"—is an
impassioned assertion of both presence and absence: for David
affirms his paternity even as he mourns the lost one who is no
longer his son. Sutpen repeats and extends only David's failure. Insisting that Bon's very existence is a mistake, Sutpen
grants him neither presence nor absence, neither name nor
merest gesture, and so inspires the act of rebellion that des-
troys them all. In contradistinction to the novel's present
narrators, Sutpen's greatest failure is that of imagination, a
refusal to conceive of what he has already conceived: the son
whose existence he would erase like an erroneous ledger entry.
The absent cry of relationship and loss—proclaimed by the
title and always expected by the shadowy Bon to whom it
would grant nativity and name—sounds silently throughout
the novel and the hollow vision at its core.[29]

That Bon is indeed his father's son, or shadow, is underscored repeatedly.[30] "He came into that isolated puritan country
household almost like Sutpen himself came into Jefferson:
apparently complete, without background or past or childhood"; Bon too "must have appeared almost phoenix-like,
fullsprung from no childhood, born of no woman and impervious to time." Though they initiate the novel's two cycles of
action, both father and son are essentially passive, fatalistic

spectators of their own lives—their innocence shocked into consciousness at the door of a mansion where they expect at least to be heard. Bon himself unconsciously draws the parallel when he refers to Sutpen's sending "me a message like you send a command by a nigger servant to a beggar or a tramp to clear out." Sutpen has orphaned them both, denied them solidity, identity—even death. Rosa cannot believe in either's demise. To Sutpen's corpse she responds: " 'Dead?' I cried. 'Dead? You? You lie; you're not dead; heaven cannot, and hell dare not, have you!'" Bon, whom she loves without ever seeing, remains for her "the abstraction which we had nailed into a box. . . . He was absent, and he was; he returned, and he was not; three women put something into the earth and covered it, and he had never been." Just as, during Quentin's and Shreve's narration, "neither of them said 'Bon,' " so Bon is the one subject never mentioned, between his death and war's end, by the three women awaiting Sutpen—that shell return- ing to a shell: he "came home with nothing, to nothing, to four years less than nothing." Bon becomes voided, like his father, as his father means him to be—"as though as a man he did not exist at all." He is a pure imaginative projection for Rosa who, though one of his pallbearers, cannot determine if anything is really in his coffin: "I had never seen him," she says. "(I never saw him. I never even saw him dead. I heard a name, I saw a photograph, I helped to make a grave: and that was all.)" Later she adds: "we had buried nothing." For all his desperate attempt to found a line, Sutpen is the negative progenitor of negative progeny—"his own ironic fecundity of dragon's teeth." Henry says of Judith, Bon, and himself that "the three of us are just illusions that he begot," while Bon alludes to his negative birth "out of the shadow of whose absence my spirit's posthumeity has never escaped." No wonder Judith has the same blank reaction to both deaths—"no tears, no bereave- ment this time too"—as if nothing had happened.

Of all Faulkner's protagonists, Bon most resembles Joe Christmas in *Light in August*, that other novel originally called "A Dark House" (see Blotner, pp. 701, 828). Both seem unreal,

shadowy, and passive, simultaneously desperate for certitude
about their origins and, through their actions, underscoring
their lack rather than overcoming it. Denied identity and
name, they remain hovering and undefined; forever unable to
begin their lives, they can only trigger the fatal crisis. Yet Bon is
paradigmatic rather than unique, for everyone in *Absalom,
Absalom!* is incorporeal, ethereal, illusory. Sutpen is a ghostly
presence, a phantom who haunts his own life and others. Ellen
"even while alive had moved but without life ... as if she had
never lived at all." Her death is imperceptible, "the substanceless shell, the shade impervious to any alteration of dissolution
because of its very weightlessness: no body to be buried: just
the shape, the recollection." Their children are also hollow,
voids, shades: Judith—"the blank shape, the empty vessel"—
exists as if unborn, displaces no air, "dreaming, not living";
Henry, an illusion who inhabits a "fairy balloon-vacuum," is
more shadowy than the dead Bon, "already a corpse" while still
alive. The composite, "the conventional family group of the
period, [exists] with formal and lifeless decorum [in a] fading
and ancient photograph." Unsurprisingly, the shell they
inhabit, a "desolation and decay as if the wood of which it was
built were flesh," was designed by "a condemned and conscien-
tious ghost" and is now guarded by Sutpen's mulatto daughter:
the sexless, ageless Clytie, "the cold Cerberus of his private
hell." The only solidity to the family are two thousand-pound
marble monuments that Sutpen, incredibly, imports from Italy
during the war and carries around with him for a year (the
troops "speaking of the two stones as 'Colonel' and 'Mrs.
Colonel' ")—finally setting one "above the faint grassy depression which Judith told him was Ellen's grave" while reserving
the other for his own imminent need. Yet these stones too
partake of Sutpen evanescence: "Both the flat slabs were
cracked across the middle by their own weight (and vanishing
into the hole)."

Negative characters performing negative action define not
only *Absalom, Absalom!*'s substance but also its structure, for
everything in it is absent, displaced, denied—existing *"in some*

curious serene suspension." Not only Rosa's life, fixed in "impotent and static rage" as the novel's first page indicates, but its basis too is suspended, withheld—until Shreve, the furthest removed of narrators, finally reveals, on page 177, what Sutpen proposed to her. Both Sutpen and Rosa, traumatized into consciousness and reaction by a key confrontation, remain frozen in their own lives, transfixed by the defining rebuff, able only to replay it with variations. Just as the Civil War confounds action for Henry and Bon—serving as hiatus until defeat signals their return to time—so the novel's method of narrating, as if bent on *not* telling its stories, obscures and suspends events. On page 87, for example, Wash Jones comes screaming out Rosa's name at her gate, but does not reveal his news—"Henry has done shot that durn French feller. Kilt him dead as a beef"—until page 133. On page 185 Sutpen scorns the daughter he has with Wash's granddaughter—repeating in even more outrageous form the insult to Rosa—though knowledge of the baby's sex is denied us for over one hundred pages (292).

The novel begins with Rosa and Quentin poised to visit Sutpen's Hundred, a trip whose purpose is concealed until, halfway through the book, we learn that she initiated it on discovering, somehow, that "There's something in that house. ... Something living in it. Hidden in it. It has been out there for four years, living hidden in that house" (172). That "something" (actually, Henry as an old man) remains hidden almost to the end, for Rosa and Quentin continue poised—and then, instead of their actually going, Quentin, months later in Cambridge, recalls their having gone (362-73). In the meantime, as Rosa and Quentin wait for it to be "dark enough to suit Miss Coldfield," Mr. Compson repeats the pattern. He tells Quentin *his* version of the Henry/Bon relationship, which he bases largely on conjecture—"or perhaps (I like to think this)"—and Bon's last, and only surviving, letter to Judith. She had given the letter to Quentin's grandmother as a way of asserting that what happened matters, that in fact something *had* happened: "maybe if you could go to someone, the stranger the better, and

give them something—a scrap of paper—something, anything, it not to mean anything in itself and them not even to
read it or keep it, not even bother to throw it away or destroy it,
at least it would be something just because it would have
happened, be remembered even if only from passing from one
hand to another, one mind to another, and it would be at least a
scratch, something, something that might make a mark on
something that *was* once for the reason that it can die someday" (127). Mr. Compson's narrative—all the narratives—are
attempts to fulfill Judith's implicit injunction to compel meaning "out of the ragtag and bob ends of old tales and talking"—
received and imagined, withheld and passed on. Thus, he first
offers Quentin the letter on page 89, alludes to it throughout
section 4, dismisses letters and old tales as inadequate to
explain the past (100-101), teases us with a sentence from it
that speaks our own impatience—*"We have waited long
enough"* (101)—then finally allows Quentin to take it (128)
and us to read it with him (129-32), "the dead tongue
speaking."

Sutpen's early life is revealed through the greatest complex
of narrative layering. Quentin receives a letter from his father
that, though first mentioned on page 31, does not begin until
pages 173-74: *"Miss Rosa Coldfield was buried yesterday."*
Itself suspended (and not finished until the novel's penultimate page) as Quentin continues to stare at it, brood over it,
the letter triggers and frames Quentin's memory of the evening he spent with Rosa, as well as imagined and received
memories. Perhaps most notable within that suspension is
Sutpen's self-revelation—while hunting his escaped
architect—to General Compson about his early years. Sutpen's
story suspends that of the hunt, and is in turn suspended by its
end: "It was thirty years before Sutpen told Grandfather any
more of it." Then, though this is left implicit, General Compson must have told the story to his son so that he could tell
Quentin, who is now both telling Shreve and hearing it back
from him. Yet that process is necessarily partial—"Grandfather
didn't tell him all of it either, like Sutpen never told Grand-

father quite all of it"—its product acquiring layers as it changes hands.

Self-conscious about negating both its characters and stories, *Absalom* (like Sutpen) at times attempts to fix in stable, aesthetic terms what is forever elusive. Rosa's first vision of Sutpen is that "he would abrupt (man-horse-demon) upon a scene peaceful and decorous as a schoolprize water color"—the conditional implying both past and future, fixity and repetition, of the initial act. Characters are often isolated and framed, seen as inhabitants of pictures, photographs, "broken cinema film." Such envisioning, however, only confirms their lifelessness, their existence as artifact, figures on an urn. But the novel's central aesthetic metaphor, as Shreve mockingly emphasizes, is theatrical: "Jesus, the South is fine, isn't it. It's better than the theatre, isn't it. It's better than Ben Hur, isn't it." Its characters are both spectators in their own lives and role-players desperate to perform well, and always failing. Henry, waiting in the wings, "had not yet returned to play his final part in his family's doom" (86), while Quentin, miscast in his own life, comes increasingly to play Henry stuck repeating the lead in an unsuccessful version of an ancient tragedy: "that gaunt tragic dramatic self-hypnotized youthful face like the tragedian in a college play, an academic Hamlet waked from some trancement of the curtain's falling and blundering across the dusty stage from which the rest of the cast had departed last Commencement" (174).

Ellen, her life indistinguishable from her role and therefore long over before her death, "escaped at last into a world of pure illusion ..., speaking her bright set meaningless phrases out of the part which she had written for herself ... — a woman who, if she had had the fortitude to bear sorrow and trouble, might have risen to actual stardom in the role of the matriarch." And Sutpen, *"a walking shadow,"* appears to Rosa not as a unique individual, but one lacking distinctive features, "like the mask in Greek tragedy, interchangeable not only from scene to scene, but from actor to actor and behind which the events and occasions took place without chronology or sequence." He "acted his role ... unaware ... that while he was still playing the scene to the audience, behind him Fate, destiny, retribution, irony—the stage manager, call him what you will—was already striking the set and dragging on the synthetic and spurious shadows and shapes of the next one."

The image of the stage being struck for the *next* failure even as the current one unfolds is especially appropriate to this novel of inadequate actors and authors. Sutpen's own self-revelation—with its minimal "regard for cause and effect even if none for logical sequence and continuity"—simply will not play. His attitude toward its events is one of aesthetic removedness: "he was not talking about himself. He was telling a story. He was not bragging about something he had done; he was just telling a story about something a man named Thomas Sutpen had experienced, which would still have been the same story if the man had had no name at all" (247). Rosa, who, like Judith, "displaced no air, gave off no betraying sound," ill-fits her own life and story. She wears her small body "like a costume borrowed at the last moment and of necessity for a masquerade which she did not want to attend." Born old and useless, she is worse off even than Bon—he "miscast for the time and knowing it, accepting it"—her very life out of joint, every season inapt: *"That was the miscast summer of my barren youth."*

Mr. Compson's narrative and imagination—predicated on "a few old mouth-to-mouth tales ... letters without salutation or signature ... the paper old and faded and falling to pieces, the writing faded, almost indecipherable, yet meaningful"—ultimately come up short, repeating Rosa's failure. He sees Henry loving both Judith and Bon—seducing them to the engagement and abandoning home and family when his father forbids the wedding—yet killing "Bon to keep them from marrying," and Bon—who watches with "fatalistic and impenetrable imperturbability" all the players including himself—finally insisting on the marriage to the point of provoking Henry to kill him. "Something is missing," Mr. Compson insists, all the pieces are brought together but they fail to fit:

"It's just incredible. It just does not explain. Or perhaps that's it: they dont explain and we are not supposed to know."

His narrative offers both less and more than he intends. He offers less because he speculates on people's motives not knowing he lacks certain key information (for example, he knows about Bon's octoroon wife but not that he is Sutpen's son) and more because his language and imagery often anticipate later revelations: he parallels Sutpen's and Bon's entries into Jefferson; he finds Bon, without knowing why, always "a little out of place," "too old to be where he was." He also represents Henry to Quentin in a way that replays past failure and suggests the origins of his son's own fatal obsession, explicit in *The Sound and the Fury* and implicit here: Henry, Mr. Compson tells him, "may have been conscious that his fierce provincial's pride in his sister's virginity was a false quantity which must incorporate in itself an inability to endure in order to be precious, to exist, and so must depend upon its loss, absence, to have existed at all. In fact, perhaps this is the pure and perfect incest: the brother realizing that the sister's virginity must be destroyed in order to have existed at all, taking that virginity in the person of the brother-in-law, the man whom he would be if he could become, metamorphose into, the lover, the husband" (96). And for all his cynicism and fatalism, Mr. Compson speculates, "with a sort of astonishment" and startling inappropriateness, that what he calls "the old virtues" may explain human behavior.

His temporarily resuscitated son, inheritor and agent of Southern doom and his own, is less a character than a conduit—recipient and conveyor of others' failures of action and narrative, all of which resonate with his own as he recounts them in his "flat, curiously dead voice."[31] Experience for Quentin is a contradiction in terms, something he receives only indirectly: through Rosa's story "Quentin seemed to watch" Sutpen's assault on the Yoknapatawpha wilderness; his father enables him to witness Sutpen's brief visit home during the war: "He could see it; he might even have been there. Then he thought *No. If I had been there I could not have*

seen it this plain"; his father's letter and Shreve's narrative
repeatedly evoke Rosa's final visit to Sutpen's Hundred:
"Quentin could see it. . . . He, Quentin, could see it. . . . he
(Quentin) could see her, them; he had not been there but he
could see her" (375-76). Quentin suggests that "Maybe
nothing ever happens once and is finished"—a declaration
that may be read as having two distinct parts, separated as well
as joined by the conjunction, both equally valid: "Maybe
nothing ever happens once" and "Maybe nothing ever is
finished."

Quentin's roommate, the mocking outsider Shreve, preempts
Quentin's narrative with "Let me play a while now." Echoing
Rosa and anticipating Ratliff in the Snopes trilogy, Shreve
asserts necessity as authority, maintaining "how there are
some things that just have to be whether they are or not, have
to be a damn sight more than some other things that maybe
are and it dont matter a damn whether they are or not" (322).
So it is Shreve who finally reveals—or imagines—not only
Sutpen's affront to Rosa, but also that Bon is Sutpen's son
(265) and that Sutpen told this to Henry (293). Further, for all
his cynicism, Shreve convincingly argues that Bon loved
Judith, that he replaced Judith's picture in the metal case she
had given him with that of the octoroon so that Judith would
find it if Henry really did kill him: "It was because he said to
himself, 'If Henry dont mean what he said, it will be all right; I
can take it out and destroy it. But if he does mean what he said,
it will be the only way I will have to say to her, *I was no good;
do not grieve for me.*'" And Quentin, who had earlier denied
the love, can only assent as Shreve formulates this surprising
and congenial truth.

After emphasizing their differences, the novel is at pains to
conflate Quentin and Shreve: "both born within the same year
. . . born half a continent apart yet joined, connected after a
fashion [by] the geologic umbilical" of the Mississippi River.
They breathe the same air, Shreve in fact breathing it first
since Southern air blows down from Canada. Becoming "free
now of flesh" and interchangeable with Henry and Bon, both

become voices indistinguishable first from Mr. Compson's and then from each other's: "It was Shreve speaking, though . . . it might have been either of them and was in a sense both: both thinking as one, the voice which happened to be speaking the thought only the thinking become audible, vocal; the two of them creating between them . . . people who perhaps had never existed at all anywhere" (303). Yet the union between Quentin and Shreve, and between them and the earlier pair they repeat and create, is necessarily temporary. It gives "way to violent ambivalence" as Quentin frantically denies hating the South while Shreve taunts him about its legacy: the howling, coal-black idiot grandson of Bon (the only survivor of the burning House of Sutpen) who, Shreve insists, will "conquer the western hemisphere . . . in a few thousand years."[32]

As the novel nears its end, we anticipate a sense of completion, yet the narrative progression—Rosa, Mr. Compson, Quentin, Shreve—displaces us increasingly from action's unknowable, reiterated, and receding center. Faulkner then offers, in an appended "Chronology" and "Geneology," a seemingly straightforward final narrator—one totally removed from his haunted "Dark Houses"—but the cited "facts" clash startlingly with what has been revealed in the text—so that this account proves least acceptable of all.[33] It serves, consequently, to remind us that, when Quentin and Shreve give freest rein to their fancy, the characters and scenes they imagine are *reliably* represented: "they had invented [what] was probably true enough." This notion is crucial to Faulkner's stance and achievement not only in and toward *Absalom, Absalom!*, this remarkable concatenation of fiction and truth, but to all his work.

4

Visions and Versions: *As I Lay Dying, Light in August*

Both *As I Lay Dying* (1930) and *Light in August* (1932), anomalies within the Faulkner canon, are unique, unrepeated experiments with time, perspective, and tonal antitheses. With the contradictions inherent in their multiple revelations, their comic and tragic elements, and their double resolutions, neither of them tells or concludes quite the story it seems to intend. In both cases, the whole is other than the mere sum of its parts—since the latter are never simply totaled and subsumed but remain in animated suspension, different with each twist of the kaleidoscope.

With its fifty-nine sections narrated by fifteen different characters, *As I Lay Dying* would seem impossibly fragmented, disjointed, and subjective, yet there is also unity in its temporal focus (it is more intensely and monolithically present, more oblivious of the past, than any other Yoknapatawpha novel); in the close connections among the speakers (seven narrators of forty-three sections are members of one family, almost all the rest are their rural neighbors); and especially in the central action of the journey to Jefferson that the family undertakes. The journey perfectly climaxes the stalemated marital battle between Addie and Anse, whose

domestic failure represents a typical if extreme version of
Faulknerian marriage. Each seems to have imposed the journey on the other—Addie in order to be buried with her own
family, Anse in order to get a new set of teeth (and also, we
learn at the end, a new wife)—as a kind of ultimate revenge:
Anse's hollow pride and stubborn persistence regardless of
cost to others negates not only his own claim to dignity but
death's as well; Addie's rotting corpse, in turn, mocks and
nearly overwhelms its bearers. The novel's double rhythm, as
David Minter suggests, concerns both its content and its
overall construction. It is a story of family disintegration
(paralleling that of Addie's body) and ironic reconstitution:
with Addie finally buried and Darl sent to an insane asylum,
the novel ends with the remaining children—and the reader—
being introduced to the next Mrs. Bundren.[1] Thus, while the
form of the novel stresses tragic fragmentation, its action
stresses comic continuity—and the whole becomes a kind of
sustained dance between the two.

The atypicality of *Light in August* on the other hand, lies in
the serene, almost motionless journey of its framing story: that
of the pregnant and then maternal Lena Grove, traveling
ostensibly to find her baby's father, her alliance with natural
fecundity told against the violent and destructive action at the
center of the novel. The past-obsessed stories of Joe Christmas,
Joanna Burden, and Gail Hightower are not only implicitly
morbid and sterile, they explicitly counterpoint Lena's and
Byron Bunch's healthy focus on the present, their harmonious
relationship with the world around them and ultimately with
each other, and what Faulkner calls "the basic possibility for
happiness and goodness" (*F in U*, 97). In this case, the novel of
Gothic horror and the novel of pastoral romance—antithetical
versions of perception and being—negotiate an intricate if
strained arrangement that sustains the independent telling of
each.

As I Lay Dying

The structure and design of both *As I Lay Dying* and *Light in August* are determined by the motif of the journey or quest—though only the first of these is monolithic in its plotting. For this reason, and because it is narrated wholly through various limited perspectives, *As I Lay Dying* is the most accessible, the most circumscribed, and the least commented upon—by both Faulkner and critics—of his generally acknowledged masterpieces. Faulkner himself encouraged readers to take a limiting view of the novel when, despite the fact that he did make substantial revisions, he said that its writing was remarkably easy and enjoyable, essentially a trick: *As I Lay Dying* was a "*tour de force*. I knew when I put down the first word what the last word of that would be. . . . *As I Lay Dying* I wrote in about six weeks without changing any of it" (*F in U*, 207). Its story, though "played out against a background of cosmic scale,"[2] is easily summarized: Addie Bundren dies; her husband, Anse, and her children (Cash, Darl, Jewel, Dewey Dell, and Vardaman) surmount numerous obstacles to cart her rotting corpse to her family's plot in Jefferson where, in accord with her wishes, she is finally buried ten days after her death. The novel's fragmentary narration affords all members of the family, as well as some of those they encounter, opportunity to comment on both their quest and the family itself. Yet despite its straightforward plotting and structure, *As I Lay Dying*, as Faulkner also implies, is a work of intricate interweaving, "a book by which, at a pinch, I can stand or fall if I never touch ink again."[3] The book's dense patterning results largely from numerous semantic elements that are often other than what they first seem, that do not fit into the larger scheme as it seems they will, and that clash in a variety of troubling ways. Together, they define a surprisingly rich complex of verbal and imagistic repetition and variation that rewards the closest and most careful scrutiny.

Because its events are entirely reflected through its characters, *As I Lay Dying* lacks the ballast and stability pro-

vided by the Dilsey section of *The Sound and the Fury*, or by
the distance and reliability of *Light in August*'s unnamed
narrator. The various sections and characters are linked by
exactly what separates them: the absolute isolation of each
unique perspective, their failures to communicate and connect,
or even, at times, to inhabit the same worlds. Since all the
perspectives are subjective and partial, something approximating truth and validity can emerge—both within a single
character's accounting and between different versions of the
same event—only where consistency and coherence exist.
How the characters repeat, echo, and "correct" not only themselves but each other reveals much about each of them, about
their relationships, and about the overall quality of the novel.

Through speculating endlessly on Bundren family dynamics
and invariably getting them wrong, Cora Tull, a sanctimonious
busybody, goes furthest in undermining her own version of
events. Convincing evidence is offered that she errs about
almost everything she pretends to know: that Anse sent a
reluctant Darl on a lumber-hauling job as Addie was about to
die (it was Darl who, *knowing* that Addie would die before
their return, insisted on going); that Jewel rather than Darl
was after the three dollars they would earn; that the journey to
town was entirely Anse's idea; that Addie truly loved Darl and
not Jewel (Cora contradicts herself on this); that Addie was "a
faithful wife"; that the Rev. Whitfield (Addie's secret lover
and Jewel's father) was "pure religious"; that Jewel "never
loved her" (his one section expresses his fierce obsession with
her), and so on.

A healthy corrective to Cora's skewed reality is offered by
her long-suffering husband, who tries to balance her distorting
self-righteousness with skepticism and humor (he is something of a punster), and to minimize her interfering in their
neighbors' lives. Tull manages to get her away from Addie
long enough for the latter to die peacefully, and to keep her
from returning to do what she calls "my duty" until he is
certain that the death has in fact occurred. The tone of his
references to Cora is resigned, yet often sardonic:

I reckon I am blessed in having a wife that ever strives for sanctity and well-being like she says I am. . . . I reckon if there's ere a man or woman anywhere that He could turn it all over to and go away with His mind at rest, it would be Cora. And I reckon she would make a few changes, no matter how He was running it. And I reckon they would be for man's good. Leastways, we would have to like them. Leastways, we might as well go on and make like we did.

In his six sections (twice as many as Cora has), Tull is a model of neighborliness, amiability, and decency. Though unwilling to intrude or be solemn, Tull invariably assists others—especially Anse—during times of need. He comments on the latter's crop, "I tell him again I will help him out if he gets into a tight, with her sick and all. Like most folks around here, I done holp him so much already I cant quit now." Nor is he beyond self-mockery; having just helped Anse, Dewey Dell, and Vardaman to cross the bridge half-submerged by flood waters, he looks back in astonishment:

Like it couldn't be me here, because I'd have had better sense than to done what I just done. And when I looked back and saw the other . . . and knew that I'd have to get back there someway, I knew it couldn't be, because I just couldn't think of anything that could make me cross that bridge ever even once. Yet here I was, and the fellow that could make himself cross it twice, couldn't be me, not even if Cora told him to.

Much of what Tull recounts confirms what we learn from others' sections. For example, along with Vardaman and Darl he notes the package and basket that Dewey Dell insists on carrying to town. Whitfield's section ends with the words, " 'God's grace upon this house,' I said" (171); Tull quotes Whitfield's words almost exactly: "His grace be upon this house" (83). Tull's description of the upending of the Bundren wagon by a log in the swollen river essentially repeats Darl's of a few pages earlier. Of greater significance, because realistically inexplicable, are occasional metaphorical echoes: for example, Dewey Dell says that Anse "rouses up, like a steer that's been kneeling in a pond and you run at it" (59); Tull likens Anse to "a steer standing knee-deep in a pond and somebody come by and set the pond up on edge and he aint missed it yet" (69).

Tull's geniality and seeming reliability give his reiterated defense of Darl's sanity particular force and authority. "I have said and I say again, that's ever living thing the matter with Darl: he just thinks by himself too much. Cora's right when she says all he needs is a wife to straighten him out." Yet this statement immediately assumes ironic overtones when, with clear reference to his own situation, he wryly adds, "And when I think about that, I think that if nothing but being married will help a man, he's durn nigh hopeless." Tull also remarks that Darl's queerness resides in his eyes: "I always say it aint never been what he done so much or said or anything so much as how he looks at you. It's like he had got into the inside of you, someway. Like somehow you was looking at yourself and your doings outen his eyes." Yet, surprisingly, Tull later quotes Cora as saying to him, "you're one of the folks that says Darl is the queer one."

Tull also participates in several other contradictions, the most blatant of which concerns the bridge to Jefferson. First Tull quotes Whitfield: "I was late because the bridge has gone. I went down to the old ford and swum my horse over, the Lord protecting me" (83). As if to reiterate the point, Tull immediately metaphorizes the incident in describing Whitfield's preaching: "His voice is bigger than him. . . . It's like he is one, and his voice is one, swimming on two horses side by side across the ford" (86). And Whitfield, in his only section, offers corroborative description of his crossing the river (169-70). Yet when Tull and the Bundrens arrive there and see the apparently impassible bridge, Tull responds to Dewey Dell's plaintive "Mr Whitfield crossed it" with agreement rather than with denial: " 'He was a-horseback,' I say. 'And three days ago. It's riz five foot since' " (119)—thus contradicting (and for no discernible reason) what we learn elsewhere.

Failing us after seeming wholly dependable, Tull's version of events necessarily casts even greater doubt upon the less obviously trustworthy accounts—especially those of the self-obsessed Bundrens that form the bulk of the novel. Failure in *As I Lay Dying* is that of perspective and communication even more than of action. In their accounts all the Bundrens are either narrowly focused to the point of monomania (Anse on the promise of new teeth and keeping his word to Addie, Dewey Dell on obtaining an abortion, Jewel on his horse, Cash on his carpentry) or visionaries narrating what is beyond their ken:[4] the mad Darl, whose nineteen sections comprise almost one-third of the total and something of a comprehensive family history; the child Vardaman, distraught over his mother's death, who has the second-most sections; and the dead Addie, who, like one of the minor characters, has only one. I will consider each of these last three in some detail.

Darl's eyes, whose strangeness Tull notes, are, according to Dewey Dell and Anse, "full of the land": they see further and deeper than anyone's. Darl not only knows that Addie will die while he and Jewel are away, but he also describes in detail the death, the family's reaction, and Cash's completion of the coffin as if he were present. He alone knows, "without the words," both that Jewel is Addie's child from her affair with Whitfield and that Dewey Dell is pregnant and frantic about it: "And then I knew that I knew. I knew that as plain on that day as I knew about Dewey Dell on that day." Desperate for any kind of contact with his family, he mocks and, against his own interest, increasingly antagonizes both Dewey Dell and Jewel throughout the book—until they turn on him with fury and hatred at the end.

His narrative is powerful and poetic both in itself and in its impact on those of others, for many of them echo his thoughts, descriptions, and language in ways that seem literally impossible. Yet such linguistic repetition—which is unique to this novel—is ultimately a sign of rupture rather than the connection it seems to promise. This failure is especially true of Darl's relationship with his sister, for, as Cash says, "him and Dewey Dell kind of knowed things betwixt them." It is Darl, not Dewey Dell, who first expresses her intense, silent appeal for help to Dr. Peabody: "You could do so much for me if you just

would. If you just knew." Darl first sees the sign, "New Hope
Church. 3 mi.," that she translates into her forlorn, reiterated,
"New Hope. 3 mi. New Hope. 3 mi.," and then, "New Hope.
Was 3 mi. Was 3 mi." She uses his language, natural imagery,
and alliteration; for example, Darl's description of Cash viewing the suddenly dead Addie—"He is *l*ooking *down* at her
peaceful, rigid *face fading* into the *d*usk as though *darkness*
were a precursor of the *u*ltimate *earth, u*ntil at *l*ast the *face*
seems to *f*loat *d*etached *upon* it, *lightly* as the reflection of a
*dead l*eaf" (49)—becomes for her: "The sky *l*ies *flat down* the
slope, *upon* the secret clumps. Beyond the hill sheet-*lightning*
stains *up*ward and *fades*. The *dead* air shapes the *dead earth* in
the *dead darkness,* further away than seeing shapes the *dead
earth*. It *l*ies *dead* and warm *upon* me" (61; my emphasis).
Both of them also represent falling asleep as erasure of self, an
entry into nonbeing, a blurring of waking distinctions. Darl
says: "you must empty yourself for sleep. And before you are
emptied for sleep, what are you. And when you are emptied for
sleep, you are not. And when you are filled with sleep, you
never were. I dont know what I am. I dont know if I am or not"
(76); and she: *"I had a nightmare once I thought I was awake
but I couldn't see and couldn't feel I couldn't feel the bed under
me and I couldn't think what I was I couldn't think of my name
I couldn't even think I am a girl I couldn't even think I . . . then
all of a sudden . . . it was like the wind came and blew me back
from where it was I was not"* (115). In these instances and
others, Darl tacitly establishes the pattern that she unknowingly repeats in her own terms.

The relationship between Darl and Dewey Dell, desperate
children of disastrous parents, is as intense and destructive as
that of Quentin and Caddy in *The Sound and the Fury* or
Henry and Judith in *Absalom, Absalom!,* and more so than
that of Horace and Narcissa in *Flags in the Dust* and *Sanctuary*
or Jody and Eula Varner in *The Hamlet.* In perhaps the book's
central thematic statement, Darl recognizes the repetition and
failure that, fatalistically, he sees defining both the history of
humankind and the family on their outrageous journey: "How

do our lives ravel out into the no-wind, no-sound, the weary
gestures wearily recapitulant: echoes of old compulsions with
no-hand on no-strings: in sunset we fall into furious attitudes,
dead gestures of dolls." The key phrase, itself one more weary
gesture, is recapitulated, echoed, a page later: "If you could just
ravel out into time. That would be nice. It would be nice if you
could just ravel out into time" (198). Darl associates life's
circular progress with the contours of the land: "Life was
created in the valleys. It blew up onto the hills on the old
terrors, the old lusts, the old despairs. That's why you must
walk up the hills so you can ride down" (217)—contours
repeated in the body of Dewey Dell, that most aptly named
and, by her brother, most intimately visualized of all Faulknerian females. Darl regards with titillation and horror "those
mammalian ludicrosities which are the horizons and the valley
of the earth" (156) and, lower down, "that lever which moves
the world; one of that caliper which measures the length and
breadth of life" (97-98). She responds—fantasy or memory?—
with a description of being stripped by Darl's eyes: "The land
runs out of Darl's eyes; they swim to pinpoints. They begin at
my feet and rise along my body to my face, and then my dress is
gone; I sit naked on the seat above the unhurrying miles, above
the travail" (115). Whether or not incest has literally trans-
pired remains uncertain, but lust and despair and proximity
together seem to explain this, the most intense of the book's
relationships: their mutual fixation, her insistence that *"He'll
do as I say. He always does. I can persuade him to anything,"*
her vision of killing him, his bitter mocking of her pregnancy,
and her betrayal and fierce attack on him at the end.[5]

Darl's aberrance manifests itself in various ways even
before it emerges full-blown late in the book: describing himself in the third person; hearing the flood waters (134) and
then Addie's corpse (202) talk to him; his maniacal laughter.
Yet with "the supreme lucidity of the mad,"[6] Darl perceives
the greater madness of the journey and tries to halt it: he
refuses to help rescue Addie's coffin from the flood and he
desperately fires Gillespie's barn in hopes of destroying it.

Failing totally, he weeps in despair, elicits exactly the wrong kind of solicitude from the misapprehending Vardaman— "You needn't to cry. . . . Jewel got her out"—and succeeds only in providing the rationale for the family's having him committed since the alternative is to pay for the barn. Inevitably, his powerful, odd presence has great impact on Vardaman, the family's youngest, who often echoes and repeats Darl's ideas and phrases, even his extrasensory perception. For example, Darl describes the scene of his taking Vardaman to hear Addie's corpse speak: "The breeze was setting up from the barn, so we put her under the apple tree, where the moonlight can dapple the apple tree upon the long slumbering flanks within which now and then she talks in little trickling bursts of secret and murmurous bubbling. I took Vardaman to listen. When we came up the cat leaped down from it and flicked away with silver claw and silver eye into the shadow" (202). Vardaman's version uncannily recounts the experience in nearly identical terms: "She was under the apple tree and Darl and I go across the moon and the cat jumps down and runs and we can hear her inside the wood. . . . I put my ear close and I can hear her. Only I cant tell what she is saying" (204). Even more striking, Darl's beginning his last section with "Darl has gone to Jackson" *follows* rather than precedes Vardaman's reiterated *"Darl went to Jackson. . . . He went crazy and went to Jackson both* (239-42) in the previous section. It is almost as if Vardaman has been training all along to succeed his farsighted brother—and does so at the end.

Just as Darl's narrative impossibly transcends time and space, so Vardaman's employs a language and insight impossible for a five-year-old. Shaken both by catching a large fish and by Addie's death, two nearly simultaneous occurrences, he confounds them in his reiterated, "My mother is a fish." Instinctively denying what he can neither comprehend nor accept, Vardaman hysterically demands to know whether Cash will nail her in his coffin, insists that "It was not her. . . . It was not my mother" lying there not moving, opens the window and then bores holes in the coffin for her to breathe (thereby putting two in her face). Addie, he maintains, would resist what they are doing to her, "And so if she lets him it is not her." In fact, he adds, "I was there. I saw when it did not be her"; therefore, everything is changed, different from what it was, especially Addie and the fish: "It was not her because it was laying right yonder in the dirt. And now it's all chopped up. I chopped it up. It's laying in the kitchen in the bleeding pan, waiting to be cooked and et. Then it wasn't and she was, and now it is and she wasn't."

Having driven off Dr. Peabody's horses for bringing him, as he thinks, to kill her ("she was all right but he came and did it"), he now seeks out Tull who, having been first to describe the fish, could confirm the moment when it lay in the dust and Addie was still alive. Tull quotes Vardaman, having come through the stormy night, as saying: "You was there. You seen it laying there. Cash is fixing to nail her up, and it was a-laying right there on the ground. You seen it. You seen the mark in the dirt. The rain never come up till after I was a-coming here. So we can get back in time" (67). Consciously or not, Vardaman seems to mean several complex things: he wants Tull to help prevent Cash from nailing Addie in the coffin since she could then still be alive; he wants Tull to confirm the enduring existence of that moment they shared before time stopped; and he wants to return to time as it worked before Addie's death ruptured it. But his failure to achieve anything is as great as Darl's; in fact, it reiterates the pattern shared by all the siblings on this journey of loss, for Cash breaks his leg (again), Jewel sacrifices his horse (the only living thing he loved), Dewey Dell fails to get an abortion. Only Anse and Addie, disastrous failures as parents and ostensibly mere creatures of words, translate desire into consummation.

Addie seems, at first, capable of occupying the novel's moral center. Her plight evokes sympathetic attention, as do both her marriage to the parasitical Anse and her frustrated attempt to establish any significant human contact: she whipped her pupils when she was a teacher in order to put her mark on them; she responds genuinely—with pain, fear, pride—to childbirth and mothering; she passionately commits the "utter and terrible" sin with Whitfield. Her intense, active attachment to life remains great even after her death; as Brooks says: "it is obviously her still-vital, implacable energy that enables her family to complete their mission and holds them together as a family until her body is finally deposited in the stipulated grave."[7] Further, Addie alone seems fully to value deeds as opposed to mere intentions, thoughts, mouthings. Sin and salvation, she knows, are just words for Cora; Whitfield fatuously believes he can substitute the will for moral action; Anse, who never sweats, always uses others while denying dependence or obligation: " 'We wouldn't be beholden,' Bundren says. 'I thank you kindly.' " Mastering language so effectively that she can use it over a hundred pages after her death to declare her centrality in the cortege, Addie nonetheless asserts language's failure or limitations as well as her own isolation, for, as Brooks puts it, "With Addie, the loss of community is at the same time a loss of communication. Language seems to her empty and drained and ineffectual."[8] Addie says "that words are no good; that words dont ever fit even what they are trying to say at. . . . I would think how words go straight up in a thin line, quick and harmless, and how terribly doing goes along the earth, clinging to it, so that after a while the two lines are too far apart for the same person to straddle from one to the other."[9]

Addie's use of verticals and horizontals contrasts and reverses Anse's earlier defense of inertia:

the Lord put roads for travelling: why He laid them down flat on the earth. When He aims for something to be always a-moving, He makes it longways, like a road or a horse or a wagon, but when He aims for something to stay put, He makes it up-and-down ways, like a tree or a man. . . . if He'd a aimed for man to be always a-moving and going somewheres else, wouldn't He a put him longways on his belly, like a snake? It stands to reason He would. (34-35)

Dr. Peabody, without knowing the connection, repeats and deflates Anse's nonsense with this tacit refinement: "Too bad the Lord made the mistake of giving trees roots and giving the

Anse Bundrens He makes feet and legs. If He'd just swapped them, there wouldn't ever be a worry about this country being deforested someday. Or any other country" (41). Yet Anse, who incessantly invokes a spirituality everything in his life denies, blames horizontals for Addie's condition: "She was well and hale as ere a woman ever were, except for that road." Similarly, he sees Darl, with "his eyes full of the land,"as crazed by this earth, by restless doing, the opposite of Tull who, with sympathy at least but perhaps no greater insight, maintains, "that's ever living thing the matter with Darl: he just thinks by himself too much."

Anse, who seems nothing but "the shape and echo of his word," is dead for Addie long before she is for him, only "He did not know he was dead" (166). Never fully alive in his self-centered and bullying passivity, Anse understands life no more than he does death; for him, both are things to be used, as he uses his tortured children and Addie's stinking corpse to get to Jefferson—where new teeth and "a kind of duck-shaped woman . . . with . . . hard-looking pop eyes," the new Mrs. Bundren, await him. Addie, despairing of the world to which she clings, twice quotes with approval her father's saying "that the reason for living was to get ready to stay dead a long time," an image of the vertical metamorphosed into the horizontal. She knows about life and death, and about the relationship between them, and that they require doing and being, an active and literal assertion of selfhood against all mortal odds.

Yet Addie's failure as moral model is signaled from the book's title, with its tension between the dynamic and static, active and passive. It evokes Homer's Agamemnon, another victim of both external and internal forces who, impossibly, reflects on his own death. During his visit to the Underworld in book 11 of *The Odyssey,* an amazed Odysseus hears the shade of the once mighty Agamemnon relate how, on his return home, he was both murdered and scorned by the faithless Clytemnestra: "as I lay dying with a sword through my body: the bitch turned her back, she would not take the trouble to draw down my eyelids or to close my mouth in death."⁹ Like Clytemnestra, Addie seeks an ultimate retribution from the man who has violated and betrayed her: "my revenge would be that he would never know I was taking revenge. And when Darl was born I asked Anse to promise to take me back to Jefferson when I died" (164-65). Like Agamemnon. however, Addie, while in the extraordinarily powerful position of narrating death first-hand and retrospectively, can destroy only her children and not the spouse she hates. Reduced first to a rotting corpse and then to words, Addie not only fails to gain her revenge, she becomes, ironically, Anse's means of triumphing in the end.

As I Lay Dying demands many things of its readers: acceptance of multiple impossible narrations, concern for its numerous unappealing characters, vicarious participation in their desperate odyssey and destructive parody of family life. In compensation, it offers ease of access into variously disturbed minds, a clear pattern of external events and a more subtle one of verbal and imagistic complexity, and much grotesque humor. The result, a pattern that both Brooks and Minter find simultaneously heroic and preposterous,¹⁰ inevitably creates a good deal of uneasiness—for both narrative structure and characterization disorient and hold us at a distance, as Faulkner clearly intended, but at greater cost to our sympathetic engagement with both the characters and their travails than some readers may be willing to pay. *As I Lay Dying* is the most accessible of Faulkner's major novels but it is, ultimately, the least compelling.

Light in August

Light in August is unique among Faulkner's novels not in its obsessive, reiterated failures but in the framing context in which its gothic horrors occur: kindliness, serenity, motion that is linear and progressive, natural fecundity. The novel begins and ends with Lena Grove—first pregnant then, lighter in August, a mother—as she journeys, aided only by the instinctive generosity of strangers, from Alabama to Mississippi (where the novel's action occurs) and then to Tennessee. Tracking Lucas Burch, her baby's father, she seems almost indifferent to his fleeing from her when they finally meet in the novel as he had after impregnating her. Her serenity, in fact, is threatened only when, right after the birth, it seems that she might actually reclaim Lucas and lose Byron Bunch, the novel's quixotic hero who, on sight, falls hopelessly in love with her. By the end, Lucas has come to seem far more traveling's excuse than its goal, the putative quest for respectability allowing Lena—as the amused furniture dealer who narrates the last chapter in bed to his wife expresses it—"to travel a little further and see as much as she could, since I reckon she knew that when she settled down this time, it would likely be for the rest of her life."

Settling down, domesticity, is exactly what fails all of the other major characters in the novel, and vice versa; burdened with inherited visions of disaster and doom, they are incapable of defining viable roles for themselves as spouses, parents, or children.[11] They remain outsiders, strangers, wherever they live, and consequently destroy those closest to them and themselves. Lacking the immediacy of parental influence, Joe Christmas, Joanna Burden, and the Reverend Gail Hightower are all literally or figuratively haunted by monomaniacal grandfathers who seem bent on denying them the unique origins and individuality common to the rest of humankind.[12]

Faulkner has said that he began the novel with the placid image of Lena en route to give birth but that Christmas, most obsessed of all his characters with his origins and most ignorant of them, defines "the tragic, central idea of the story—that he didn't know what he was, and there was no way possible in life for him to find out. Which to me is the most tragic condition a man could find himself in—not to know what he is and to know that he will never know" (F in U, 72). His grandfather Hines, we learn late in the novel, had killed his daughter's lover because he was convinced he had black blood;

he then refused his daughter a doctor, and so caused her to die in childbirth. Left on the doorstep of an orphanage on Christmas eve, the baby received the name that marks him as an alien, a pariah, all his life:

"Is he a foreigner?"
"Did you ever hear of a white man named Christmas?" the foreman said.
"I never heard of nobody a-tall named it," the other said. (29)

Joe's years in the orphanage are literally watched over "with a profound and unflagging attention" by the "mad eyes" of Hines whose presence, as janitor, thus sets Joe apart from the other children, who ridicule him with the taunt of "nigger." Adopted at the age of five by the Calvinist Simon McEachern, Joe moves from one religious fanaticism to another. Enduring a harsh upbringing (he is beaten when he fails, or refuses, to learn the catechism), he acquires neither self-understanding nor knowledge of how to survive in a world of ambivalent demands and offers, but only the self-stigmatizing label "nigger" that he claims for himself at the most inconvenient times. When actually asked directly, however, he acknowledges ignorance, and then wryly adds, "If I'm not, damned if I wasted haven't a lot of time" (241).

Not surprisingly, Joe's greatest failures are with females, whom he finds totally unpredictable and, therefore, untrustworthy: the girl in the orphanage who befriends him and then suddenly disappears; the dietician who frightens him with a bribe to keep quiet about her sex in the afternoon when he, ignorant of what he has witnessed, expects to be punished for spying; Mrs. McEachern whose "soft kindness" he finds far more threatening than his foster father's dependable beatings; the black girl whose sexuality confuses him at fourteen, and whom he beats rather than partake of communal copulation; Bobbie, the waitress/prostitute who introduces him to sex but then, in a shock to his naïvete, refuses to marry him after he has beaten and perhaps killed McEachern when the latter finds them at a dance; and, finally, Joanna Burden whose fierce

carnality had corrupted *him* for two years and whose subsequent religiosity, arousing old desperation, spurs him to
murder her and leads to his own death. Such a pattern, explica-
ble as neither accident nor coincidence, would seem to validate
the obsessive attacks by Joe's grandfather and foster father on
what they call "womanflesh" and "bitchery," for Joe is the
perfect product and exemplar of both in action—except that,
as the novel also emphasizes, they have created him as a kind
of justification, a self-fulfilling prophecy: his life and death
validate their visions and actions.

Joe thus remains variously defined and distanced throughout
the novel, the unwilling recipient of numerous imposed
identities. As Alfred Kazin puts it: "he is seen as what others
say about him, he is only a thought in other people's minds. . . .
Joe Christmas is an abstraction seeking to become a human
being. . . . Everyone wants to play God to the orphan Joe
Christmas."[13] A tabula rasa, he is constantly being created by
others but never actually allowed to exist. Consequently,
"Almost everything we learn about Joe Christmas comes to us
in the form of hearsay, accusation, the tortured memories of
others; even his death is told as an incident in the life of his
murderer, Percy Grimm. All these reports about the stranger
sufficiently suggest his alienation. But in themselves they also
create that stillness, that depth of meditation into which all the
characters are plunged."[14] No character in the book plunges
more desperately than Joe into both thought and action; but,
remaining peripheral and fragmented, he never manages to
make them cohere.

Though Joanna Burden, too, ultimately seeks to have her
will of him, her story strongly parallels Joe's and is inextricably
linked to it. She has lived all her life in the house in which "she
was born, yet she is still a stranger, a foreigner whose people
moved in from the North during Reconstruction." Like Joe's,
her grandfather, aptly named Calvin Burden, had killed in
self-righteous defense of his beliefs and bullied his family
about hell and damnation, beating "the loving God" into his
children. Murdered along with Joanna's brother by Colonel

Sartoris for defending Negro voting rights after the Civil War, he leaves Joanna burdened by his passion and vision. She devotes herself not only to improving Negro education throughout the South, but also to assisting neighboring blacks who bring her their personal problems. She is, in fact, shunned locally as a "nigger lover"—though as soon as her death is discovered, the town righteously determines to lynch *her* "nigger lover." Like Joe, Joanna continually initiates the actions that victimize her: her rape by Joe, their violent and corrupting sensuality, her death. Once the "imperious and fierce" sex between them is finished and she finally surrenders her lust for damnation, she turns to her grandfather's religiosity and attempts both to make Joe pray and to impose on him what he has ostensibly sought all along: identity as a Negro. But Joe's need is for certitude, not merely a role to play—and certainly not for an imposed one—and he reacts, as they both surely knew he would, as though their fates were long since determined.

Although we learn this later, Joe's murder of Joanna and his setting fire to her house occur almost exactly as the novel begins, for Lena's first sight of Jefferson the next morning is of a sky filled with smoke (26). The murder is, in fact, one of those key Faulknerian moments that is always past or imminent but never present, always envisioned or revised rather than actually represented. Thus, the image of that smoke— "impregnable as a monument" (277)—pervades the novel's present even before we know its significance, and the murder is recounted by several characters, none of whom witnessed it; yet its occurrence is forestalled by flashback and inertia, and then elided at the crucial moment. In Chapter 4, Byron tells Hightower about the murder and the fire; Chapter 5, which concerns Joe's actions leading up to them, builds on the refrain *"Something is going to happen to me. I am going to do something"* (97, 110; Faulkner's italics)—which recurs on page 261 after a long temporal suspension, initiated by "Memory believes before knowing remembers" (111) that focuses first on Joe's and then on Joanna's past. The phrase

"Then it was time" (266) both clicks us back into the present and signals that it is time for the murder. Yet even when we finally come to it, we experience not the event itself but a false tableau—Joanna about to shoot Joe—followed by a gap and then his flight. Only before and after do we learn that during that gap he slit her throat after the gun misfired. Thus, as often occurs in Faulkner, the climactic moment is both inevitable and avoided, so much determined by historical processes and the atemporal dance of Faulkner's narrative that it seems long past, long since become grist for revisionist scrutiny, without ever bothering simply to occur. And this absence at the center of the novel's action parallels that at the center of Joe Christmas—the doomed quester seeking an unknowable identity.

Like other Faulkner characters who embody such inevitability—he and Joanna "would not let one another alone"—Joe despairs of human initiative: "he believed with calm paradox that he was the volitionless servant of the fatality in which he believed that he did not believe. He was saying to himself *I had to do it* already in the past tense; *I had to do it. She said so herself*" (264). Past and future blur, become one: " 'Maybe I have already done it,' he thought. 'Maybe it is no longer now waiting to be done' " (104). Paradoxically, such a perspective, instead of denying the present, ultimately denies all else. "There is no such thing as *was*—only *is*," Faulkner has said (*Lion*, 255). Time becomes spatial when all moments become contemporaneous "since all that had ever been was the same as all that was to be, since tomorrow to-be and had-been would be the same" (266).

Joe, then, is both free and trapped. He is released for flight with the death of Joanna's corrupting constraints, relieved of responsibility for a murder that she and fate willed and contrived, beyond time's orderly progression (as indicated by sudden shifts in verb tenses) and such regular needs as food and sleep. Yet his journey, unlike Lena's, is circular, regressive. Hers is predicated on self-knowledge and serendipity, openness to new experience; his is a desperate hurtling toward

certitude and identity that, once found, will both define and
doom him: "It seemed to him that he could see himself being
hunted by white men at last into the black abyss which had
been waiting, trying, for thirty years to drown him and into
which now and at last he had actually entered, bearing now
upon his ankles [he has just donned Negro brogans to fool the
bloodhounds on his trail] the definite and ineradicable gauge
of its upward moving" (313). That image of negritude rising
from the ground to claim him is repeated with a vengeance
just before Joe's capture, which he had sought, is announced:
" 'I have been further in these seven days than in all the thirty
years,' he thinks. 'But I have never got outside that circle. I have
never broken out of the ring of what I have already done and
cannot ever undo,' he thinks quietly, . . . the black shoes
smelling of negro: that mark on his ankles the gauge definite
and ineradicable of the black tide creeping up his legs, moving
from his feet upward as death moves" (321). The circle closes
with the reappearance of his grandfather Hines—"coldly and
violently fanatical and a little crazed." Still obsessed with Joe
and his begetting—"It's God's abomination of womanflesh!"—he strikes him and tries to arouse a lynch mob, and so
sets the stage for Joe's final flight to castration, death, and
identity: "from out the slashed garments about his hips and
loins the pent *black* blood seemed to rush like a released
breath.... upon that *black* blast the man seemed to rise soaring
into their memories forever and ever" (440; my italics). Only
in journey's end does this lost soul—who could live neither
within nor "outside the human race" (*F in U*, 118)—achieve a
Lena-like harmony and meaning, for his memory, we are told,
"will be there, musing, quiet, steadfast, not fading and not
particularly threatful, but of itself alone serene, of itself alone
triumphant."

Gail Hightower's is yet another version of the novel's
central story, and since it is told in the novel's third and
penultimate chapters, it serves as a kind of double counterpoint: a frame within a frame. Like Joe and Joanna, Hightower
inherits and inhabits a grandfather's vision rather than

imagines one of his own—"as though the seed which his grandfather had transmitted to him had been on the horse too that night and had been killed too and time had stopped there and then for the seed and nothing had happened in time since, not even him" (59). He came to Jefferson as "toward the consummation of his life" (456), it being where his swashbuckling grandfather had died, only to fail disastrously himself: "It was as if he couldn't get religion and that galloping cavalry and his dead grandfather shot from the galloping horse untangled from each other, even in the pulpit" (56). Having first driven his wife to madness, illicit sex, and suicide, and then lost both his church and *the* Church, Hightower refuses to leave Jefferson even after he is threatened and beaten. Byron knows what holds him: "A man will talk about how he'd like to escape from living folks. But it's the dead folks that do him the damage. It's the dead ones that lay quiet in one place and dont try to hold him, that he can't escape from." Like Joe, Hightower had vainly sought a separate peace, the kind implicit in the surname half of his divided self: "it seemed to him that he could see his future, his life, intact and on all sides complete and inviolable, like a classic and serene vase, where the spirit could be born anew sheltered from the harsh *gale* of living" (453; my italics). But this ethereal self-image clashes impossibly with Hightower's failure to find peace and meaning in being the son of his father, a man of contradictions whose actions often negated his coldly uncompromising convictions. He was "a minister without a church and a soldier without an enemy," whose abhorrence of slavery compelled him neither to "eat food grown and cooked by, nor sleep in a bed prepared by, a negro slave" but which somehow allowed him to participate— albeit as a noncombatant—in the long and bloody struggle to perpetuate slavery. He lived a life that, for Hightower, was devoid of purpose and, therefore, no more real for him than Joanna's father was for her. Instead, like Faulkner's South itself, Hightower expresses a forlorn, prelapsarian identity, "full of galloping cavalry and defeat and glory," one associated with his grandfather's "swagger, his bluff and simple adherence to a simple code." " 'So it's no wonder,' he thinks, 'that I skipped a generation. It's no wonder that I had no father and that I had already died one night twenty years before I saw light. And that my only salvation must be to return to the place to die where my life had already ceased before it began' " (452).

But Hightower's story becomes a repetition with a difference, for unlike Joe and Joanna he undergoes a kind of gestation during the course of the novel. Recipient of Byron's confidences and startling news about Lena and Christmas, Hightower at first remains passive and then rejects reinvolving himself in human affairs: "I am not in life anymore." Furthermore, he urges Byron to flee Lena and mocks him as "the guardian of public weal and morality." But in the end, and despite his name and instincts, Gail Hightower is neither obsessed nor aloof; he responds not only to Byron's goodness but to Byron's evocation of his own: he silently blesses Byron for ignoring his advice, successfully delivers Lena's baby, and later tries to save Joe after earlier having refused to do so. After the birth Hightower feels triumphant and purposeful for the first time in twenty-five years ("Life comes to the old man yet"), foresees many more babies for Lena—by Byron, and mourns Joanna: "Poor, barren woman. To have not lived only a week longer, until luck returned to this place" (385). And though he weeps like a newborn at his forced reentry into life, he finally does what Joe never could: confronts the truth about his grandfather (a murderer and a chicken thief) and about what he had done to his wife: "I became her seducer and her murderer, author and instrument of her shame and death" (462). He had offered his congregation, he now realizes, not pity and love but "a swaggering and unchastened bravo killed with a shotgun in a peaceful henhouse, in a temporary hiatus of his own avocation of killing" (462). The book's last view of Hightower is ambiguous, for, thinking he is dying, he hears again "the wild bugles and the clashing sabres and the dying thunder of hooves"—though it may be that Hightower does survive (as Faulkner insists in an interview [*F in U,* 75]) while the sound in his head finally dies, and that he is at last free to envision some viable identity of his own.

The novel ends more or less where it began—with Lena Grove on the road, passively bemused by experience, reiterating her sense of wonder and openness: "My, my. A body does get around" (26, 94, 480)—though now toting her infant and accompanied by Byron who *"had done desperated himself up"* enough to cast his lot with her (479). The novel began with a tableau, a vision of terrific immobility: "Sitting beside the road, watching the wagon mount the hill toward her, Lena thinks, 'I have come from Alabama: a fur piece. All the way from Alabama a-walking. A fur piece.' Thinking . . ."—the four present participles in the first four lines serving to link active and passive modes, action and contemplation, momentum and stasis—inertia in both its senses. The language associated with Lena throughout has this same double quality: "Her voice is quiet, dogged. Yet it is serene"; "Her face is calm as stone, but not hard", tranquil and hearty decorum"; "serene pride"; "interested, tranquil"—the language not of tidal waves or hurricanes, but of "the untroubled unhaste of a change of season": incremental, unnoticed, inevitable. Her journey is "like something moving forever and without progress across an urn," almost a reversal of motion: "backrolling now behind her a long monotonous succession of peaceful and undeviating changes from day to dark and dark to day again." She and the wagon that is about to contain her "draw slowly together as the wagon crawls terrifically toward her in its slow palpable aura of somnolence and red dust." And with her in it, "The wagon goes on, slow, timeless."

The vision is one compounded of intense summer heat, vast quantities of dust, and "a lambence, a luminous quality to the light, as though it came not from just today but from back in the old classic times. It might have fauns and satyrs and the gods. . . . Maybe the connection was with Lena Grove, who had something of that pagan quality of being able to assume everything" (*F in U*, 199). Lena represents not the obsessive repetition of past failures—as do Christmas, Burden, and Hightower—but the repetition of seasons, waves, fecundity, the reiterated ancient rhythms that endure man's violence and disasters. Lena's story and vision do not, unfortunately, negate these others, but they provide them a structural and thematic context, a mode of containment. Faulkner takes a great risk here, for we might be tempted to assume that Lena's unreflective and sheeplike progress is meant as a moral exemplum; but he is not so simple as to advocate that we eschew evil and self-destruction by becoming as are the beasts of the fields. Lena is, after all, more comic caricature than believable character, an assurance that life has its triumphs despite, if not because, of all man's efforts. It may be a weakness of *Light in August*—as the most common criticism of the book maintains[15]—that its contradictory stories live together most uncomfortably, but this is no truer within its confines than outside of them.

tion as a form of recreation, of play or trial—accounts not only for the relationship between *Sanctuary* and *Requiem,* but also for much that occurs within each of them, since virtually everything in them is variously repeated. At the beginning of *Sanctuary,* for example, we get a typical pairing: not just one visit to the Old Frenchman place but two—first that of Horace Benbow, and second that of Gowan Stevens and Temple Drake—and then numerous retellings of both. A series of echoes of the first visit in the second creates a pattern of repetition, though always with a difference. Retrospectively, we see that both the initial visit—for all the ominousness with which it is depicted—and its retellings are trivial, minor versions of the second, which it foreshadows. Thus, Horace's indiscreet and incessant talk amazes Ruby, who thinks he is crazy; and Tommy, later telling Gowan of Horace's visit, expresses a similar reaction: "He sho was a talker, now. Kep on tellin how he up and quit his wife." But Gowan's and Temple's talk is far more indiscreet and dangerous (especially, as it turns out, for Tommy, who is killed by Popeye while they are there), and several unsuccessful efforts are made to silence them before violence explodes. A verbal echo is heard in Ruby's casually thinking that Horace is a fool, and then both her and Goodwin angrily calling Temple "fool" when things begin to get out of control during her stay. Yet another: Horace at the beginning threatens to run from Popeye but instead passively accepts being temporarily his prisoner, and so receives both food and a ride into Jefferson. In contrast, Temple "rigidly and quietly" watches as Gowan, "apparently looking straight ahead, drove into the tree at twenty miles an hour," and then begins her running at exactly the wrong moment, when it compels the wrong kind of attention. Consequently, she gets raped instead of fed, and driven not home to Jefferson but to a brothel in Memphis.

The two visits are also radically different in their recountings. Allusions to the first are few and insignificant, having no more portentousness than a misremembered date or a casual lie. Popeye, for example, tells Ruby that Horace had asked him if he read books (*S,* 94) when, in fact, it was Popeye who had asked Horace (*S*, 4). But the status of the second visit, and especially of Temple's rape in the corncrib by the impotent Popeye using a corncob, is of a different order: it expands like a myth with each retelling. Even within *Sanctuary*, Temple's rape occurs not just once, but over and over, in a number of forms, variously imagined and expressed. First, Temple previews and even provokes it through her alternately incessant talking and running, both her hysterical fear and what the narrator calls her "taut, toothed, coquetry," what Ruby calls her "Playing at it"—turning it into a kind of game suggestive of storytelling. Then the description of the rape simultaneously suggests both despair and fulfillment on Temple's part, a fearful future become a triumphant present: "She could hear silence in a thick rustling as he [Popeye] moved toward her through it, thrusting it aside, and she began to say Something is going to happen to me. . . . 'Something is happening to me!' she screamed. . . . 'I told you it was!' she screamed, voiding the words like hot silent bubbles into the bright silence about them." Subsequently, we are offered no less than four reconstructions, all different, of the event. First, in a narrative framed by Horace's frenzied insistence that Temple "was all right" (he uses the phrase four times in one short paragraph on page 156, three times on page 160), Ruby recounts what occurred at the Old Frenchman place while Temple was there—though it is uncertain whether she tells Horace of the rape. Later, after Horace discovers her in Miss Reba's brothel, Temple turns the experience into self-dramatization, delivering what the sexist narrator calls "one of those bright, chatty monologues which women can carry on when they realise that they have the center of the stage; suddenly Horace realised that she was recounting the experience with actual pride, a sort of naive and impersonal vanity, as though she were making it up" (208-209).

Third, upon returning to Jefferson and looking at the picture of Little Belle, his lovely adolescent step-daughter toward whom he feels both desire and guilty responsibility, Horace finds his vivid imagination confusing and confounding Temple and Little Belle, himself and Popeye, the past and the fearfully possible. Feeling suddenly ill, he rushes to the bathroom and, in one of the book's most audacious passages, he enters empathetically into both Temple's rape and also imagined future ones:

> He opened the door running and fumbled at the light. But he had not time to find it and he gave over and plunged forward and struck the lavatory and leaned upon his braced arms while the shucks set up a terrific uproar beneath her thighs. Lying with her head lifted slightly, her chin depressed like a figure lifted down from a crucifix, she watched something black and furious go roaring out of her pale body. She was bound naked on her back on a flat car moving at speed through a black tunnel, the blackness streaming in rigid threads overhead, a roar of iron wheels in her ears. The car shot bodily from the tunnel in a long upward slant, the darkness overhead now shredded with parallel attenuations of living fire, toward a crescendo like a held breath, an interval in which she would swing faintly and lazily in nothingness filled with pale, myriad points of light. Far beneath her she could hear the faint, furious uproar of the shucks.[2] (216)

Sanctuary's final version—which, in fact, ultimately provokes yet further retellings in *Requiem*—is offered at Goodwin's trial, during which Temple again holds center stage and again reconstructs the rape—only this time "making it up" with a vengeance, so that Goodwin rather than Popeye is condemned, and then lynched, both for the rape and the murder of Tommy.

The double visitation to the Old Frenchman place early in *Sanctuary*—with only the second actually fulfilling its implicit promise of dire consequences—also parallels and prepares for the two trials and deaths at the end of the novel—only the first of which is horrific and meaningful. The two are identical in some ways: neither Goodwin nor Popeye, at their respective trials, makes any effort to defend himself against false charges, and both are found guilty by juries that take exactly eight minutes to reach a verdict (284, 304). But after Goodwin is murdered and mutilated by a lynch mob, Popeye's execution—

for a murder he did not commit rather than for one of the two he did—is anticlimactic, almost a casual afterthought, and it lacks reverberations. Goodwin's fate, on the other hand, not only shocks Horace into returning to his disastrous marriage in the penultimate chapter of *Sanctuary*, but it also ultimately requires its own recounting: the trial by confession of Temple Drake Stevens, which forms, the bulk of the dramatic parts of *Requiem*.

A trial is, in a sense, a narrative, an attempt to tell a story (or rather to retell it, since its rough outline, at least, is usually known to its participants) in order to arrive at truth, or at least an acceptable version of it—or perhaps only justice. Like a story, then, a trial is never a vision but only a revision, or a version of history, the creating of an official order or meaning out of relics called evidence, conflicting stories called testimony, the rhetoric of partisans. Trials are also tests—a practical "interpreting" of the participants' mettle as well as veracity, or at least credibility, a civilized version of chivalric combat. For all these reasons Faulkner finds legal trials both appropriate and impossible as vehicles for representing the truth about the past—as witness, for example, the zany and inconclusive trials in *The Hamlet, Knight's Gambit*, and the wonderful story, "Barn Burning."

Both *Requiem* and its two trials are not only sequels to *Sanctuary* and its trials, but also, in large part, the same experiences reimagined—though from different points of view, with different intentions, differently motivated and shaped. In essence, the same impulse lies behind *Requiem* as led to the multiple retelling of Caddy Compson's story in *The Sound and the Fury* and Eula Varner's in the Snopes trilogy. The Gavin Stevens we see in the trilogy is entranced by pubescent girls and, as Chick Mallison, his nephew and co-narrator, puts it in *The Mansion*, females "had to be alive for him to notice them, and they had to be in motion to be alive, and the only moment of motion which caught his attention, his eye, was that one at which they entered puberty" (197). As if this description were of himself, Faulkner sets about to create a roll call of repeating young females throughout his fiction: not only Caddy Compson but her daughter Quentin; not only Eula Varner but her daughter Linda; not only Temple Drake in *Sanctuary* but Narcissa Benbow in *Sartoris/Flags in the Dust*, the wonderfully named Dewey Dell in *As I Lay Dying*, and the placidly fertile Lena Grove in *Light in August*. But Faulkner is fascinated by the doubleness of puberty's rhythm—not only the "how" and "why" of the transitional moment into adulthood, but also where it goes: the "so what" and "whither." First the telling, then, and years later, for most of them, the telling yet again in other ways and other contexts.

The linkage I am suggesting here between Faulkner and Gavin Stevens (who is, it should be noted, modeled on Faulkner's mentor, Phil Stone, and not on Faulkner himself) makes it especially appropriate that the themes and values of *Requiem* are largely expressed by Gavin, who appears, with his biography slightly altered, throughout much of the Yoknapatawpha saga. The first stage direction describes him as a seeker and speaker of the good and the noble: "He looks more like a poet than a lawyer and actually is: a bachelor, descendant of one of the pioneer Yoknapatawpha County families, Harvard and Heidelberg educated, and returned to his native soil to be a sort of bucolic Cincinnatus, champion not so much of truth as of justice, or of justice as he sees it, constantly involving himself, often for no pay, in affairs of equity and passion and even crime too among his people, white and Negro both, sometimes directly contrary to his office of County Attorney which he has held for years, as is the present business." In this "present business" Gavin places himself in the odd role of a prosecutor playing defense attorney, a position doubly peculiar since the murder victim is his great-niece and he knows that his client, Nancy Mannigoe, is guilty.

Gavin is, in many ways, a repetition of Horace Benbow of *Sanctuary*. Almost the same age, both are lawyers who defend hopeless causes for the sake of justice; rhetorically excessive speakers whose tongues often get them in trouble; foolish romanticizers who, feeling little love and less desire, become second husbands to totally inappropriate women whom they fail to understand. They are, in effect, one character with two

names. Faulkner's failure to "look up" occurrences in previous
novels leads to such discrepancies as the following: at a crucial
point in telling her story to the governor in *Requiem*, Temple
speaks of her discovery of evil within herself. "It was eight
years ago that Uncle Gavin said—oh yes, he was there too; . . .
said how there is a corruption even in just looking at evil, even
by accident; that you can't haggle, traffic, with putrefaction—
you can't, you don't dare—" (*RN*, 129). Actually, of course, it
was not Gavin but Horace who "was there" in *Sanctuary* and
who said: "there's a corruption about even looking upon evil,
even by accident; you cannot haggle, traffic, with putrefaction"
(*S*, 125). Not surprisingly, then, it is Gavin who speaks the
central thesis of *Requiem:* "The past is never dead. It's not
even past"— one which both justifies and requires Temple to
become a kind of oral historian, struggling to express what she
has experienced but, until now, never confronted.

Requiem for a Nun, which was being written simultaneously as both novel and play, represents the most radical
formalistic experiment of the entire Yoknapatawpha saga:
two counterpointed sections—one narrative, one dramatic—
each divided into three interwoven parts. As always, Faulkner
maintains, perhaps slightly disingenuously, that his experimentation was solely for the purposes of telling his story,
and not for its own sake: "that was the best way to tell that
story. That the story of those people fell into the hard simple
give-and-take of dialogue. The longer—I don't know what you
would call those interludes, the prefaces, preambles, whatever
they are—was necessary to give it the contrapuntal effect
which comes in orchestration, that the hard give-and-take of
the dialogue was played against something that was a little
mystical, made it sharper, more effective, in my opinion. It was
not experimentation, it was simply because to me that seemed
the most effective way to tell that story" (*F in U*, 122).

The three prose sections or prefaces in *Requiem* ("The
Courthouse," "The Golden Dome," and "The Jail") provide
historical and physical context for the dramatic sections—
since the latter, all set in the present and thus at the end of the
process chronicled in the narrative, take place, respectively, in

the courthouse in Jefferson, the Capitol (or golden dome) in Jackson, and the jail in Jefferson. Thus, the narrative anticipates and validates the dramatic, just as, in turn, the dramatic assumes and fulfills the narrative: how and why each of the settings came to be, how they have evolved, what they represent in the life of the community. Further, the two modes intersect and overlap: the dramatic is mainly in the form of a trial, and therefore implies story or narrative; the narrative depicts characters in conflict who, confusedly, attempt to sort out what is happening and why, and who do so in a world they inhabit "like a stage."

The prose sections, with their multifarious, disembodied narrators, are as close as we get to objective chronicling in the book, perhaps in all of Faulkner; but they are, nevertheless, a blend of the tangible and the fanciful, the known and the problematical, what the novel calls "the ephemerae of facts" (*RN*,235), whether concerning the South's past or earlier Faulkner recountings. Their central concern is with history, which for Faulkner is created as much in the present as in the past—or even more so: more an assertion of will and imagination than of events confined to one time and place. The obsession in the first preface, for example, is with records, not because this "meagre, fading, dogeared, uncorrelated, at times illiterate sheaf" contains received or observed wisdom or truth, but because its very existence, the mere fact of its having been accumulated until it becomes "a minuscule of archive," is an act of communal self-assertion that adds up first to a settlement and then, with time and accretion, to a town, and finally to a city. Removed in time and mood from the past, the ever-receding present creates its history in its own terms, so that the fortuitous and obscure sequence by which past becomes present is transformed into something solid, inevitable, the stuff of what the first preface calls "fading corrupted legend." Similarly, the future is a matter of proclamation or pronouncement, the settlement "dubbing itself city as Napoleon dubbed himself emperor and defending the expedient by padding its census rolls." That a specific fact or account may clash with another seems to matter very little, if at all. Four times in the

first preface we are told that there were either three or four
bandits in the jail (5, 6, 7, 32) and that, despite subsequent
legend, it "was impossible" that any of them could have been
the infamous Big Harpe; the preface to Act Three, however,
asserts that there were precisely "four highwaymen, one of
whom might have been the murderer, Wiley Harpe" (229).
The arrival of the mail, we are variously told, occurs every two
weeks (17), bi-monthly (9, 26), "every two or three weeks"
(35), "tri-weekly" (219), or not always "every two weeks, nor
even always every month" (9). Again, what matters is not a
detail or two—when the mail arrives or even its contents—but
that it happens at all: its more or less regular arrival—carried,
amazingly, by an unarmed rider blowing a tin horn through
the "still almost pathless wilderness" that armed parties tra-
verse only with great stealth and trepidation—representing a
kind of validation: the United States in Jefferson, and vice
versa.

The preface to Act Two—"The Golden Dome (Beginning
Was the Word)"—is the most blatant example in the book of
Faulkner's juxtaposing of the factual and the fanciful, and may,
for that reason, be its weakest section. It is half almanac
data—numbers, facts, dates—relating to Jackson, the capital of
Mississippi, and half a poeticization of the world's evolution
from "one vast incubant ejaculation already fissionating in one
boiling moil of litter from the celestial experimental Work
Bench" until the moment of writing: A.D. 1950. Joseph Blotner
says of this section that

In writing "The Golden Dome" he had help ready at hand. Taking
from his bookshelf a copy of *Mississippi: A Guide to the Magnolia
State*, he transcribed almost directly many of the historical facts.
Others he changed or disregarded, such as the fact that the actual
statehouse dome was silver, not gold. The segment requiring nothing
from the guidebook was the best: Faulkner's own tracing of the
evolution from earliest creation of this spot where eventually "this
rounded knob, this gilded pustule" (99) would stand.... He borrowed
from the guidebook at the end when he listed the diversions he called
"chronic": the annual festivals, tournaments, and pageants. He borrowed from no one in the very last line.... he wrote, "Diversions:
acute: Religion, Politics (111)." (Blotner, 1379)

The narrator of this preface is, in a double sense, merely recapitulating what is already written—not only in the guidebook but also in the earth itself, "that long signatureless chronicle," which is time's scratching of a record on what he calls "the broad blank midcontinental page." Thus, the capitol building serves as an appropriate setting for the recapitulation that occurs there in the second dramatic section: Temple's retelling of the *Sanctuary* events for the purpose not of truth or justice or even to save Nancy's life, but for the sake of story itself. "For no more than that," Temple says in amazement. "For no better reason than that. Just to get it told, breathed aloud, into words, sound. Just to be heard by, told to, someone, anyone, any stranger none of whose business it is, can possibly be, simply because he is capable of hearing, comprehending it." And so later she tells the governor: "I can't even bargain with you. You haven't even said yes or no yet, whether you can save her or not, whether you want to save her or not, will consider saving her or not." As Temple knows, saving Nancy's life is the excuse not the goal: "I've got to say it all, or I wouldn't be here. But unless I can still believe that you might say yes, I don't see how I can."

The preface to Act Three brings us full circle, for its locale is again Jefferson and it begins by repeating, with a difference, the opening of the first preface. The book's first line is "The courthouse is less old than the town"; the third preface begins: "So, although in a sense the jail was both older and less old than the courthouse, in actuality, in time, in observation and memory, it was older even than the town itself. Because there was no town until there was a courthouse." The final preface, for all its nostalgia for the South's legendary past and what it calls "the old deathless Lost Cause," is largely the story of the homogenization of the South, the displacement of legend by progress, relentless in all its manifestations: the railroad, the automobile, radio ("one air, one nation"), machines destructive of the family farm, the Depression and federal programs, two world wars, electricity, television, and so on. Qualities once magnificent in scope, if often morally dubious, and that

enabled men with names like Compson and Sartoris and
Ratcliffe and Peabody and Sutpen to conquer a continent and
tame a wilderness are now reduced to a kind of self-parody, to
social decorousness: "the old deathless Lost Cause had become
a faded (though still select) social club or caste, or form of
behavior." Yet the narrator of this preface, perhaps preparing
us for what R. P. Adams calls "Nancy's bare, intransitive
injunction, 'Believe' "[3] in the last dramatic section, asserts a
strong sense of values enduring beneath the faded veneer:
"that steadfast and durable and unhurryable continuity against
or across which the vain and glittering ephemerae of progress
and alteration washed in substanceless repetitive evanescent
scarless waves."

All three prefaces are obsessed with records, versions of
history, the way the past becomes legend. In the first, Ratcliffe
(the ancestor of V. K. Ratliff, Faulkner's major speaker in the
Snopes trilogy) offers the wondrously simple solution to the
surreal problem of Alec Holston's lock, lost during the jail
escape that the narrator calls "a thing not just fantastical but
incomprehensible, not just whimsical but a little terrifying"
since both the huge fifteen-pound lock and an entire wall are
gone. His solution is the one Faulkner attempted all his life:
" 'Put it on the Book,' Ratcliffe said—the Book: not a ledger,
but *the* ledger." That the solution first fails and then succeeds
results from the intrusion of Thomas Jefferson Pettigrew, the
mail carrier. He invokes a greater record than Ratcliffe's
"Book," an Act of the U.S. Congress, to oppose the expediency
of turning the lock into entries on a page, but then acquiesces
in the act's legitimacy as the settlement deems itself a town
through building a courthouse and giving itself *his* name.

The second preface also focuses on the paradoxical struggle
to legislate, and thereby to retell, what is already fixed and
therefore inevitable. Although "this rounded knob, this gilded
pustule" was decreed in the beginning of time, this section
nonetheless details the actions of "men with mouths full of
law" as they fail to accommodate themselves to that inevitable
"until in 1832, perhaps in simple self-defense or perhaps in

simple weariness, a constitution was written designating Jackson as the capital"—thus legislating what was, in a sense, always already there.

The third preface employs the format of a fairy tale, telling and retelling the story of the daughter of the town jailer, "a failed farmer" who had "for his patronymic the designation of the vocation at which he was to fail: Farmer." Like an imprisoned medieval princess, she stands idle and hopeless within "the bower framing a window ... —musing, not even waiting for anyone or anything, as far as the town knew, not even pensive, as far as the town knew: just musing amid her blonde hair in the window facing the country town street, day after day and month after month and—as the town remembered it—year after year for what must have been three or four of them, inscribing at some moment the fragile and indelible signature of her meditation in one of the panes of it (the window): her frail and workless name, scratched by a diamond ring in her frail and workless hand, and the date: *Cecelia Farmer April 16th 1861*." And then a "soldier, gaunt and tattered, battle-grimed and fleeing and undefeated," with whom she exchanges only a momentary look, returns to claim her after the war, carries her off on his big mule—"the frail useless hands whose only strength seemed to be that sufficient to fold the wedding license into the bosom of her dress and then cling to the belt around his waist"—carries her to "Alabama and the small hill farm which had been his father's," where she would bear a dozen sons, "bequeathing to them in their matronymic the heritage of that invincible inviolable ineptitude." But at least as important is her bequeathing of a name and a date on the jail window as a kind of landmark or sign for the curious visitor or implied reader, someone the narrator refers to as "you, a stranger, an outlander say from the East or the North or the Far West" who seeks to read and to understand. For in that scrawl is a story, told and heard over that century in the girl's own idiom—"that voice, that whisper, murmur, frailer than the scent of lavender"—still summonable "out of the town's composite heritage of remembering that long back, told, repeated, inherited." The mere facts, "the roster and chronicle," seem disproportionate, trivial, very much not the stuff of fairy tale—the face at the window unequal to the siren's charm with which it compels a fleeing soldier, the scrawl on the pane inadequate to capture "the will and hope and dream and imagination" of "yourself the stranger, the outlander with a B.A. or (perhaps even) M.A. from Harvard or Northwestern or Stanford, passing through Jefferson by chance or accident on the way to somewhere else." And yet the very disproportion, the inappropriateness, is central: "so vast, so limitless in capacity is man's imagination to disperse and burn away the rubble-dross of fact and probability, leaving only truth and dream."

All of this would seem to suggest an attitude toward facts that is cavalier or whimsical or even contemptuous. Yet Faulkner is quite clear and consistent about facts in *Requiem*, at least about the novel's two central facts: Nancy's killing of Temple's baby and her consequent execution. The first stage direction presents Nancy thus: "She is—or until recently, two months ago to be exact—a domestic servant, nurse to two white children, the second of whom, an infact, she smothered in its cradel two months ago, for which act she is now on trial for her life." But this last is somewhat misleading, for the trial is already completed and, in virtually the first words spoken in Act One, Scene One, the judge pronounces sentence on Nancy: death by hanging. Nowhere in the novel is either Nancy's action or execution ever in doubt; the facts are solid, monumental, twin columns supporting the portico of an antebellum mansion, now reduced to anachronism, to mere façade, in a world that is run on law and order rather than, as Nancy's action seems to urge, on spiritual values. Indeed, the two events have a kind of other-worldly quality, transcending both the common decorum of human behavior and, since they are not actually depicted, the book itself. The novel's dramatic sections are, in fact, framed and confined by death: the acts of infanticide and execution, which (though the killing of the child is recalled in the flashback scene, Act Two, Scene Two) occur outside its boundaries.

What is at stake in *Requiem for a Nun,* then, is neither fact nor act, but coherence and interpretation, motivation and meaning—not what Nancy did but why, and why it serves to compel Temple's narrative. It is not uncommon to see the relationship of *Sanctuary* to *Requiem* as crime and punishment or sin and expiation or innocence and experience—an endless reprise, as Gavin, speaking Temple's thought, puts it, of the seminal moment in *Sanctuary:* "he [Gowan] will wreck the car again against the wrong tree, in the wrong place, and you will have to forgive him again, for the next eight years until he can wreck the car again in the wrong place, against the wrong tree" (*RN,* 206). But for all Temple's efforts to keep the focus on the past, the eight years separating the events of the two novels—with her marriage to Gowan and the birth of their two children—have already witnessed a communally sanctioned form of expiation, while allowing the truth to remain hidden. And it is not the arrival of Pete, Red's younger brother, who comes to blackmail Temple with the letters she wrote to Red in *Sanctuary,* that triggers the disaster in *Requiem,* but rather Temple's response: not horror but fascination, not shame or regret for actions committed but her reawakened desire to repeat them—even at the cost of the marriage and family that had seemed to restore the moral equilibrium. By going off with Pete, then, Temple seeks not to expunge the consequences of her past actions (as she could by paying him blackmail) but to validate them, to reclaim and proclaim them—and she thereby sets in motion the events that lead to the death of her second child and, finally, to the full recounting of the past.

In a sense, then, *Requiem* is both independent of *Sanctuary*—since it contains its own complete cycle of action—and a closely related sequel, since it seeks, at last, to tell the earlier novel straight. This suggests why, despite the form of the dramatic sections of *Requiem,* they are virtually all talk and no action—although, as the prose sections have implied, under certain circumstances talk may well be a kind of supreme action or creative force: "Beginning was the Word." Through-

out both books, in fact, characters are revealed largely by
how—or even whether—they talk, usually with authority and
quantity of talk inversely related. For example, in *Sanctuary*,
Horace's impotence in every action he undertakes is reflected
in his incessant, indiscreet chatter. His sister, Narcissa, on the
other hand, who is thoroughly petty and mean-spirited, "had
never been given to talking, living a life of serene vegetation,"
a life of decorum, fear, and small-town biases. Popeye uses
silence as a weapon, a means of dominance and control. The
old man (Pap) who haunts the first section of *Sanctuary*, seems
horrific not only because he is "Blind and deef both," but also
because he is mute.

Of all the characters in these two books, Temple has the
most interesting, the most complex, relationship to language.
In *Sanctuary* she is a raver, a screamer, and a liar. As if testing
all the possibilities of human speech, putting them on trial,
"Temple moved her mouth as though she were experimenting
with words, tasting them." Her misuse of language is never
more blatant or absurd than in the irrelevant appeal to authority, family, and civilization in her increasingly hysterical
refrain: "My father's a judge" (*S*, 50, 52, 54). As discussed
above, she is also a storyteller, taking great pleasure in recounting various versions of her rape. Ruby, who scorns Temple for
what she calls "Playing at it," for being too gutless to love or
fear, sees her as living *only* in words: "You'll have something
to tell them now, when you get back. Wont you?" But storytelling, for all its power and authority, is a mixed blessing, a tool
more than a goal, and it can serve various purposes; what it
distorts and corrupts in *Sanctuary* it seeks to clarify and reviv-
ify in *Requiem*, but it must be complete, comprehensive, or it
fails the mark. Thus, to Temple's repeated question, "How
much will I have to tell?" the answer is always "Everything"—
and in the end she does. Such story as Temple offers us in the
sequel cannot save the world, or even the one life which is its
ostensible purpose—for Nancy's execution, since it is always
to happen, is in a sense already past. But that death—like
Scheherazade's in *The Arabian Nights*—cannot occur so long

as narration continues. Thus, Temple's finally facing and retelling the *Sanctuary* events, with all their implications and consequences, represents both a hiatus between actions and also a bridge connecting them—for it not only defines the distance that separates them by filling it, but also connects what would otherwise remain void, empty of meaning. The book itself, or at least its dramatic sections, occupies the space between two indissolubly linked actions and thereby suspends causality, for Nancy must remain alive so long as Temple continues to speak. Her extended disquisition, therefore, holds the execution in abeyance until such time as Nancy's action is, if not justified, fully explained and understood, provided with its appropriate moral and verbal validation.

What, finally, are we to make of Nancy, the nun of the title? A "nigger dope-fiend whore," as she is repeatedly called, she serves as link between the past that was and the future that might be. Although both Gowan and Temple would like to believe that their taking her into their home is an act inspired by what Gavin mockingly calls "simple pity and humanity" (*RN*, 69; also 118), both they and we know better. Rather, Nancy represents for Temple both the *Sanctuary* events and their continuance in talk, in recounting. She is Temple's confidante because, as Temple puts it, "Temple Drake, the white woman, the all-Mississippi debutant, descendant of long lines of statesmen and soldiers high and proud in the high proud annals of our sovereign state, couldn't find anybody except a nigger dopefiend whore that could speak her language." But this pattern of reiteration is precisely the one that Nancy—having gotten religion, morality, and thereby become dangerous—seeks to break. Temple's going off with Pete, the novel seems to argue, would be a validation of the *Sanctuary* events and an assertion of a future in its image; Nancy's murder of the infant child who should represent the future—in order to keep Temple, Gowan, and the surviving child together as a family—is the act of a holy fool, of someone who seeks to impose a new message on the world rather than read the one already inscribed there. But is that an unequivocally good thing, as Nancy suggests? Is a devastated home necessarily better than a broken one? Are Nancy's actions, her unblinking serenity in confronting infanticide and execution, her monosyllabic proclamation of faith—in *what,* she cannot or will not say—are these meant to establish a new standard for living and dying? The presence, at the end, of the obtuse jailer who mocks Nancy's faith, mocks her for having faith, seems to provide a final validation for her act—since he is all too easy to reject—and emphasizes the book's rather neat answers to these questions. Yet they remain, for such ultimate questions can never be fully resolved, only answered. And Nancy's action and purpose, as well as her abdication of speech, are both surely terrible.

Requiem is, in many ways, curiously unsatisfactory: the narrative and dramatic sections, though linked, are less than wholly integrated; the drama, purposely devoid of any action, is undramatic; Nancy, who suggests both such other nurturing blacks as Dilsey in *The Sound and the Fury* and an avenging fury, is not so much a fully realized character as a set of postures, a natural force; and the reenvisioning of the *Sanctuary* events—rendering explicit what is subtle and insidious there—sometimes reduces them to formulae and cliché, a moral injunction to choose good and eschew evil. *Requiem*'s duality of intention—both play and novel, both self-contained and a sequel, both historical and contemporary, both intense psychodrama and almanac data—is a source of weakness as well as strength. There are, finally, both power and a kind of hollowness—like a sounding drum—in its restless energy, its attempt to tell a story against the odds, its struggle to assert a rather simple understanding of what Gavin repeatedly calls truth. Faulkner has said that "Failure brings me stimulation to try to do better in each new book. I have something to say, but I know I will not have time to write all the books I want."[4] In the end *Requiem for a Nun,* impossible in its conception and improbable in execution, is, in Faulkner's precise sense of the word and like every trial, a failure.

6

Twice-Told Tales: *The Unvanquished, The Wild Palms, Go Down, Moses*

More than most writers, Faulkner wrote a great deal of what might be called "twice-told tales"[1]—fiction first published as stories in magazines and subsequently revised to become sections of books that are variously called "composites," or "fragmentary novels," or simply collections—though usually their contents interconnect since Faulkner thought "that a book of short stories should be linked together by characters or chronology."[2] Faulkner's motivation was a mixture of the pragmatic and the instinctual: he was, on the one hand, desperate throughout much of his life for whatever cash his stories would bring (since he lived by his two writing careers and sought to minimize his dependency on what he considered his hack work in Hollywood); on the other, he naturally combined the talents of a mosaicist and a weaver, intricately juxtaposing and interweaving the numerous pieces and threads that came to make up the world of Yoknapatawpha. Leslie A. Fiedler goes so far as to assert that "Faulkner is essentially a short story writer,"[3] but the now generally held view is that Faulkner's greatest achievement is the Yoknapatawpha saga as a whole. With "his panoramic vision and his microscopic sight,"[4] Faulkner is at once a miniaturist and a painter of the largest of literary canvases.

117

Of Faulkner's books created by accretion, some are indeed relatively conventional short-story collections. Both *These 13* (1931) and *Doctor Martino and Other Stories* (1934) contain thematically unconnected stories, most of which had been conceived and published separately (Faulkner's inclusion of previously rejected material reflects what Blotner calls "two familiar characteristics: frugality and a dogged confidence in his own work" [Blotner, 693]), and all of which—except for two of *Doctor Martino*'s fourteen stories—are reprinted in Faulkner's *Collected Stories*. Yet even this last named work, containing forty-two distinct and unlinked stories, is printed not in order of the stories' compositions (as such collections often are) but in six thematic or topographical sections: "The Country," "The Village," "The Wilderness," "The Wasteland," "The Middle Ground," "Beyond"—for, as Faulkner maintains, "even to a collection of short stories, form, integration, is as important as to a novel—an entity of its own, single, set for one pitch, contrapuntal in integration, toward one end, one finale" (*Letters*, 278).

Collected Stories (1950) does include several self-contained stories that were first published in magazines and then reworked into novels ("Wash" from *Absalom, Absalom!;* "Centaur in Brass" and "Mule in the Yard" from *The Town*); and it includes one story ("A Bear Hunt") that, with only one change, became part of *Big Woods* (1955). A quasi novel despite being subtitled "The Hunting Stories of William Faulkner," *Big Woods* comprises four stories, including "The Bear" (without section 4)[5] and "The Old People" from *Go Down, Moses,* and "Race at Morning," previously published in magazine form only. The stories alternate with a framing commentary (which Faulkner called "interrupted catalysts" [Blotner, 1522]), which is mostly excerpted from such other works as *Requiem for a Nun,* "Red Leaves," "A Justice," an essay entitled "Mississippi," and "Delta Autumn" again from *Go Down, Moses.* As in *The Portable Faulkner,* which Malcolm Cowley conceived of as "The Saga of Yoknapatawpha County, 1820—1950," Faulkner drew freely on old material in order to create a new thing. *Big Woods* is unified both by its illustrations of hunting and by the thematic connections of its stories: from the ritual hunt and killing of the totemic Old Ben in "The Bear" to the hunting, but sparing, of the magnificent though nonmystical deer in "Race at Morning" so that it may be hunted again the next year. But this hopeful pattern is counterpointed by the book's third feature: the linking commentary, which traces the decline and fall of the South as symbolized by the wilderness—"which man has deswamped and denuded and derivered"—and then concludes the book with this despairing comment drawn from "Delta Autumn": "No wonder the ruined words I used to know don't cry for retribution. The very people who destroyed them will accomplish their revenge." The book, while attractive both conceptually and visually, does not represent a significant achievement; rather, much of the recast material in *Big Woods* (especially that taken from the more carefully integrated *Go Down, Moses*) works better in its earlier context.

Despite occasional exceptions, such as those noted above, Faulkner's adaptation of material generally went from magazine publication (or reject box) to book, not from book to book. In fact, that was his basic creative method during a dozen years that might be called his middle period. Between *Absalom, Absalom!* (1936) and *Intruder in the Dust* (1948) Faulkner failed to write what Blotner calls "a unitary novel controlled by a dominating vision. *The Wild Palms* had paired two stories, whereas *The Unvanquished, The Hamlet,* and *Go Down, Moses* had for the most part comprised disparate units written earlier—scrupulously rewritten and unified though they were" (Blotner, 1179). Often desperate for money, Faulkner naturally sought double publication and payment for his stories; but he also found it creatively congenial to reformulate material already published—usually with "the comic note . . . gradually muted until the dark tone predominated" (Blotner, 1033)—and make it part of a fiction that evolved over three and a half decades. But Faulkner was not straitjacketed by this procedure: "Barn Burning," one of his finest stories, was rejected not only by half a dozen magazines before *Harper's* accepted it, but also by Faulkner himself who, having initially intended it for the opening section of *The Hamlet,* found it tonally inappropriate when he actually came to create the first of his Snopes novels. Something from every novel of this period is included in *The Portable Faulkner* (a first attempt to *un*weave the Yoknapatawpha material so as to tell its story chronologically) but none of them is represented in *Collected Stories*—which may suggest that Faulkner no longer thought of their sections as separate stories. *Knight's Gambit* (1949), a collection of detective stories about Gavin Stevens, is represented in neither *The Portable Faulkner* nor *Collected Stories.* Clearly, then, Faulkner's apprehension of his mythical country developed continuously over the course of his career: he came, with time, to see it increasingly steady and increasingly whole.

The Unvanquished

The Unvanquished is the most upbeat of Faulknerian titles, poles apart from the defeat and despair proclaimed on the covers of such earlier novels as *The Sound and the Fury, As I Lay Dying,* and *Absalom, Absalom!* The book begins not far removed from childhood innocence for the narrator, Bayard Sartoris (Old Bayard of the earlier *Flags in the Dust*), and Ringo, his intimate black companion: "Ringo and I had been born in the same month and had both fed at the same breast and had slept together and eaten together for so long that Ringo called Granny 'Granny' just like I did, until maybe he wasn't a nigger anymore or maybe I wasn't a white boy anymore, the two of us neither, not even people any longer." All of the book's stories except the last two take place during the Civil War and, therefore, represent stages both in the crumbling and defeat of the South and in the maturation primarily of Bayard and, secondarily, of Ringo. In the final section, both Bayard (now a law student) and the South must reevaluate how to live: by continuing to kill and die for the immoral Lost Cause or by transcending the cycle of destruction and death. Unarmed, Bayard courageously stares down his father's killer, and so breaks the pattern of revenge.

In the first of the book's seven sections, "Ambuscade," the two boys, who have been playing at the war the men are off fighting in earnest, ambush a Yankee soldier using the long, heavy "captured musket which [Colonel Sartoris] had brought home from Virginia two years ago." They are saved from Union troops by hiding under Granny's skirts, by her denying their very existence, and by the Yankee colonel's gallant willingness to believe the blatant lie. Yet even this lightest of episodes (light because, having killed horse rather than rider, the boys are in no real danger) has its serious overtones—not only the fact that it ends with Granny's praying forgiveness for her lying and washing out the boys' mouths for cursing (actions repeated like refrains in later episodes), but, more importantly, for its initiating the novel's three most powerful themes: men going off to war, and war coming home to those left behind; the education of Bayard and his fall into experience (which he ultimately transcends in the book's final section); the translation of myth into history.

Even in this first episode the older Bayard expresses this double perspective when he describes his father: "He was not big; it was just the things he did, that we knew he was doing, had been doing in Virginia and Tennessee, that made him seem big to us." As with sight, so too with smell—"that odor in his clothes and beard and flesh too which I believed was the smell of powder and glory, the elected victorious but know better now: know now to have been only the will to endure." From near but never total idolatry for his father Bayard, in the key moment of mature choice in the book's final section, ultimately repudiates and transcends all he represents. The pattern established in the first six sections is one of success mocked or reduced to an "ash pile"—like the plantation house in section 2, the burning of which follows two remarkable triumphs: the accidental capture of a Yankee camp by Colonel Sartoris and the two boys, and Granny's managing to return home with her wagon and treasure chest after the theft of her mule team.

Though the emphasis in the book, as compared to the earlier stories, is far more on "destruction and death" (Blotner, 1033), its tone is still often comic, especially in the sequence concerning Granny's conning of hundreds of mules from the Union Army in order to sell them back, and in the boys' innocent (though changing) perspectives on adult matters like violence and sex. There is humor in the outrageous success of these three partners in crime, just as there is in the fury and frustration of the Yankee lieutenant who finally puts them out of business: " 'I'd rather engage Forrest's whole brigade every morning for six months than spend that same length of time trying to protect United States property from defenseless Southern women and niggers and children. Defenseless!' he shouted. 'Defenseless!' " And there is humor in the lieutenant's plea that Granny not turn the ten-dollar voucher he gives her for damaging her corral into one for a thousand dollars that he, a poor man, would have to make good—for it acknowledges her ability to continue manipulating an invading army as she wishes.

But Granny's authority rests on faith and morality, not comic caricature, qualities in scarce supply in Faulkner's South or Civil War—where even the septuagenarian Uncles Buck and Buddy, so far ahead of their time in their treatment of both blacks and poor whites that the South lacks a name for it, are eager to kill Yankees. It is, perhaps, comic that Granny washes the boys' mouths with soap every time they utter so much as a damn, but it is profoundly serious when, revealing her motives, she prays in the most uncompromising terms for forgiveness for the sins she has caused them to commit: " 'I did not sin for gain or for greed,' Granny said. 'I did not sin for revenge. I defy You or anyone to say I did. I sinned first for justice. And . . . I sinned for the sake of food and clothes for Your own creatures who could not help themselves—for children who had given their fathers, for wives who had given their husbands, for old people who had given their sons to a holy cause, even though You have seen fit to make it a lost cause.' " The irony of Granny's situation lies not only in the ultimate futility of seeking to assert human concern in the midst of conflagration (especially one whose cause is mistakenly read as morally justifiable), but that she is first betrayed to the Union Army by a Southerner, Ab Snopes, and then murdered by Grumby's Independents, a gang of Southern looters, preying on women, old men, and blacks.

Granny, who had seemed at first merely a genius of comic invention, proves herself a tragic anachronism before her death. Repeating the folly of the South as a whole, "she still believed that what side of a war a man fought on made him what he is"—yet the Yankees who catch her red-handed treat her gallantly; Southerners, whom she presumes share her sense of honor and decency, kill her. Her revenge, accomplished by Bayard and Ringo, is inevitable in the context of the Southern code, easy because merely physical (the real challenge, Bayard knows, was to prevent her walking into the trap), futile since it only validates the repeated pattern of death and negation, and yet ultimately traumatic—as recollections of it in the last section of the novel emphasize. Appropriately, its backdrop is the end of the war—another defeat.

The book's last two sections concern war's aftermath: the Southern pretense that it never happened—despite the "burned towns and houses and ruined plantations and fields inhabited only by women"—that nothing has changed. The women still maintain the mythical "heritage of courageous men and spotless women," the men their cowardly dominance over the powerless: Colonel Sartoris murders two federal officials sent to assure Negro voting rights and he insures that the vote goes openly and unanimously against the black candidate, while surviving soldiers of the "lost cause" mindlessly cheer him on. Ringo has it right when he pronounces, "This war ain't over. Hit just started good."

The final section, "An Odor of Verbena," begins with Bayard's being summoned home from law school by Ringo, who informs him that his father has been killed. The counterpoint of this section, climaxing in Bayard's confrontation with Redmond, his father's killer, juxtaposes pressures for and against revenge. Expected to behave as what he now is, "The Sartoris," and as his father would, and as he himself did in killing Grumby and nailing his body to a door in order to avenge his grandmother's murder, Bayard increasingly acknowledges other truths, other codes: *"Who lives by the sword shall die by it"* and *"Thou shalt not kill."* During the ride home, Bayard recalls the various killings his father had committed, his organizing night riders to keep the blacks subjugated, and his destroying the partnership and friendship with Redmond due to "Father's violent and ruthless dictatorialness and will to dominate." Learning that his father died in a fair fight, Bayard is confirmed in his determination to confront Redmond alone and unarmed despite the expectations of his father's widow— "the hysterical priestess of a rite, a destructive force, she urges upon Bayard the dueling pistols with which to avenge his father"[6]—and his old army troops. The real danger for Bayard is not that he will succumb to external pressures he considers invalid but that in rejecting them he will seem—or be—a coward.

Bayard realizes almost from the first of "An Odor of Verbena" that killing Redmond or being killed by him is really not the issue for him; but confronting him fearlessly is. He thinks, self-reflexively, "who would not die (I knew that) but who maybe forever after could never again hold up his head." And in the frozen moment of confrontation the pattern established by the book's first six sections and by the South itself— startling triumphs fashioned out of myth, and always followed by disastrous defeats—is challenged and perhaps shattered: "we did not speak; I just walked steadily toward him as the pistol rose from the desk. I watched it, I could see the foreshortened slant of the barrel and I knew it would miss me though his hand did not tremble." After firing two shots that hit nothing, Redmond walks bravely through the crowd of Sartoris supporters that thinks he has killed Bayard, never looks back, and simply leaves Jefferson and Mississippi forever. Bayard's action may be viewed as extraordinarily foolish but, as Brooks says, it "is the culminating step in his initiation into manhood and moral responsibility."[7] What Bayard gains are not only personal accolades but an acknowledgment not unlike that which terminates the revenge pattern of *The Oresteia:* "Maybe you're right, maybe there has been enough killing in your family." Though lacking divine intervention, Bayard's reversal of the ancient mythic pattern of revenge, if not a repudiation of all that has gone before, is an especially admirable refusal to keep on replicating it. As death and defeat are finally turned to triumph, the book's title, seemingly ironic in each of the first six sections, gains powerful validation.

The Wild Palms

Faulkner's next book, *The Wild Palms,* is even more oddly constructed than *The Unvanquished,* a *Bildungsroman* in the guise of a short-story collection. *The Wild Palms* contains ten sections, five alternating chapters each from two stories, "Wild Palms" and "Old Man," that are unconnected in terms of time, setting, tone, and characters. Yet despite its structure, this novel is *not* an amalgam of earlier stories, nor is it one that Faulkner intended to write in this strange double form. What happened, he says, is that "When I reached the end of what is now the first section of *The Wild Palms,* I realized suddenly that something was missing, it needed emphasis, something to lift it like counterpoint in music. So I wrote on the 'Old Man' story until the 'Wild Palms' story rose back to pitch. Then I stopped the 'Old Man' story at what is now its first section, and took up the 'Wild Palms' story until it began to sag. Then I raised it to pitch again with another section of its antithesis" (*Lion,* 247). Faulkner's musical metaphor is not inappropriate to describe the relationship between these two stories; certainly it is more valid than his assertion that they share the theme of love. "Wild Palms," he has misleadingly said, is "the story of Charlotte Rittenmeyer and Harry Wilbourne, who sacrificed everything for love, and then lost that" while "Old Man" "is the story of a man who got his love and spent the rest of the book fleeing from it, even to the extent of voluntarily

going back to jail where he would be safe" (*Lion,* 247-48).
While the first part of this statement is reasonably accurate,
the second, as Blotner has indicated, is surely ironic, for "the
pregnant woman rescued by the protagonist was not his
choice, let alone his love" (Blotner, 980). In fact, he had never
met her before and though, in a sense, they share more in two
weeks than most married couples of fifty years, they never
become intimate. More accurately, if still too neat, Blotner
suggests that the pairing is of "the man who had given up
everything he had known for freedom and love, and the man
who wanted only to return to the safe confinement he knew"
(Blotner, 990). What the stories do share is a conflict between
the main characters and the vast forces arrayed against them.
Charlotte and Harry, who in many ways echo Hemingway's
lovers in *A Farewell to Arms* (as well as Faulkner's extended
but ultimately hopeless affair with Meta Carpenter[8]), declare
not a separate peace but a separate war—against marriage,
family, respectability, domesticity, whatever society, determined
to force them "to conform, or die," opposes to "bright wild
passion." The unnamed convict of "Old Man," who in many
ways anticipates Hemingway's protagonist in *The Old Man
and the Sea,* battles valiantly against natural forces—flood,
poisonous snakes, alligators, female fecundity—not for love or
even freedom, but merely for survival. Both stories are mythic,
literary, in their use of coincidence, outsized action, denial of
linear time, naturalistic imagery, treatment of women, and
cosmic reverberations of the events.

About halfway through the novel, Harry says, "Of course
we cant beat Them; we are doomed of course; that's why I am
afraid." We know he is right because the novel begins in
medias res, with Charlotte already dying from the infection
caused by the abortion she demanded that he perform. Her
pregnancy occurred because they had fled security and society,
believing that "it's got to be all honeymoon, always" and "that
when people loved, hard, really loved each other, they didn't
have children, the seed got burned up in the love, the passion."
It is all larger than life: Harry and Charlotte fall in love, or at

least passion, at first sight; despair of their love because her Catholic husband will not countenance divorce and because they have no money; run off together (with the husband's connivance) when Harry fortuitously finds a wallet crammed with money (abandoning his medical career just as it is about to begin); live idyllically, knowing money will always be there; flee civilization's bourgeois confines to live like innocents on the frontier until the botched abortion kills her. Harry, accepting responsibility for her death (caused, he believes, by love), rejects both flight and suicide out of a sense of desperate loyalty to her, because *"when she became not then half of memory became not and if I become not then all of remembering will cease to be.—Yes, he thought, between grief and nothing I will take grief."*[9] And so he accepts society's justice for having loved her: "a sentence at hard labor in the State Penitentiary at Parchman for a period of not less than fifty years."

All this is the stuff of pulp fiction—of the sort that Harry writes successfully for a time and that the convict of "Old Man" reads. In fact, such literature is responsible for the latter's being in Parchman to begin with, his hopeless life imitating a poor art form, since his reading of dime novels had inspired him to commit an abortive train robbery in order to impress a girl who, after he was imprisoned, visited him once only, flirted openly with a guard, and then, seven months later, sent him a postcard which read: *"This is where were hon-nymonning at. Your friend (Mrs) Vernon Waldrip."* "Old Man," too, is the stuff of fantastical fiction: it begins, fairy-tale-like, with "Once . . . there were two convicts"—the tall one seduced by popular romances, the plump one sentenced to 199 years—"this incredible and impossible period of punishment or restraint itself carrying a vicious and fabulous quality." The tall convict, described as Herculean at one point, undergoes a series of extraordinary labors or trials after he is sent out to assist flood victims: apparent drowning, enforced fasting, suprahuman endurance, being shot at twice when seeking help, a birth, hunting alligators bare-handed, all while clinging throughout seven weeks to the skiff the state entrusted to him in order, in the end, to surrender it and himself with the wonderful understatement: "Yonder's your boat, and here's the woman. But I never did find that bastard on the cotton-house." The ultimate irony of the story is that the system that had commended him as a hero when it believed him drowned now, though knowing better, sentences him to an additional ten years for attempted escape because his survival proves to be a political inconvenience.

Numerous parallels do exist between these two stories of men who, truly alive for the first and only times in their lives, must somehow deal with what seems to them the fabulous world of women, and specifically with a pregnant woman. The abortion and the birth are both mysteries beyond the men's abilities to cope or understand; both experiences represent violations of fundamental societal rules, and therefore lead to long sentences in Parchman—to which both men seem equally indifferent. Whether these echoes—and others that might be cited—are sufficient to link these two very different stories remains an open question. Certainly some readers are convinced that Faulkner failed to create a novel out of two separate stories. One might do best to read them twice—once as published, and then each story on its own—before deciding.

Go Down, Moses

Just as "Wild Palms" may be read as a parodic *A Farewell to Arms*—or a reductio ad absurdum: the beloved dying not in childbirth but from a botched abortion reluctantly performed by the desperate lover—and "Old Man" as a precursOr of *The Old Man and the Sea*, the protagonist battling mightily against natural forces and ultimately, in Hemingway's phrase, "destroyed but not defeated," so "The Short Happy Life of Francis Macomber" may be viewed as underlying "The Long Unhappy Dying of Ike McCaslin," which I take to be the central theme of Faulkner's finest composite novel, *Go Down, Moses*.

Ike McCaslin, the protagonist of Faulkner's "The Bear" (as well as of *Go Down, Moses*, the book of which it is the

keystone), would seem, by training and instinct, to be all that
Macomber seeks to emulate, and yet his fate, which is, initially
and ultimately, the crucial issue of *Go Down, Moses,* strikes me
as far worse. The book's first story, "Was," begins with this
static, verbless assertion about the significance of what
happens to Ike; the first paragraph, in its entirety, reads: "Isaac
McCaslin, 'Uncle Ike,' past seventy and nearer eighty than he
ever corroborated any more, a widower now and uncle to half a
county and father to no one"—a condition and subject to which
everything in the book may be said to refer, even the seemingly
irrelevant title story with which the book ends. In "Delta
Autumn," the penultimate story and the last in which Ike
appears, the girl (a mulatto, distant cousin) who confronts Ike
and appeals in vain for his sympathy and support concludes
with these damning words: "Old man, . . . have you lived so
long and forgotten so much that you dont remember anything
you ever knew or felt or even heard about love?" Thus, Ike's
fate is central to the book, his *Bildungsroman,* from first to
almost last; it is also problematical, a subject on which critics
divide sharply. Whatever position one takes about it, however,
requires consideration of three related matters: Ike's education
in the woods, his decision in the commissary in section 4 of
"The Bear," and what happens to him as a consequence. The
key question seems to me, why does Ike, with such a propitious
beginning as he has, go so wrong (as I think he does)—that is,
why does he choose to live the life he does and why does it have
such dire results?

   "The Bear," as Faulkner maintains, is two different stories
(two of his finest)—it can be read on its own or as part of *Go
Down, Moses.* "That story was part of a novel. . . . the pursuit
of the bear was simply what you might call a dangling clause in
the description of that man when he was a young boy. When it
was taken from the book and printed as a short story . . . I
would have said, Take this [section 4] out, this doesn't belong
in this as a short story, it's a part of the novel but not part of the
story" (*F in U,* 273; also 4). That is, "The Bear" may be read as
the story of Ike's education, the hunt that culminates in the

killing of Old Ben, and the destruction of the woods through the industrialization of the once rural South (a story told in sections 1-3 and 5), *or* as a story which *includes* these events but whose far broader focus is archetypal: the whole history and mythos of the South, its fall from innocence to experience through the act of taking possession of land and people, and the necessity for survivors to learn to live well in a world of contingency, frustration, and suffering.

Yet this distinction itself is a bit misleading since "The Bear" (even with the omission of section 4) is much less a straightforward hunting story than are, say, "Lion" (an earlier version of "The Bear")[10] and "The Old People"—the story in *Go Down, Moses* that immediately precedes "The Bear" and in which Ike, at age twelve, successfully kills his first deer and is marked with its blood by Sam Fathers, his mentor. That initiatory experience is scarcely mentioned in "The Bear" and it is given no significance whatever; instead the emphasis throughout much of the later story—even if it is read as a hunt—is on passivity, on the abnegation of action, on, for example, learning *not* to shoot.

"The Bear" begins in 1883, the year when Ike was sixteen and Ben was killed, but almost immediately it shifts back six years in order to trace Ike's education in the woods from his first experience, at age ten, of the annual hunt to the climactic moment in section 3 when Lion and Boon kill the old bear. Three major, interrelated themes are established early on. First, that the ownership of the woods is conferred not through "any recorded document," but "It was of the men, not white nor black nor red but men, hunters, with the will and hardihood to endure and the humility and skill to survive, and the dogs and the bear and deer juxtaposed and reliefed against it": deeds, then, not a deed. Second, the deeds in the woods take the form of a dangerous game, "the best game of all, the best of all breathing and forever the best of all listening," "the yearly pageant-rite of the old bear's furious immortality." The terms, firmly prescribed by setting and tradition, are "ordered and compelled by and within the wilderness in the ancient and unremitting contest according to the ancient and immitigable rules." And third, the goal of the contest is the right to a name, such as Old Ben—who "had earned a name such as a human man could have worn and not been sorry"—already possesses, or that might yet accrue to a rather fearful hound who, according to Sam, knew "all the time that sooner or later she would have to be brave once so she could keep on calling herself a dog."

All three themes converge in Ike who, under the tutelage or priesthood of Sam Fathers, ritualistically passes all the tests the wilderness requires of its initiates—and so attains the name of hunter, as well as, presumably, such knowledge and wisdom as it can offer about the world it represents and about himself. "He entered his novitiate to the true wilderness with Sam beside him as he had begun his apprenticeship in miniature to manhood after the rabbits and such with Sam beside him. . . . It seemed to him that at the age of ten he was witnessing his own birth." Sam teaches Ike both the lore of the woods and the requisite virtues (humility and patience and courage and pride) so that by age thirteen Ike was already "a better woodsman than most grown men" and at sixteen, on the day of the final hunt for Ben, he is honored by being given the best mount—the only one the old bear cannot spook. Ike's education had proceeded steadily, directly, beyond even Sam: "If Sam Fathers had been his mentor and the backyard rabbits and squirrels his kindergarten, then the wilderness the old bear ran was his college and the old male bear itself, so long unwifed and childless as to have become its own ungendered progenitor, was his alma mater." By thirteen, Ike "knew game trails that even Sam Fathers had never seen"; more significantly, he had become mentor to himself, his "own ungendered progenitor": "he was teaching himself to be better than a fair woodsman without even knowing he was doing it." Thus, when Sam, the guardian of the rules of the hunt, tells Ike that he will never see Ben so long as he carries his gun—" 'You will have to choose,' Sam said"—Ike is able to relinquish what, through earning the name of hunter, he has come both to personify and to transcend: "He had left the gun; by his own will and relinquishment he had accepted not a gambit, not a choice, but a condition in which not only the bear's heretofore inviolable anonymity but all the ancient rules and balances of hunter and hunted had been abrogated." And then, realizing that "He was still tainted," he surrenders even more—his watch and his compass—and so gains a kind of ultimate accolade: the soundless, motionless, "dimensionless" confrontation with Old Ben. In Ike, then, validation through deeds, ritual, and naming appear to be well met, and yet they are simultaneously undermined and betrayed throughout—and to a large extent by Ike himself.

Major de Spain, who buys and sells the woods, would seem primarily responsible for the demise of the world entrusted to his care. The woods, we are told, are "bigger and older than any recorded document:—of white men fatuous enough to believe he had bought any fragment of it, of Indian ruthless enough to pretend that any fragment of it had been his to convey; bigger than Major de Spain and the scrap he pretended to, knowing better." Society maintains a ritual pretense of ownership, and men who hope to prove worthy of the name return as claimants—through "the will and hardihood to endure and the humility and skill to survive"—in the annual ritual hunt. But the pretense itself is *only* pretense, the ownership embodied in a deed all too real, and the claim of the hunters self-deceptive and invalid; and for all the insistence that the woods are timeless, "markless," indifferent to "the little puny humans [who] swarmed and hacked at [it] in a fury of abhorrence and fear like pygmies about the ankles of a drowsing elephant," it is to a "doomed wilderness" that Ike returns for the last time in section 5 of "The Bear" since Major de Spain "had sold the timber-rights to a Memphis lumber company." Earlier it was this same de Spain who, through right of ownership, had arrogated to himself the Jehovah-like authority of apocalyptic judgment. Ben, he asserted, has killed a colt, and all is changed: "He has broken the rules. I didn't think he would have done that. He has killed mine and McCaslin's dogs, but that was all right. We gambled the dogs against him; we gave each other warning. But now he has come into my house and destroyed my property, out of season too. He broke the rules." And the last hunt—participated in by a curious rabble of townspeople, farmers, loggers, poor white trash—becomes a repetition with a difference: parodic of the Southern cause or the final charge of an already defeated army, "so that when they went into the woods this morning Major de Spain led a party almost as strong, excepting that some of them were not armed, as some he had led in the last darkening days of '64 and '65."

But just as the South—as myth or nation—is doomed, with or without de Spain to lead it, so too are the wilderness and the bear, already anachronistic, "out of an old dead time, a phantom, epitome and apotheosis of the old wild life," by the time Ike is ten. Ike and Sam Fathers, men of the wilderness par excellence, play their curiously central parts (curious because passive) in the demise of Old Ben and the woods he symbolizes. The refrain in the first part of the story is "So he [Ike] should have hated and feared Lion" (209, 212, 226)—and yet Ben's ultimate conqueror is welcomed and trained for the job. On the other hand, Ike already knows at the age of ten that he will never fire his gun at Old Ben; so that his subsequent relinquishment of it in order to encounter the bear is no sacrifice of a usable weapon. Yet Ike and Sam agree between them that Ben's killer "must be one of us," and when de Spain pronounces his doom on Old Ben, Sam (Ike realizes) *"was glad. . . . He was old. . . . It was almost over now and he was glad"* (215; Faulkner's italics). Ike also welcomes his own part in the demise of what cannot endure, of what (since its end is inevitable) is in a sense already dead: "It seemed to him that there was a fatality in it. It seemed to him that something, he didn't know what, was beginning; had already begun. It was like the last act on a set stage. It was the beginning of the end of something, he didn't know what except that he would not grieve. He would be humble and proud that he had been found worthy to be a part of it too or even just to see it too." That last phrase is revealing, for when it comes to it both Ike and Sam

are inactive, voyeurs at the kill. Ike has learned well the lessons
of the master—humility and patience and abnegation, all the
negative virtues—so that at the climactic moment both of
them are, in effect, absent—or worse: Sam, in fact, collapses
fatally, though "markless" as the dying wilderness, at the
moment the bear falls. It is no wonder, then, that Ike's one
resolute action in all of Go Down, Moses should be one of
relinquishment—an acknowledgment of failure that repeats
his relinquishment in the woods but in morally disastrous
terms—and that what he relinquishes is his patrimony, his
inherited identity: that which gives him a name and a link to
the past, and therefore a future as well.

The central story of "The Bear" as part of the novel concerns not only Ike's education in the woods under the tutelage
of Sam Fathers but his subsequent attempt, in section 4, to
apply what he has learned to the world beyond the woods; and
most of the rest of Go Down, Moses concerns the consequences of Ike's action in that section—the vacuous and helpless life
his choice there initiates and defines. Ike's repudiation of "the
tamed land which was to have been his heritage" is, like his
laying by of watch and compass, an attempt to remove a taint,
for the ledgers of ownership are a record of injustice and
corruption, a "chronicle which was a whole land in miniature,
which multiplied and compounded was the entire South." But
what Ike brings from the woods is also largely negative—a fact
that is emphasized if, for the moment, we reverse sections 4
and 5, and read them in the order in which events happen
rather than as they are printed. When Ike returns to "the
doomed wilderness" for the last time (section 5), it is two years
before the scene in the commissary (section 4). Its events—
culminating in his encountering the hysterical Boon screaming his frenzied claim to ownership of the squirrels while
trying desperately to fix the jammed gun with which he has
never yet shot anything ("Dont touch them! Dont touch a one
of them! They're mine!")—will then be clearly seen for what it
is: both direct consequence of the final hunt and also antecedent to, and therefore the context for, Ike's renunciation in

section 4. Thus, the result of Faulkner's inversion of these two sections is that the destruction and madness of section 5 (the only wilderness experience that Ike omits to mention in speaking to Cass in the commissary) both precede and follow Ike's repudiation of his patrimony—and therefore seem both its effect and cause.

The failures and losses and betrayals occurring in the woods leave Ike with nothing to replace what he repudiates—except the self-deception implied by the tools he buys "because if the Nazarene had found carpentering good for the life and ends He had assumed and elected to serve, it would be all right too for Isaac McCaslin." But Ike's tools prove as useless as his gun, for, as Gary Lee Stonum writes, "in repudiating the McCaslin plantation, Ike also relinquishes a future. He finds himself isolated in the world and powerless to speak or act with any consqence. His eventual situation as a childless figure living on the fringes of his world is oddly like that of the fliers in *Pylon,* Faulkner's most striking representatives of dispersion."[11]

The climax of the confrontation between Ike and his cousin in the commissary occurs when Cass demonstrates the central flaw in Ike's logic: that the land is rightfully Ike's *whether or not* he repudiates his inheritance. "You said how on that instant when Ikkemotubbe realised that he could sell the land to Grandfather, it ceased forever to have been his. All right; go on: Then it belonged to Sam Fathers, old Ikkemotubbe's son. And who inherited from Sam Fathers, if not you? co-heir perhaps with Boon, if not of his life maybe, at least of his quitting it?" But Ike, like his black cousin Fonsiba who reverts to a kind of inert squalor and degradation ("she did not even seem to breathe or to be alive except her eyes watching him"), has no answer except to proclaim himself free: "I am free. . . . Sam Fathers set me free." Ike is indeed free, but also irrelevant, himself repudiated or, worse, ignored by the South as it struggles to come to terms with its past, for those inclined toward the good who yet deny responsibility for rectifying evil help to perpetuate it by leaving the running of the world to their

moral inferiors. This is the view not only of the other descendants of Lucius Quintus Carothers McCaslin (Cass, obviously,
and also Lucas Beauchamp in "The Fire and the Hearth" and
the young woman in "Delta Autumn"), but also of General
Compson, perhaps the most trustworthy judge of action in the
novel. Although paralleled to Major de Spain in several ways
(both former Civil War leaders whose birthdays are celebrated
together at the hunting camp), Compson is his moral antithesis; and it is he who pronounces Ike worthy of the best mount
on the final hunt and who trusts him enough, without knowing his reason, to defend his staying behind in the woods with
the fallen Sam when the others prepare to depart. So Compson, loving and trusting Ike, has the right to doubt and to
question Ike's relinquishment of responsibility: "I don't
believe you just quit. It looks like you just quit but I have
watched you in the woods too much and I dont believe you just
quit even if it does look damn like it." But quit is exactly what
Ike has done, as Faulkner himself complains in an interview: "I
think a man ought to do more than just repudiate. He should
have been more affirmative instead of just shunning people."[12]
And Ike also knows this truth, knowing "long since that no
man is ever free and probably could not bear it if he were." No
woonder, then, that in the end, through both denial and
self-deception, he becomes merely Uncle Ike—not only lacking surname, but also having surrendered both the active role
of husband that he played for a time and the even more active
one of father that, for all his desiring a son, he could never
manage to fulfill. Thus, all the negatives accrue to Ike: proper-
tyless, powerless, nameless, childless. Only the long, extended
dying remains.

7

"Jest another Snopes": *The Hamlet, The Town, The Mansion*

The Snopes trilogy—*The Hamlet, The Town,* and *The Mansion*—is a large and complex multivolume novel within the much larger and much more complex multivolume novel that is the entire Yoknapatawpha saga. Taken as single work, the Snopes trilogy is Faulkner's most ambitious and intricate experiment in narrative technique, yet it is a logical extension of his earlier fiction. Conceived and written over a period of three and a half decades, the trilogy nonetheless functions as a unit,[1] though at first glance the structures of its three books seem to have little in common. The four sections of *The Hamlet* are all told by a voice commonly called the omniscient narrator, though Faulkner offers us V. K. Ratliff as commentator within that frame. The twenty-four chapters of *The Town* are all subjective statements: ten by Charles (Chick) Mallison, eight by Gavin Stevens, and six by Ratliff. *The Mansion* seems a whimsical combination of these two modes. None of its three main sections is narrated by the title characters: Mink Snopes (five chapters), Linda Snopes Kohl (six), and Flem Snopes (seven)—but two of Mink's chapters have personal narrators (one each by Ratliff and Montgomery Ward Snopes) as do all of Linda's (three by Chick, two by Ratliff, one by Gavin). Such a narrative structure suggests chaos rather than unity, a failure of all the disparate pieces that went into the trilogy to cohere.

The trilogy's macrocosm concerns the South's changing from an agrarian and village society into the commercial, urban twentieth century. This is one of Faulkner's central themes from first to last: "In 'Father Abraham,' which contained the seeds of his Snopes saga, he began engaging the social, economic, and political developments that were transforming the South."[2] From this as yet unpublished manuscript written in the late nineteen-twenties, Snopeses began proliferating, like rats or vermin, throughout Faulkner's fiction and landscape: the countryside, the hamlet of Frenchman's Bend, and then the town of Jefferson—and despite the ironic impotence of the patriarch, Flem Snopes. Snopeses and Snopesism become both cause and consequence of the South's second fall from grace: "a family who by petty chicanery and unscrupulous politics, take possession of the country town of Jefferson, Miss. They creep over it lahk mold over cheese and destroy its traditions and whatever lav'liness there was in the place" (*Lion*, 39). In horror and amazement, the trilogy's appalled narrators recount Flem's rise from obscure poverty to riches, respectability, and power; his reverse Midas touch—contaminating everything he touches along the way; the hollowness at the core of his achievements; and then his sudden and appropriate demise at the height of his success as Snopeses destroy Snopeses.

Warren Beck, one of Faulkner's most interesting commentators, writes of the trilogy this way: "The three books not only complement but blend into each other. The omniscience of *The Hamlet* richly furnishes the stage and gives the narrative its tremendous impetus; the first person reports which make up *The Town* turn illuminative speculation upon emergent facets of character and action; *The Mansion* emphasizes theme and resolution by apposing the two methods. . . . By alternating third person omniscient narrative method, like that of *The Hamlet,* with extended first person accounts like those which make up *The Town, The Mansion* achieves a wider range of tone than either of the preceding volumes, while echoing and fulfilling them."[3] Actually, as I argue, it is a remarkably subjective and often dramatized, though still anonymous, multifarious voice with which Faulkner begins and concludes and unites the Snopes trilogy.

The unnamed narrator of *The Hamlet* demonstrates his humanity by articulating the shared values and perspective—though not always the language and imagery—of the choric-like gallery inhabitants. He says, for instance: "A few days later they learned that the new smith was living in the house where his cousin (or whatever the relationship was: nobody ever knew for certain) Flem lived." Typically, the narrative voice tells us only what "they" see and know and feel. Thus, his portrayal of Eula Varner, Jefferson's budding Venus, expresses the presumably common emotional reaction the narrator himself shares; further, such passages are often ascribed, directly or indirectly, to a particular character. Here, for instance, is Eula in the classroom: "By merely walking down the aisle between them she would transform the very wooden desks and benches themselves into a grove of Venus and fetch every male in the room ... importunate each for precedence in immolation." In this section the narrator has taken us inside Labove, Eula's pedantic and frustrated schoolmaster; appropriately, then, the language, imagery, and sentiments perfectly express both his pedantry and his frustration.

The narrator performs a second major function in treating Ratliff as just a character, and also as something more. Ratliff remains in the third person throughout *The Hamlet,* but in what might be termed third-person subjective: he is the only individual we get significantly inside of in *The Hamlet,* and the only one who comments with anything like consistent authority. The frame narrator emphasizes that we should pay close attention to Ratliff: "If he had lived in Frenchman's Bend itself . . . he would have known no more." Ratliff knows all anyone can know, perhaps all there is to know.

The multifarious narrator of *The Mansion* similarly plays a double role: he both voices the communal values of Jefferson and speaks as the consciousness of a major character, in this case Mink Snopes. Thus in both *The Hamlet* and *The Mansion* the multifarious narrator is neither omniscient nor objective: he takes stances, adopts perspectives, enters into the fray. To this extent he is as limited, involved, and unreliable as any named narrator.

Within the framework of the multifarious perspective lie the single-faceted narrators, most notably Ratliff, Gavin Stevens, and Chick Mallison. Their voices are those of participants since they are both actors and narrators. Ratliff is central because of his moral perspective, his relative reliability, and (since he alone appears in all three novels) his serving as a unifying device. Shrewd, bland, cool, and yet deeply humane, Ratliff is the most sensitive, incisive, and trustworthy narrator in the trilogy, the closest to a touchstone of enduring and instinctive human understanding. Only he, we are told, will recognize the returned Mink after thirty-eight years: "Ratliff alone out of Yoknapatawpha County would know Mink on sight. To be unschooled, untravelled, and to an extent unread, Ratliff had a terrifying capacity for knowledge or local information or acquaintanceship to match the need of any local crisis" (*M*, 381). It is Ratliff who both points a moral in Flem's story (he **got** what he deserved) and then, in the appropriate note of mocking sympathy, sums up Gavin Stevens's experience: "I don't know if [Linda's] already got a daughter stashed out somewhere, or if she jest aint got around to one yet. But when she does I jest hope for Old Lang Zyne's sake she dont never bring it back to Jefferson. You done already been through two Eula Varners and I dont think you can stand another one" (*M*, 434).

Ratliff's actions similarly reflect the communal values he shares with Faulkner's implied author and presumably with Faulkner himself: he warns Frenchman's Bend against Flem's ponies; he separates Ike Snopes from his cow;[4] he refuses to go to New York to celebrate Linda's shacking up with Barton

Kohl, but goes happily to the wedding; he unfashionably insists that Stalin is as evil and dangerous as Hitler and Mussolini. Yet Ratliff never embodies omniscience, absoluteness; his wisdom and understanding emerge from the context of mortal confines—even domestic ones: he is an unabashedly good cook, seamstress, housekeeper. In *The Hamlet*, Ratliff's serious illness and his falling for "the oldest trick in the book" in buying the Old Frenchman place from Flem for its supposed buried treasure (after his having warned the others against Flem's ponies) emphasize his limitation as character.

His reconstruction, in *The Mansion*, of Eula's impregnation (which occurs in *The Hamlet*) makes explicit that his narrative often transcends the factual. "I think what I prefer is, that them five timorous local stallions actively brought about the very exact thing they finally nerved their desperation up to try to prevent. . . . I wont have nothing else for the simple dramatic verities except that ever thing happened right there that night and all at once . . . that it taken all six of them even to ravage that citadel, let alone seed them loins with a child." And Ratliff adds: "my conjecture is jest as good as yourn, maybe better since I'm a interested party, being as I got what the feller calls a theorem to prove. . . . I dont even insist or argue that it happened that way. I jest simply decline to have it any other way except that one because there aint no acceptable degrees between what has got to be right and what jest can possibly be" (*M*, 119—24). Ratliff's position—that having a conjecture to prove (that is, being involved with events rather than removed from them) makes him more reliable than passive observers—represents a repudiation of omniscience. There may be paradox in Ratliff's implied aesthetics, but his view nonetheless is central to the tradition of the modern novel. It is, further, Ratliff's way of affirming what Faulkner calls the verities. In response to Bookwright's cynicism about God, Ratliff says, "I dont know as I would believe that, even if I knowed it was true" (*H*, 83). In *The Town*, he says, "between what did happen and what ought to happened, I dont never have trouble picking ought." For Ratliff "ought" is truer than "did" or "is"—truer morally, truer aesthetically, truer humanly.

As might be expected, Ratliff is at times as inadequate in narration as in the action concerning the Old Frenchman place. He is, for example, at a loss to explain Flem's failure to free Montgomery Ward from prison; he is wrong in speculating on why Linda, in her senior year of high school, avoided meeting Gavin (it was Gavin, fearing a growing intimacy, who avoided Linda); and he offers us boredom as the identical, glib, and, at best, superficial explanation for Eula's and Flem's deaths.[5] And yet Ratliff—having been burned once, having learned not to "tangle with Flem"—not only completely regains and thereafter maintains his equilibrium, his reputation for sagacity, but he also enters into another business arrangement with another Snopes (Wallstreet Panic, this time), and with success; to this extent, he serves if not as check then at least as counterweight to Flem's rise.

What emerges, I think, is a somewhat mixed picture of an unusual but very real and therefore limited human being. And if Ratliff—"too damned innocent, too damned intelligent" (T, 33)—is this far from being the trilogy's definitive speaker, how much further are the more obviously flawed single-faceted narrators? The most important of these, Gavin Stevens and Chick Mallison, narrate with much force, convincingness, and reliability. They are rendered largely sympathetic because, from the inside looking out, we are made to see—and mostly share—their attitudes toward Snopesism, Eula and Linda, Ratliff, America's wars, and so on. And yet it is absurd to condemn Faulkner, as some have done, for failing to make them perfect authorial mouthpieces when it is clear from the novels that they were never conceived as such. Gavin Stevens, for one, commits so many acts of perverse folly and willful self-blinding—the feud with de Spain, his pseudochivalric and feeble posturing toward Eula and Linda, his adopting Montgomery Ward as his protégé, his despairing surender (of not only himself but his whole generation) before the threat of Clarence Snopes, his refusal to acknowledge Linda's motive for freeing Mink—that we tend to lose track of them and to adopt Ratliff's attitude of frustrated and patronizing, if sympathetic, bemusement.

Irving Howe offers us an easier view: that Faulkner's artistry failed him. "How else," he asks rhetorically, "can one explain the frantic verbal outpourings of Gavin Stevens, the District Attorney with a degree from Heidelberg and a passion for rant, who serves so disastrously as Faulkner's 'alter ego'?"[6] One could do worse, however, than note Faulkner's response to this very question, a response dismissive of glib author-character equations: "you don't really have time to identify yourself with a character except at certain moments when the character is in a position to express truthfully things which you yourself believe to be true. Then you'll put your own ideas in his mouth, but . . . when you do that they'll become his. . . . It just happens that this man agrees with you on this particular point and so he says it." And Faulkner goes on specifically to suggest Gavin Stevens's inadequacies in *The Town:* "Well, he had got out of his depth. . . . He got into a real world in which people anguished and suffered, not simply did things which they shouldn't do. And he wasn't as prepared to cope with people who were following their own bent, not for a profit but simply because they had to. That is, he knew a good deal less about people than he knew about the law and about ways of evidence and drawing the right conclusions from what he saw with his legal mind. When he had to deal with people he was an amateur" (*F in U*, 25—26, 140). This seems to me a valid if redundant statement. For the trilogy makes unambiguously clear that Gavin, for all we may like and sympathize with him, was conceived and created as an inadequate speaker for inadequate views. As Brooks indicates, Faulkner knows what he is about: "Gavin again and again in the novel is made to play the fool. As a Snopes killer, he is not impressive, and in much of this novel [*The Town*] we are invited to smile at his follies."[7]

So far from being Faulkner's mouthpiece, Gavin is his mirror image for Flem's impotence. On this subject Brooks notes that "Gavin's conduct seems so strange that some com-

mentators have concluded that he is impotent; but his behavior throughout the novel is not that of an impotent man."[8] Yet
Brooks, despite his convincing treatment of Gavin as a de
Rougemont Tristan, offers little evidence of his potency.[9] The
only solid piece is Gavin's eventual marriage to Melisandre
Backus, but as Brooks himself says, "his marriage involves
friendship and even affection, but presumably not much passion.... there is in the marriage none of the anguished passion
that Gavin associates with his Helens and Iseults. It may well
have been a happy marriage, but the very fact of happiness
would for the gun-shy Gavin have removed the possibility of a
romance in the grand manner."[10] The lack of passion is
obvious; one wonders about even the friendship and affection.
The marriage receives little treatment; that it has the force and
form of a digression suggests its relative insignificance and
negative impact on Gavin's life. He hates his wife's expensive
wedding present and pedigreed horses. "At first his wife's
money was a problem," the narrator (mildly amused because
distanced) relates. "In fact, if it hadn't been for the greater
hysteria of the war, the lesser hysteria of that much sudden
money could have been a serious one" (*M*, 363). Chick Mallison also compares Gavin's marriage to the war when he says,
"By which time I was married too, to a bombsight." When
Gavin himself speaks of his wife, he tells Linda it is nonsense
to think she will be jealous (jealousy, after all, exists only where
there is passion); and when he speaks *to* her as he goes off to
see Linda, he says, "I love you.... Yes. No. I dont know. Dont
wait up." There is something far more ambivalent in this
relationship than in Eula's with the impotent Flem.

Faulkner comments that Gavin "was probably afraid to be
married. He might get too involved with the human race if he
married one of them" (*F in U*, 141). Gavin's marriage to
Melisandre represents a reversion, a flight to the past, to the
girl who had preceded Linda as his protégée. Gavin had earlier
vicariously identified himself with Hoak MacCarron (*T*, 135,
342—343) and therefore as Linda's father. Given Gavin's
convoluted logic, this may well be anticipatory rationalization

to preclude his later having to marry Linda. Chick's view is that "his Uncle Gavin might already have been a grandfather before he even became a bride" (*M*, 356). But Gavin never has any children, and he seems incapable of having any. His most intimate female relationships are with prepubescent girls and postmenopausal mothers; his most obsessive emotions focus on hollow chivalry and Flem's impotence. How pathetically revealing of his own masculine feebleness is his comment that Eula, always ready "for anything that just wore pants," was like any woman always ready for "anything in pants just named Gavin Stevens" (*T*, 192). Regardless of the physiological technicalities, Gavin is really worse off than the unambiguous Flem, and the reader tends to ask, along with Chick, "is it virginity or just celibacy?"—in the exact non sequitur tone that is used whenever someone (Gavin, *T*, 94; Montgomery Ward, *M*, 70) realizes that Flem is impotent.

For all its romantic trappings, Gavin's relationship with Linda is no more a vital or positive expression of mature heterosexual love than Gavin's marriage. Its symbol is the wall separating their otherwise co-joined beds the night they spend in a hotel (*M*, 250—53). For both Linda and Gavin, the relationship is remarkably static—in fact, sterile. Playing at omniscient narrator, Gavin had pronounced Linda's fate. Ratliff tells him: "Doomed to fidelity and grief, you said. To love once quick and lose him quick and for the rest of her life to be faithful and to grieve." As character, Gavin acts on the apparent assumption that his pronouncement represents a revealed truth. Ratliff knows better: "it wasn't her that was doomed, she would likely do fine; it was the one that was recipient of the fidelity and the monogamy and the love, and the one that was the proprietor of the responsibility." For all his claims of victimization, Gavin has willed or allowed his own fate, for Linda is remarkably consistent in her proffers not merely of her body (her mother's offer), but of love (with or without marriage). Even at the end—after her marriage, Barton's death, Gavin's marriage, Flem's death—she can still say: "I love you. . . . I have never loved anybody but you" (425).[11] But

Gavin cannot allow himself to hear this any more than he can alow himself to hear her say he can do what he calls "the explicit word" to her. In fact, Gavin censors the word out of his narrative just as he has effaced the act from his life.[12] He registers his shock to Linda's explicit offer (or plea) by blushing and hastily writing: *"because we are the 2 in all the world who can love each other without having to"* (239; Faulkner's italics), and by trying to block it out, as he does later with the image-destroying knowledge of her motive in helping to free Mink from prison (she knows he will kill Flem).

Linda's deafness, Chick tells us, removes her from the flux of time and motion, renders her (like the bride on Keats's Grecian urn) "immobilised by a thunderclap into silence . . . , herself no mere moment's child but the inviolate bride of silence, inviolable in maidenhead, fixed, forever safe from change and alteration" (203). Yet Linda does hear the noises of the world and tries to improve it, and she is extraordinarily articulate on the fullness of time continuously evolving the present from the past; while Gavin (embodying and reflecting Linda's deafness as much as he does Flem's impotence) evades the reality Linda embodies and retreats into stasis. Chick says of his uncle that females "had to be alive for him to notice them, and they had to be in motion to be alive, and the only moment of motion which caught his attention, his eye, was that one at which they entered puberty" (197). Gavin's marriage, then, is an imaginative construct not unlike his relationships with Eula and Linda; for Gavin, as Ratliff tells us, is bound by the self-willed imposition of his own blinkered vision upon reality. "It was his fate. He jest got run over by coincidence. . . . It wasn't that he was born too soon or too late or even in the wrong place. He was born at exactly the right time, only in the wrong envelope" (128). That is, to be Gavin Stevens is to be doomed to be Gavin Stevens. It is as simple, and complex, as that.

For all his intensity and energy, Gavin initiates surprisingly little action. Such actions as do involve him—the feud with de Spain, the beating by Matt Levitt, the "adoption" of Montgomery Ward—not only defeat but also humiliate him. There is one significant exception, one wholly successful act, yet it too winds up tasting like failure. Gavin had looked absurdly foolish during the rise and fall of Clarence Snopes because (playing again at prophetic voice or omniscient narrator) he had made one of his typically sweeping and erroneous pronouncements to Ratliff: "it's too late for us now. . . . we are just too old. Call it just tired, too tired to be afraid any longer of losing. Just to hate evil is not enough. You—somebody—has got to do something about it. Only now it will have to be somebody else. . . . it wont be us" (307). Yet immediately after Ratliff's successful exorcising of Clarence, Gavin himself, apparently having learned the lesson of the master, acts and defeats the inevitable next Snopes, Orestes. But the upshot only reinforces his sense of frustration and impotent bitterness. "It's hopeless. Even when you get rid of one Snopes, there's already another one behind you even before you can turn around." And he lapses back into an unfecund lassitude that leaves him floundering and foolish before the coming of Mink. Ratliff agrees with this thesis— " ' That's right,' Ratliff said serenely. 'As soon as you look, you see right away it aint nothing but jest another Snopes' " (349)—but the tone and emphasis are utterly different: calm, broad in vision, actively satisfied without being complacent, believing in the meaningfulness (if not always the efficacy) of human values and action, and therefore never defeated or despairing over mortality. "Fate, and destiny, and luck, and hope," Ratliff says, "and all of us mixed up in it . . . until cant none of us tell begin. . . . I used to think that hope was about all folks e had, only now I'm beginning to believe that that's about all anybody needs—jest hope" (373-74).

In the end, Gavin is hope*less* (both enfeebled and devoid of hope): a failed humanist and self-convicted coward; absurdly irrelevant first on Mink's cosmic significance ("By God, God Himself is not so busy that a homicidal maniac with only ten dollars in the world can hitchhike a hundred miles and buy a gun for ten dollars then hitchhike another hundred miles and shoot another man with it" [389]), and then on Mink's

imagined "death"; willfully self-deceiving about Linda's motivation; feebly denying her pitying: "You haven't had very
much, have you. No, that's wrong. You haven't had anything.
You have had nothing." And finally, telling Ratliff that Flem
was impotent, Gavin sounds like he is confessing something
from the depths of his own being: "When he got in bed with a
woman all he could do was go to sleep.—Yes! . . . The poor
sons of bitches that have to cause all the grief and anguish they
have to cause! Drive on!" Worn out, used up, Gavin "was too
old now and the real tragedy of age is that no anguish is any
longer grievous enough to demand, justify, any sacrifice"
(392).

Yet Gavin was already old and exhausted in *The Town*. He
ages during the course of that novel without maturing; in fact,
the mocking horn of Matt Levitt's car and the beating Gavin
takes from him (a replay in miniature and parody of the de
Spain feud) suggests enfeeblement rather than maturation.
The regressive note had been sounded earlier, when Gavin,
after his abortive attempt to impeach de Spain, cries out,
"What must I do now, Papa? Papa, what can I do now?" (*T*,
99). Gavin may learn some things along the way but he is
essentially unaltered by events. At the beginning he seems
younger even than Chick (who is unborn as yet); after a while,
he is suddenly old, older than anyone else, older than anyone
has any right to be; and at the end of *The Town* he seems not
to have grown up, but only to have gone through it all.

In chapter 20 of *The Town*, his most introspective chapter,
Gavin expresses a sense of being old beyond time. He recounts
his frustration over Eula's summons (*"Why cant you let me
alone? What more can you want of me than I have already
failed to do?"*), a briefly calm view of sunset from a hill with all
of mortality "supine beneath you," followed by a very untrans-
cendent statement that "life itself is always premature which is
why it aches and anguishes"; and then the final meeting with
Eula during which he again refuses to marry Linda (*T*, 319—
34). In this long and intricately constructed chapter, Gavin
presents himself at his most compelling and also most self-

pitying. We are meant to sympathize, even identify, yet if we do so completely and then subsequently resent having yielded to Gavin's self-indulgent sentimentality, we have only ourselves to blame. Faulkner's multifarious narrator, though he likes Gavin, knows better than to take him simply at face value: he frames the entire chapter with the same mockingbird voice that (along with Ratliff and Mrs. Littlejohn) offered ironic commentary on those bidding for Flem's ponies in *The Hamlet* (*T*, 310, 334).

Throughout the trilogy, Ratliff is often referred to as a know-it-all minding everyone's business but his own; yet Ratliff himself calls Gavin a meddler. The difference lies in Ratliff's ability, generally, to play his role without imposing or doing harm. His one major lapse is his being duped by Flem over the salting of the Old Frenchman place at the end of *The Hamlet;* but as he suggests, if he had not been there to allow Flem his egress to Jefferson there would have been someone else. Other than that, he involves himself with Snopeses and Snopesism only through purposeful and morally impelled acts of volition: removing Ike's cow, his partnership with Wall, helping Gavin sanction Linda's marriage, and the like. In virtually all he says and does, Ratliff demonstrates his interest in people and their "active" values ("he always said active for actual," Gavin tells us). Gavin, however, is concerned only with those who somehow touch his life: he does not simply hate Snopesism for its evil power, he is obsessed with it because, like Don Quixote attacking windmills, he feels it as a direct and personal affront to his beautiful and doomed vision of reality. An impassioned if sterile romantic, Gavin can be objective about nothing, and thus often rushes blindly in where Ratliff is too wary to tread. Thus he winds up playing impossible vicarious roles—Eula's outraged husband; Linda's high school sweetheart *and* protective father; in general, Jefferson's self-appointed guardian of puritanical virtue—and looking absurd in the process.

Far from being Faulkner's mouthpiece, Gavin is the most pathetic of the developed characters in *The Town*, in fact in the entire trilogy. Yet because of his gallant championing of stasis, his often inept attempt to frame and maintain verities in the unequal battle with continual flux—as well as his intense, if not always wholly honest, introspection—Gavin is also the trilogy's most complex and interesting human being. Ratliff may be the most incisive and attractive, Flem the most awesome, Eula the most compelling, Chick the most impressionable and impressionistic—but Gavin is the most tortured, the most beseiged, and he alone borders on the tragic.

The third major participant voice in the Snopes trilogy is that of Chick Mallison. Like Gavin, he has been viewed as an authorial spokesman—with Faulkner praised or condemned according to how well or badly Chick is considered to succeed in this role.[13] Yet as both narrator and character Chick is no more trustworthy than Gavin—and perhaps a good deal less.[14] Each of the first three chapters Chick narrates in *The Town* begins with his emphasizing that "I wasn't born yet," and Ratliff later underscores the warning when he implies that Chick was "doomed to be too young" (*M*, 218).[15] Further, he receives most of his information from his cousin Gowan, who was himself first too young and then too peripheral to the events he speaks of to know or care what they were really about. Chick himself comments: "But then Gowan was seventeen; he had a few other things to do, whether grown people believed it or not.... he didn't always listen to all Ratliff would be saying ... so that afterward he couldn't even say just how it was or when that Ratliff put it into his mind and he even got interested in it like a game, a contest or even a battle, a war, that Snopeses had to be watched constantly like an invasion of snakes or wildcats" (*T*, 95—96). Chick, then, so far from being an omniscient or multifarious narrator, is triply removed in both time and space from much of what he narrates. His role is that of an artist uncertain of his relationship to his materials. "I was only thirteen," he tells us, "when Mrs Snopes shot herself that night so I still dont know how much I saw and remembered and how much was compelled onto or into me from Uncle Gavin, being, as Ratliff put it, as I had spent the first

eleven or twelve years of my existence in the middle of Uncle
Gavin, thinking what he thought and seeing what he saw" (*M*,
211). He might have said "filtered" as well as "compelled"—
because the process includes Gavin's experiencing (sometimes
vicariously through Ratliff and others), recreating, and trans-
mitting, followed by Chick's own ingesting, reenvisaging, and
now attempting to communicate.

Chick is additionally removed from events by the moral
perspective he adopts as his own. On the first page of *The
Town* he says, "when I say 'we' and 'we thought' what I mean is
Jefferson and what Jefferson thought." And what are the
values inherent in that perspective? "We were his [de Spain's]
allies, his confederates; our whole town was accessory to that
cuckolding.... It was not because we were against Mr Snopes
.... Nor were we really in favor of adultery, sin: we were
simply in favor of de Spain and Eula Snopes, for what Uncle
Gavin called the divinity of simple unadulterated uninhibited
immortal lust which they represented... ours the pride that
Jefferson would supply their battleground." Chick then parallels and displaces the multifarious narrator of *The Hamlet*, for
just as his predecessor spoke the communal voice of Frenchman's Bend, Chick speaks that of Jefferson. In this context,
many of his prejudices and predilections may be seen as not
merely adolescent pseudosophistication, but small-town and
southern narrowness—like the fear and hatred of the outsider
(Linda Kohl, Colonel Devries) whether he be labeled commu-
nist, Jew, or nigger-lover. Our position as reader is therefore a
treacherous one, for we tend to think events are as someone
we like describes them; but in doing so here, we would be as far
removed from a fixed center of reality as if we accepted as
literal truth the recreated past Quentin and Shreve offer in
Absalom, Absalom!

Chick's narration is in fact as intensely subjective as are
those of that earlier vorticular novel; for from his perspective,
the trilogy is a *Bildungsroman*. And a picaro on a quest for
education (like one seeking adventure) encounters not wisdom
but experience, knowledge, temptation. Faulkner suggests the

same thing when he says that Chick evolves in *The Town.* "He
grew up in that book. And of course, his point of view
changed" (*F in U,* 140). Chick's journey, which (like Tristram
Shandy's) seems to have begun long before his birth or conception, is an initiation—into the mysteries and dangers of Snopesism, women, money, war, all the traditional attractions and
threats of this world—conducted by the ally-seeking efforts of
Ratliff and Gavin.

The results for Chick are as ambivalent as they invariably
are. A third of the way through *The Mansion,* as Linda is
returning to Jefferson from the war in Spain, Ratliff pronounces Chick ready to share fully in the action. "This time he
wouldn't be no innocent infantile bystanding victim." Yet *The
Mansion* is as replete with Chick's sophomorisms as is *The
Town.* He is jealous of Gavin's relationship with Linda, yet
sees her as a whore and mockingly asks Gavin, "Is it all right
with you if I try to lay her?"; he insensitively ridicules Linda not
only for her Communism and Jewish husband, but also for her
deafness and her "dry harsh quacking voice that deaf people
learn to use"; having mocked Gavin for his "is it virginity or
just celibacy?" he then leeringly speculates on his arrange-
ments for sleeping with Linda and sardonically concludes: "So
all that remained for her and Gavin was continence. To put it
crudely, morality." And he offers a contemptuous view of the
human condition that is harsh, bleak, and cheap—"Man
stinks"—especially if we juxtapose it with the hard-earned
final view that Ratliff and Gavin wearily arrive at together:
" 'There aren't any morals,' Stevens said. 'People just do the best
they can.' 'The pore sons of bitches,' Ratliff said. 'The poor
sons of bitches,' Stevens said."

Yet Chick is also capable of learning, of real growth. At one
point, after Chick has made jokes to himself about Linda's
deafness, Gavin tells him, "When you are a little older you will
discover that people really are much more gentle and consid-
erate and kind than you want right now to believe"—and he
finds himself reluctantly agreeing. In addition, his experience
in the war had—perhaps against his own intention and

desires—effected knowledge and change: "the tragedy of war was that you brought nothing away from it but only left something valuable there; that you carried into war things which, except for the war, you could have lived out your life in peace without ever having to know they were inside you." And as a consequence, and despite all his speculative coarseness, he recognizes that Linda is not for him, and he gives up the bad attempt before he makes it.

Even more impressively, Chick becomes able to compare himself unfavorably to the uncle he has long patronized. He has considered Gavin foolish and hopelessly dense for being at a loss to explain Barton Kohl's sculpture, but standing before it, he thinks "that, if Gavin was still looking for first base, I had already struck out because I didn't even know what it was, let alone what it was doing." Chick's self-revelation here (and elsewhere) momentarily pierces his façade of cynicism and reveals it as the obverse of Gavin's romantic excesses. Just as we come to see through Gavin's posturing and to reject it as silly and hopeless (though still largely retaining sympathy for him), so *The Mansion* urges a similar response to Chick and his adolescent antiromanticizing. Faulkner strikes the right note about Gavin when he suggests that, like Quentin Compson, he creates the "sad and funny picture" of a Don Quixote defending nonexistent virtues in a world that believes in none. "It is the knight that goes out to defend somebody who don't want to be defended and don't need it. But it's a very fine quality in human nature. I hope it will always endure. It is comical and a little sad" (*F in U*, 141). Chick's climactic dual view of Gavin—because earned and apropos and quiet—is not only similarly valid but applies equally to himself: "he is a good man. Maybe I was wrong sometimes to trust and follow him but I never was wrong to love him." Even more important, this statement precisely captures Gavin and Chick as narrators as well as characters. For all their aberrations, we are impelled to trust their tales, but we do so at our peril when they lack corroboration.

What the Snopes trilogy offers, then, are three major participant voices, each (like the sections of the three Compson
brothers in *The Sound and the Fury*) confined to representing
a version of truth. "Just as," Faulkner says, "when you examine
a monument you will walk around it, you are not satisfied to
look at it from just one side. Also, it was to look at it from three
different mentalities" (*F in U*, 139—40). But the trilogy's
structure is more complex than this suggests. The "mentalities" in *The Town* are not only spatially equal perspectives but
also concentric circles: Chick speaking for community, Gavin
for "the poets," Ratliff for the oracles. On this last point, Gavin
says, "After this many years of working to establish and
maintain himself as what he uniquely was in Jefferson, Ratliff
could not afford, he did not dare, to walk the streets and not
have the answer to any and every situation which was not
really any of his business. Ratliff knew" (*T*, 141). In addition,
each of these characters moves through time not only linearly
(his own chronological aging) but also in something of a
spiraling relationship to the expanding phenomenon of Snopesism. Snopesim itself moves in complex ways. Paralleling
the Snopesian invasion of Frenchman's Bend in *The Hamlet*,
The Town at first offers a kind of peristaltic movement into
Jefferson of one Snopes after another; there then follows the
dual movement of Flem up the social and financial ladder and,
reversing the earlier process, a simultaneously contracting
gyre as other Snopeses are removed one by one from Jefferson.
The climactic moment for both phenomena occurs at the
utmost point of contraction, the "frozen moment" of Flem's
death.[16] The denouement follows as Mink fades into the West
and the earth in a final scene that completes what is, among
other things, the saga of the place detailed in the trilogy's
opening paragraph: "Hill-cradled and remote, definite yet
without boundaries, straddling into two counties and owning
allegiance to neither ... some of the once-fertile fields had long
since reverted to the cane-and-cypress jungle from which their
first master had hewed them." Back in Frenchman's Bend and
again experiencing the perspective of the frame narrator,

we—like Mink—make our peace with the ambivalent land (dual-countied, waste and fruitful, tame and wild) that first endures our struggles and then contains them.

The land, then, remains as a symbol of abiding certitude, the closest we come to eternal truth within ceaseless flux, the spatial maintaining itself against the temporal. The land itself seems to participate in the trilogy's ritual of renewal (Mink's killing of Flem), for Mink—who had felt himself owned by it and had come to fear it—at last finds peace and freedom within it. Mink's essential spatiality suggests that he could never be a narrator in any traditional sense. His dominant characteristic from the first is an indifference, even an obliviousness to time, an expansive patience that sits in ambush for Houston for "he couldn't remember how many days it had been," and then wishes "there had only been time, space, between the roar of the gun and the impact of the shot" to explain to Houston why he had to die; and that can endure thirty-eight years of prison as an instant in order to contract all time into the extended instant of Flem's death. And all of this is counterpointed by events, of the largest scope, occurring at the opposite end of the human scale—events that serve to measure not only passing but deteriorating time: the Spanish Civil War, Munich, Poland, the fall of Paris, the battle of Britain, the atomic bomb.

At the end, we see the town indifferent to its war heroes and Chick, using his uncle's imagery, asserting that the war had created social justice and economic plenty for all: "it was the fall of 1945 now and the knight had run out of tourneys and dragons, the war itself had slain them, used them up, made them obsolete" (350). This is of course wildly untrue. Only Mink, whose journey from murder to murder parallels and parodies the world's turn from war to war, slays any dragons, and only his act of destruction makes sense—first, because we have seen it in a human dimension and, second, because it is worked out as purposeful rather than chaotic: a halting but single-minded rediscovery of time and space as Mink moves with ceremonial inexorability out of the timeless aridity of

Parchman, through the modern urban wasteland of Memphis, through the gaudy veneer of Jefferson and its decadent mansion, and finally back to Frenchman's Bend and the land and cessation of time and motion. Visiting Europe in the summer of 1939, Chick had seen "a kind of composed and collected hysteria"; in contrast, Mink and Jefferson enact a controlled ritual of Greek-like necessity. And it completes the cycle and renews the world so that, regardless of what happens elsewhere, Frenchman's Bend and Jefferson endure. Brooks may have something like this in mind when he says that "In this last novel of the trilogy, Mink becomes a hero."[17]

Thus, unity and purpose determine the seemingly loosening form of the trilogy, a form that Flem, himself a central, unifying device, personifies. Fiedler notes that "In *The Town* ...Flem, though still a comic figure, loses the last vestiges of Faustian grandeur and begins to be proferred as an object of pity; revealed as impotent, and, if not chastened by the death of his never-possessed wife, at least on the verge of sensing the emptiness of his triumph."[18] Howe, on the other hand, maintains that "Faulkner has made the mistake of softening Flem," and he indulges in some condescending rewriting: "In composing *The Mansion* Faulkner seems to have been unwilling to face the possibility that Flem, having reached the top of his world, might snugly remain there, or more simply, that it would make for a better novel to let him remain there. . . . By the time Faulkner came to completing *The Mansion*, he seems to have felt a strong need to destroy Flem."[19] What Faulkner may have considered and rejected we can never fully know, but to complain that he has failed to sustain the wry, comic note of *The Hamlet* throughout the trilogy is to condemn him for not writing a different novel. Fiedler's view of Flem is more incisive and apt: "The most abiding creation of Faulkner is the Snopes family, especially Flem Snopes, that modern, American, bourgeois, ridiculous version of Faust."[20]

Faulkner's comments about the trilogy express his awareness of what he is doing, and indicate that in fact he too dislikes the change in Flem. He has a grudging admiration for Flem "until he was bitten by the bug to be respectable, and then he let me down." He can feel pity for Thomas Sutpen but none for Flem. "I never did feel sorry for him any more than one feels sorry for anyone who is ridden with an ambition or demon as base as simple vanity and rapacity and greed. I think that you can be ridden by a demon, but let it be a good demon, let it be a splendid demon, even if it is a demon, and his was a petty demon. So I don't feel sorry for Flem for that reason" (*F in U*, 33, 80, 120). The intentional fallacy proves nothing either way, but it does suggest the absurdity of a reading grounded in Faulkner's putative psychological phobias.

Even in *The Hamlet* Flem is not the "marvellous monster" Howe discerns and whose lack he deplores in the subsequent books of the trilogy. Rather, monstrosity resides largely in the panic-filled responses others make to him: for example, Jody Varner's intense fear of Flem, out of all proportion to the implicit threat of a burnt barn. Similarly, the likelihood of Flem's duping them with the spotted horses seems to impel the townspeople into public immolation in a parody of Russian show trials. Henry Armstid is only an extreme instance of one who is a pitiful fool before his encounter with Flem reduces him to a pitiable madman. Flem is not so much demonic, then, as he is demonized by timorous and insecure men who cannot deal with anything even *resembling* the force of unscrupulous and ruthless determination.

The clearest example of this reaction is Ratliff's hyperbolic nightmare vision of Flem taking over hell from the devil (*H*, 151-55). Occurring as it does early in Flem's rise, it demonstrates that Ratliff, as we might expect, sees the danger before anyone else. Fiedler says, "The voice of reason in the novel belongs to the sewing-machine salesman, Ratliffe [*sic*], who speaks for Faulkner more directly than any other character in *The Hamlet;* but it is Ratliffe who dreams, or perhaps, more properly, has a vision of Flem's Descent into Hell."[21] "Actively" knowing better, Ratliff nonetheless succumbs to the temptations Flem embodies—not, it should be noted, to an overwhelming force but to something far more treacherous:

an uncamouflaged trap. Flem's victims, as Ratliff reiterates, compete for the privilege of entering this trap: "I reckon there aint nothing under the sun or in Frenchman's Bend neither than can keep you folks from giving Flem Snopes and that Texas man your money" (282); "I never made them Snopeses and I never made the folks that cant wait to bare their backsides to them" (326). Certainly Flem, a supreme and unscrupulous opportunist, is evil, but his is not a supernatural imposition that overwhelms the good man's defenses. It is the perverse and self-willed blindness of all the others (with rare exception: Mrs. Littlejohn, Uncle Dick Bolivar) that represents the real villainy even in *The Hamlet*. Flem brings the spotted horses and seeds the Old Frenchman place, yet his function seems less the active creation of evil than the simple reaping of the inevitable fruits of human folly. Ratliff himself is the climactic example as he struggles for three days to suppress what he realizes from the first about Eustace Grimm's presence in Frenchman's Bend (355-67).

Yet Ratliff succumbs only once in the entire trilogy, and the experience teaches him a valuable moral lesson. Thereafter, Ratliff, while remaining cognizant of the very real and grave dangers Flem represents, both tries to aid Flem's victims and seeks to humanize Flem. It is thus ironic that Gavin, going off to war, "appoints" Ratliff to watch and to fight Snopesism— Ratliff was there first, equated Flem with Evil incarnate, and, having been burned, has moved beyond a purely negative response. Ratliff subsequently is most consistent in seeing Flem as merely evil—something smaller but more deadly because it is as much internal as external, insidious, unconquerable because human, very much a part of ourselves, the part Ratliff calls "nothing but jest another Snopes."

Flem, then, is not simply and unequivocally condemned even in and by *The Hamlet*—despite his being praised only by those we despise even more (like Lump Snopes). His motion is real and consistent, though it is defined more by the stages (social, economic, communal) he occupies in acquiring status and possessions than by frontal action. But as we are con-

stantly reminded, such progress is not inevitable—except in
the sense that others persist in perversely creating the moral
vacuum into which nature seems to thrust this apparently
ironic but actually most appropriately named of all Snopeses.
For all the dynamics of motion others read into him, his is the
phlegm of indolence and apathy; he cannot spit it out—and by
The Mansion he stops trying. From the moment of his initial,
passive appearance to the "frozen moment" of his death, he
embodies the qualities implicit in his name: "want of excitabil-
ity or enthusiasm; coldness, dullness, sluggishness, apathy;
coolness, calmness, self-possession, evenness of temper"
(New English Dictionary). He displays a laconic passivity
throughout: in Varner's store, at the corral, selling the Old
Frenchman place to Ratliff, in *The Hamlet;* paying for the
brass fittings, occupying restaurant, power plant, and bank,
allowing Linda to leave, in *The Town;* assuming de Spain's
role, going with Linda for whiskey, accepting his death, in *The
Mansion.* The few times he does act are memorable both
because they are rare and because they are too small and trivial
to sustain the notion of subhuman monstrosity: the scornful
five cents' worth of candy for Mrs. Armstid (*after* Armstid had
insisted on losing his money), the planting of liquor in "Atelier
Monty" (after Montgomery Ward had already been arrested),
the summoning of Varner to complain of Eula's adultery (after
he and everyone else had tacitly sanctioned it for eighteen
years), and so on.

Before he dries up and dies in the shell that is his mansion
and himself, Flem links the endings of *The Hamlet* and *The
Town* with the same act of spitting, in contempt and farewell,
as if ridding himself of those he has used and superseded. *The
Hamlet* ends with Flem spitting as he passes beyond Henry
Armstid's frenzied avarice and the narrow confines of
Frenchman's Bend: Flem takes the earth goddess Eula and,
trailing clouds of Snopeses, goes on to richer fields in Jefferson.
Near the end of *The Town,* Flem similarly spits in farewell to
Eula—whose death has brought him power, status, respecta-
bility (symbolized, respectively, by the bank presidency, de

Spain's house, and deaconship in the Baptist Church)—and, having dissipated all those clouds of Snopeses, now sends Linda off as well. Flem's characteristic spitting is as expressive as is, at the other end of the human spectrum, such an act of homage and expiation as Aufidius's royal funeral for *his* victim, Coriolanus. Flem displays utter contempt for the unending willful folly of men—and women too if we recall the parallel gesture Mrs. Armstid receives as she comes— obsequiously, grayly, impotently—to beg for the return of her hard-earned money. And who is to deny Flem his scorn when even such men as Ratliff and Bookwright are self-seduced by mindless greed?

Unlike *The Hamlet*, however, *The Town* contains an additional episode beyond the spitting, that of Byron Snopes's four wild children. Ratliff says that their departure signifies "the end of a erea.... The last and final end of Snopes out-and-out unvarnished behavior in Jefferson, if that's what I'm trying to say." But just as Ratliff's folly at the end of *The Hamlet* opens Jefferson up to Flem, his equally deluded comment at the end of *The Town* should forewarn us of Snopesism yet to come in *The Mansion*—the "unvarnished behavior" of Clarence and Orestes, and Mink's murder of Flem.

Flem succeeds in ridding himself and Jefferson of Byron's children without any significant cost, but the incident implies that, despite Flem's efforts throughout *The Town* and Ratliff's mistaken comment at its end, Snopesism will remain so long as Flem himself does—and in fact beyond, for Snopesism is always with us. Flem's lofty isolation at the end of *The Town* and throughout much of *The Mansion* is not that of a deity (or devil), but that, like Shakespeare's Richard III and Macbeth, of the dynamic impeller of action who cannot escape the consequences of the evil he has committed almost as a casual by-product of setting events in motion. Events and consequences remain with Flem as with Macbeth: they catch up to him, they destroy him in the end. Flem is, after all, impotent in more than one sense, and Eula extraordinarily insightful when, in her last comment about him (and one of the few she ever makes), she warns Gavin—and us: "You've got to be careful or you'll have to pity him. You'll have to. He couldn't bear that, and it's no use to hurt people if you don't get anything for it" (*T*, 331). What Eula tells us (and who has more right?) is that Flem is a person—a striking notion. Moreover, as a person he deserves not to be hurt gratuitously— even if it is easy and obvious and feels good. This does not, I think, mitigate or trivialize Flem's evil, but it does humanize it and afford an understandable context and perspective. And this, if we look back over the trilogy, emerges as one of Ratliff's major functions all along; for despite the numerous references to the animalism and mechanical relentlessness of Snopesism, Ratliff (an inductivist concerned with people and the on-goingness of daily life) provides understandable motivation for what often seems totally inexplicable (because not adhering to a priori assumptions) to deductivist romantics like Gavin.

Flem's death near the end of the trilogy effectively completes Faulkner's pattern—and Howe's objection to that event makes no more sense than would decrying the neatness of Macbeth's end. In one sense, Flem's death "closes" the novel, terminates both the mounting momentum of Flem's career and its subsequent contraction into the mansion. It is the ritualistic fulfillment of a revenge cycle, of a tragic progress; and yet it also occurs because, through *The Town* and *The Mansion*, Flem has been reduced to (or revealed at) the level of one who *can* die. Beck puts it this way: "The impasse at which Flem has arrived illustrates him as a flat character but also contributes to his representativeness of all those whose aggressions can brave it out only so long as their victims shrink from retaliating with equal force. And that the fellow who seemed unbeatable has come to the point where he cannot even spit marks the plainest of finalities."[22] But the novel is also "open" since Snopesism continues in all its multifarious forms. The murderous Mink heads west, perhaps to meet up with the wild, small-minded, thievish Byron; behind there remain the idiot Ike; Montgomery Ward, the pornographer (this time in the flesh rather than dirty postcards); I. O., the garrulous fool; Wat, the carpenter; Wall, the honest and successful grocer; and so on. This is far from the monolithic picture of Snopesism that (given only *The Hamlet*) we might have anticipated. It is, in fact, a fair sampling of the human spectrum.

In consequence, the Snopes trilogy seeks its unity against the grain of univocality, monolithic character, singleness of purpose and vision. None of its unities or movements is simple or simply directed. The novel revolves forward, backward, and sideways in time; expands spatially from Frenchman's Bend to Jefferson, then contracts into Flem's parody of Monticello, and yet simultaneously comes to encompass a realm of events far beyond Mississippi. Its characters (Flem most notably, but Eula, Linda, and others as well) exhibit what Lawrence calls "allotropic states," not the "old stable *ego* of the character," but shifting "states of the same simple radically unchanged element."[23] Further, the structures and tonal purposes of the trilogy's three books, though they often seem askew of each other, suggest an expanding gyre of action and concern. *The Hamlet* is the tightest and most neatly compacted of the three, but the world of Frenchman's Bend is a constricted one, and bounded by an essentially myopic vision. Thus the single viewpoint can encompass it with relative ease, and Ratliff's voice, for all its incisiveness, is as typical of Frenchman's Bend as it is uniquely his own. Jefferson inhabits a larger, more complex scale, as revealed, for instance, in the simultaneous acceptance and condemnation of Eula and de Spain, a "blend of censoriousness and indifference"[24]— followed by a tacit rewriting of eighteen years of history when Flem finally forces public acknowledgment of what the town had helped keep unexaminedly private, had in fact sanctioned. And finally, since Jefferson has been invaded not only by Flem and Snopesism but, through Gavin and Chick, by Harvard and Europe as well, *The Mansion* is the loosest, most sprawling of the trilogy because, among other things, it documents the increasing chaos of the world at large.

The greatest structural problem in *The Mansion* (perhaps in the entire trilogy) concerns Ratliff's long discursive summarizing of the past and recapitulation of the momentarily quiescent present ("a kind of Snopes doldrum") in chapters 6 and 7. What is the point of this section that adds little to what we already know from *The Hamlet* and *The Town?* For one thing, we are made to see events, if not clear, then at least whole, from a single viewpoint. And in a world of anarchic larger events this represents an affirmation of individual efficacy that, for example, allows not only for Ratliff's subsequent elimination of Clarence Snopes from the Senate race, but also validates his unique tall-tale way of narrating it.[25] Ratliff's view is not entirely "clear" because he is neither omniscient nor, ultimately, multifarious. In some ways he knows less than we: he has not read *The Hamlet* and *The Town* but only experienced some of their events. He must sometime "presume on a little more than jest evidence"—accurately enough when he imagines Eula asking Gavin to marry Linda, inaccurately when he assumes that Linda, in her senior year of high school, is avoiding Gavin rather than vice versa. In this section, then, Ratliff displays the strengths and weaknesses—and above all, the human significance—of his own intuitive faculties; in addition, he offers choric commentary on the complex of events that seems equally to fascinate all the inhabitants of Frenchman's Bend and Jefferson. Given the opportunity, each could presumably tell a similar tale, though doubtless with less good humor, articulateness, and moral suasion.

But most importantly, Ratliff's circuitous narration (like Temple's in *Requiem for a Nun*) not only reconstructs the past and helps to unify the trilogy, it actively (if momentarily) forestalls the imminent present by suspending the action that unifies and structures *The Mansion:* Mink's journey from Parchman to Jefferson. The journey itself is framed by the atemporality of Mink's life in prison and the suspended moment of Flem's death; but it gains ritual and archetypal reverberations from Ratliff's usurpation of time. Mink's journey is, among other things, an attempt to rediscover (and

therefore to create) time and space, but while Ratliff occupies
front and center, time is stayed. In a sense, this most moral of
men weds his two functions as teller and participant as he
"narratively acts" to forestall the moment when Mink—freed
from the timeless aridity of Parchman before Ratliff starts
speaking of the past, and then freed from Ratliff's atemporal
verbiage—can move out of the past and the verbiage long
enough to shoot Flem and thus complete his own cycle of
alienation from and reunion with the soil, and to end the book
and the trilogy.

But no more than Snopesism is Ratliff (or even Gavin or
Chick) defeated in the end—and not because either he or his
wisdom transcends the human, the immediate, but because the
opposite is true. Gavin, for one, had rejected an ethical pattern
in the rise and fall of Flem Snopes, but as Beck insists, "Stevens's statement that 'There aren't any morals' scarcely denies
morality, for he goes on to say people do the 'best' they can."[26]
Ratliff's position is the converse of Gavin's: for all his attempt
to point a moral, Ratliff (hoping that Gavin's future does not
include a *third* Eula Varner) reminds us in the end that there
are no ends, no close to the comic agony of the human cycle.
Ratliff's wisdom is incisive not because it is otherworldly but
because, partaking of the intensely immediate, it can live in the
most human of gestures: "Gentle and tender as a woman,
Ratliff opened the car door for Stevens to get in." Such a
gesture symbolizes a kind of paradoxical transcendence (the
kind that never gets off the ground), the nearest thing to
omniscience in the perspective of human mortality, and in that
sense perhaps the only kind we need. It is exactly that sort of
"active" wisdom for which no disembodied "omniscient"
narrator—no matter how shifting the roles he plays—could
ever find proper expression. Ratliff never becomes a multifarious narrator because, as both teller and doer, he remains
complexly and utterly true to the dualism that is himself and
all human beings.

Thus when, a quarter of the way into *The Mansion*, Ratliff
offers his version of Eula's deflowering, we know (as he does)

that it is more vital, more meaningful, than that of the multifarious narrator who prefaces his own ostensibly true account
with, "Nobody ever knew exactly what happened" (*H*, 139-
41). Similarly, though to a lesser degree, the identification with
Gavin and Chick that the novel encourages insures that, for all
their failings, we can never view them as objects, as simply
judgeable, as *other*. The multifarious narrator of *The Mansion*
seems to be seeking something of the high degree of authorita-
tiveness he embodied in *The Hamlet*, when he had center
stage pretty much to himself. But too much has happened in
the interim to allow us to partake unequivocally of the elegiac
lyricism that (paralleling the panoramic vision of the trilogy's
opening) he subsides into at the end of *The Mansion*. Mink's
heading west, while it may link him with the immortals for the
narrator, does not really change anything for those who—like
Ratliff, Gavin, and Chick—remain behind, neither disembodied nor anonymous. We grant the narrator, therefore, not the
abstract omniscience other narrators have claimed, but a
unique personal impressionism. Instead of transcending our
own prismatic vision, he claims a facet for his own. Fortu-
nately, the prism is endlessly expandable—each viewer adds
another reflector, one more to the sum of human understanding. Nameless, featureless, timeless, he is, nonetheless, one of
Faulkner's most compelling speakers and characters.

8

Worlds Elsewhere: *Soldiers' Pay, Mosquitoes, Pylon, A Fable*

Cloistered within the confines of Yoknapatawpha, Faulkner's finest and most characteristic writings scarcely acknowledge worlds elsewhere. Those who emigrate from it seem to disappear (like Caddy in *The Sound and the Fury* or Sutpen on his trip to New Orleans in *Absalom, Absalom!*); or obsessively take it with them (like Quentin Compson); or spend their time plotting to return (like Lucius in *The Reivers*). Though outside places are alluded to in the Yoknapatawpha novels, few are actually depicted: Memphis (though very little more than Miss Reba's brothel) in *Sanctuary, Go Down, Moses,* and *The Reivers;* Harvard in *The Sound and the Fury* and *Absalom, Absalom!;* Chicago, briefly, just before Bayard is killed in *Flags in the Dust,* and a few others. Most such places are represented negatively, as names lacking substantiality: Gavin Stevens's Heidelberg; Lena Grove's Alabama, from which she has come "a fur piece"; Charles Bon's New Orleans that Quentin and Shreve strive to create in *Absalom;* Linda Snopes Kohl's New York and Civil War Spain in *The Mansion;* World War I's Europe, where various characters fought (some even dying) yet which they seem never to have visited. Outside events—

the World Wars, the Spanish Civil War, the rise to power of
Hitler and Stalin—occasionally impinge, but they too seem
impossibly remote and unreal. Faulkner generally works to
create *his* world and then, through mythic, literary, and his-
toric analogues and allusions, to imply macrocosmic
significance.

Oxford, Mississippi, and its environs—or their fictional
equivalent—are the geographical referent for the term "Faulknerian." Yet Faulkner's other worlds—those outside or
beyond the small southern community central to his life and
work—are more numerous and varied than is commonly
assumed. At various times Faulkner lived and worked in
Canada, Connecticut, New York, New Orleans, Hollywood,
and Europe. In his later years he traveled a great deal—to
Japan, Europe, and South America, among others—as cultural
ambassador and to receive various honors. Finally, he became
writer-in-residence at the University of Virginia and bought a
second home in Charlottesville. It should not be surprising,
then, that—despite his rootedness in a particular place and
past—Faulkner set a fair amount of his fiction outside of his
mythical kingdom, nor that it fails to measure up to his
greatest achievements. This chapter will examine, in chronological order, Faulkner's non-Yoknapatawpha novels.

Soldiers' Pay

Soldiers' Pay (1926), Faulkner's first novel, concerns the
aftermath of World War I—the war Faulkner missed, regret-
ted, and largely effaced (though he did resurrect it for the
setting of his much later antiwar novel, *A Fable* [1954]).
Deeply and repeatedly concerned with war, the Yoknapatawpha novels return to America's war against itself, the
only one that truly mattered to Faulkner and his land. Through
his heritage, endless stories heard and told throughout his life,
its constant replay in recounting and in enduring devastation,
the Civil War became the one military experience that he
effectively entered into directly and fully. Unlike most first

novels, then, *Soldiers' Pay* is *negative* autobiography—not a fictionalized accounting of its author's early years but an imaginative construct that Faulkner imposed on paper after having failed to impose it upon his life.

The novel begins with raucous soldiers on a train returning home at war's end. The focus gradually becomes Lieutenant Donald Mahon, a victim of shell shock who bears "a dreadful scar across his brow." Little more than a mindless vegetable whose plight compels attention from all those he encounters, he is not so much the novel's protagonist as an absence at its center: the creation not only of his author but of everyone he encounters. He arouses sympathetic pity from Private Joe Gilligan and Margaret Powers, who find him on the train and take him home; frenzied revulsion from the vacuous and "epicene" fiancée he had left behind; envy from Private Julian Lowe, who self-pityingly feels that "they had stopped the war on him" and so "sat in a smoldering of disgusted sorrow"; revivified hope from the father who, having heard he was dead, thinks that his survival means that everything will return to normal; and a gamut of emotions from fascination to revulsion from his gossipy small-town neighbors.

The characters, unfortunately, are not much more fully realized than this suggests—more a set of attitudes signaled by their names than actors capable of initiative or independence from their creator's string-pulling. Lowe is callow youth, low-class and illiterate, posturing ignorantly above love, war, and death—and, therefore, about Mahon above all: "Had I been old enough or lucky enough, this might have been me, he thought jealously.... To have been him! he moaned. Just to be him. Let him take this sound body of mine! Let him take it. To have got wings on my breast, to have wings; and to have got his scar, too, I would take death to-morrow." Forlornly he asks, "Margaret, are you in love with him?' (Knowing that if he were a woman, he would be.)" He fades away as the novel progresses, writing ever shorter letters to Margaret, ever more feebly asserting his self-importance and fantasizing love for her while ignoring her indifference to him.

Margaret Powers is, as her name suggests, the novel's strongest character. Without necessarily desiring to do so, she exercises control over others, manipulates much of the action, evokes marriage proposals from various young men, and ultimately marries Mahon—presumably in order to care for him—shortly before he dies. She is haunted throughout by the first husband she had loved briefly but failed to separate herself from before it was too late; war's solution freezes her in failure:

> She thought of her husband youngly dead in France in a recurrence of fretful exasperation with having been tricked by a wanton Fate: a joke amusing to no one. Just when she had calmly decided that they had taken advantage of a universal hysteria for the purpose of getting of each other a brief ecstasy, just when she had decided calmly that they were better quit of each other with nothing to mar the memory of their three days together and had written him so, wishing him luck, she must be notified casually and impersonally that he had been killed in action.... He had not even got her letter! This in some way seemed the infidelity: having him die still believing in her, bored though they both probably were.

Still bound to the dead husband she had failed to deny, Margaret can only reiterate that relationship by marrying someone who "is practically a dead man now." Thus, marriage repeats itself as entrapment and isolation—"Married, and she had never felt so alone"—and its termination and her consequent flight connote the opposite: "Freedom comes with the decision: it does not wait for the act. She felt freer, more at peace with herself than she had felt for months." And at the end, trying to break the pattern, she refuses the ever-faithful Gilligan in order, she says, to spare him: "Bless your heart, darling. If I married you you'd be dead in a year, Joe. All the men that marry me die, you know." She thus retains her name, and all the "powers" it connotes, by refusing to exercise them for a third time.

The names of almost all the other characters might be rehearsed to the same effect. Boisterous Joe Gilligan is the stereotypical good-hearted G.I. Joe. Madden, a solider who witnessed Powers's death (he was shot "in the face at point-blank range" by one of his own men terrified of being killed) relives the trauma repeatedly, hauntingly, "maddened." January Jones, though described in vague, romantic terms—his "face was a round mirror before which fauns and nymphs might have wantoned when the world was young"—is not the youthful naïve his first name might suggest; rather, he fulfills its implication of cold calculation in his lustful pursuits. Both he and his various targets, as his surname implies, are virtually anonymous—characterless gesture lacking meaning and substance. The ill-educated Emmy, who had loved and romanticized Mahon before the war and now, still loving him, finds him utterly beyond her reach, may well echo Emma Bovary, lovelessly trapped, desperate to escape, and ultimately indifferent to her fate. Mrs. Worthington is no more than the embodiment of riches that her name connotes.

Most suggestive of all is Mahon himself—his name, its pronunciation presumably approximating "man," meant to evoke universality, the mortal realm. Always called "Loot" by Gilligan, he embodies the novel's title in the text. Spoiled by war, he is doubly its spoil: he and his condition represent both war and its proper reward. The prize for which all the others contest, he is the horrific booty for which men organize to kill and die. His own scarcely noticed death occurs as a posthumous letting go. The doctor says: "He should have been dead these three months were it not for the fact that he seems to be waiting for something. Something he has begun, but has not completed, something he has carried from his former life that he does not remember consciously. That is his only hold on life ... he will go whenever that final spark somewhere in him is no longer fed. His body is already dead." He at last becomes reconciled externally and internally—for he ceases to be "a nine-days' wonder" to his townspeople and he reexperiences and apparently accepts the moment that destroyed him: " 'That's how it happened,' he said." His funeral, which follows immediately, finally ratifies the death he survives only temporarily.

The novel is very much a thing of its moment—the wary return to peace and frenzied leisure, the cynicism and self-absorption and thin romanticism, that ushered in the "jazz age." Its tone is often archly self-conscious:

This, the spring of 1919, was the day of the Boy, of him who had been too young for soldiering. For two years he had had a dry time of it. Of course, girls had used him during the scarcity of men, but always in such a detached impersonal manner. Like committing fornication with a beautiful woman who chews gum steadily all the while. O Uniform, O Vanity. They had used him but when a uniform showed up he got the air.

Jones, a curiously literary reference informs us, "grew up in a Catholic orphanage, but like Henry James he attained verisimilitude by means of tediousness." A "disciple of the cult of boldness with women," Jones grossly and repeatedly pursues the handiest female flesh; he thinks "vulgarly" of Cecily, "I've got your number," but fails badly with her and so "knew exasperation and a puerile lust." Cecily faints on first seeing Mahon's full injury: "The light passing through her fine hair gave her a halo and lent her frail dress a fainting nimbus about her crumpling body like a stricken poplar." The rector, Mahon's father, makes speeches like this: "There is always death in the faces of the young in spirit, the eternally young. Death for themselves or for others. And dishonor. But death, surely. And why not? why should death desire only those things which life no longer has use for? Who gathers the withered rose?" And Margaret thinks things like, "It's quite romantic being reft of your love and then having him returned unexpectedly to your arms."

In these examples and throughout, the language and imagery are typically abstract and distancing, self-conscious artifice failing to vitalize character, setting, or event. This is perhaps truest in the reiterated figure of natural processes proceeding independently of the world's human inhabitants and their desperate isolation from each other. An early description represents the returned soldiers as aliens hearing "forgotten music. Caught both in the magic of change they stood feeling the spring in the cold air, as if they had but recently come into a new world, feeling their littleness and believing too that lying in wait for them was something new and strange. They were ashamed of this and silence was unbearable." Pathetically, the world of nature both excludes and expresses them: "The leaves hung lifeless and sad, as if life were being recalled from them before it was fully given, leaving only the ghosts of young leaves." All of nature, like its creatures, is stylized, abstract, redolent of decadence: "Roses were slashed upon green bushes, roses red as the mouths of courtesans, red as Cecily's mouth, shaping Don't." The action and characters, stereotypical of the twenties, conform to "the beat of the music, . . . the rhythmic troubling obscenities of saxophones," the meaningless, reiterated movement that ultimately performs not nature's or man's vitality but a shadowy dance of death.

Coming to Faulkner's first novel this late, one is perhaps most struck by isolated notes sounded more richly and fully elsewhere. Occasional descriptions—here inorganic to the plot—anticipate the oxymorons of frozen motion central to such other novels as *Light in August* and *The Mansion:* "A Negro driving a wagon passed between them, interminable as Time: he thought the wagon would never pass. . . . Niggers and mules. Afternoon lay in a coma in the street. . . . Monotonous wagons drawn by long-eared beasts crawled past. Negroes humped with sleep, portentous upon each wagon and in the wagon bed itself sat other Negroes upon chairs: a pagan catafalque under the afternoon." The rector's aesthetic/erotic question ("Who was the old pagan who kept his Byzantine goblet at his bedside and slowly wore away the rim kissing it?") initiates one of Faulkner's iterated central images. Margaret in motion—"Her long legs swept her up and onto the veranda as the pursing rain, foiled, whirled like cavalry with silver lances across the lawn"—creates a resonance, here lacking context and straining for effect, that is appropriate in *Flags in the Dust* and *Light in August;* like Henry and Bon in *Absalom, Absalom!,* she vainly hopes that war's greater catastrophe will sort out the lesser; and like Addie in *As I Lay Dying*, she finds small value in men's words: "Women know more about words than men ever will. And they knew how little they can ever possibly mean." Jones, though lacking his complexity and tragic stature, anticipates *Light in August*'s Joe Christmas in his anonymous background and accidental name: "born of whom he knew and cared not, becoming Jones alphabetically, January through a conjunction of calendar and biology." And the brief appearance of Aunt Callie, the old Negro mammy bearing the name of Faulkner's own family's Caroline Barr to whom he dedicated *Go Down, Moses*, foreshadows Dilsey in *The Sound and the Fury*. In these and other like instances, *Soldiers' Pay*, for all its many failures, initiated meanings and complexities from which Faulkner would learn and which he would exploit when he discovered his voice and his world.

Mosquitoes

Soldiers' Pay and its sequel, *Mosquitoes* (1927), frame the world that Faulkner proclaimed uniquely his own beginning with his third novel: the first book set in Charleston just after the war, the second leapfrogging to Mississippi's west—to New Orleans (primarily its Lake Pontchartrain)—in the early nineteen-twenties. Faulkner himself deprecated them in the same breath when, after completing *Flags in the Dust*, he spoke of his never again writing a book "as youngly glamorous as 'Soldiers' Pay' nor as trashily smart as 'Mosquitoes' " (*Letters*, 40). *Mosquitoes* transmutes war's drifting survivors into artists and their hangers-on—all literally adrift and then marooned on a tame sea's pleasure craft that bears, for no discernible reason, the Homeric name of *The Nausikaa*. Between its Prologue and Epilogue, the novel continuously displaces artistic achievement with incessant, empty talk about creativity, plus "masturbation, conception, constipation, evacuation, lesbianism, syphilis, and perversion" (Blotner, 514).

The trip is a joyless party performed reluctantly, often wearily, by a devitalized yacht of fools.

The sailors include the lonely and arrogant sculptor Gordon, with his "intolerant hawk's face"; the novelist Dawson Fairchild (based on Sherwood Anderson) who prattles nonstop throughout, mostly about art's inferiority to life, but who does tell comic tall tales; a woman who paints portraits and still lifes with "a bold, humorless style"; a critic, constantly referred to as "the Semitic man," "who was nurturing a reputation for cleverness"; a poetess who accurately calls the men silly and dull; a nervous and seasick bootlegger and his vacuous girlfriend Jenny, both interlopers; Mark Frost, who "with sepulchral belligerance," declares himself "the best poet in New Orleans," though the narrator comments that he "produced an occasional cerebral and obscure poem... reminding one somehow of the function of evacuation excruciatingly and incompletely performed"; and, almost as antidote, Major Ayres, a florid British eccentric who announces his schemes to cure Americans of their national blight—constipation—at the most inopportune moments.

Mrs. Maurier, the yacht's owner and the party organizer, is less Lord of Revels than puritanical restrainer who tells her guests that they "must be good children." After a barren and loveless marriage, she devotes her energies to artists with "something thwarted back of it all, something stifled, yet which won't quite die." Like her "scented upholstered bulk," her name—probably pronounced "more," as it is illiterately written by a crew member—connotes greed and excess, though all her herding efforts are ultimately unsuccessful. In theory she adores the artists and young people she accumulates and attempts to organize, but she is constantly shocked by their crude language and rudeness in evading her control; she even manages to be repeatedly surprised that the men prefer drinking on their own to dancing or bridge. Her basic motif is frustration, but then so is it for the book as a whole.[1] Nothing ever goes as it should—for her or anyone else—and yet neither actions nor consequences attain the level of significance, for their ominousness is always dissipated or denied.

Like the novel itself, the yacht loses its steering mechanism
shortly after the journey begins; but a tug eventually rescues
the latter easily from a sandbar. Gordon, the aloof yet lustful
sculptor, disappears from a rowboat during a ludicrous
attempt, organized by Fairchild, to free the yacht with a rope.
Mrs. Maurier reacts with typical despair: "Mrs. Maurier's face
became dreadful, and as the blood died swooning in her heart
she had again that brief vision of floating inert buttocks, later
to wash ashore with that inopportune and terrible im-
placability of the drowned." But Gordon later reappears as
suddenly and inexplicably as he had disappeared. Mrs. Maurier's
spoiled niece Pat, one of the novel's two objects of all the men's
lust and a repeat of Cecily in *Soldiers' Pay*, whimsically elopes
with a steward. They swim ashore from the marooned yacht;
spend a day—with truant excitement turning to confusion,
then to panic, and finally to hopelessness—tramping through
a symbolically laden jungle out of Conrad's *Heart of Darkness;*
are rescued, seemingly just this side of death, by a leering
redneck who ferries them to the yacht's yawning indifference
just in time for dinner—their return no more noteworthy than
their absence. And this is the novel's basic rhythm: rare
moments of energy trailing off into bathos and talk—much of
it epigrammatic, self-consciously clever, watered-down Oscar
Wilde—about art, life, death, sex, and drink, with all except the
drink reduced to eneffectual stratagem and conversational gam-
bits. The effect is well summarized by Fairchild's comment on
modern women, whom he sees as little more than boys in their
breastless and "uncomplex awkwardness": "Not satisfying any
more; just exciting and monotonous. And mostly monotonous."
     The theme of frustrated lust is introduced and most fully
personified by the Prufrockian Ernest Talliaferro, a man of
"obsequious courtesy," whom Blotner parallels to Januarius
Jones in *Soldiers' Pay* (515). The Prologue begins with his
unlikely assertion that "The sex instinct . . . is quite strong in
me. . . . the sex instinct is perhaps my most dominating
compulsion." The Epilogue ends, after his having become
engaged to Mrs. Maurier, with his final failure to define

women or have a sexual fling. A buyer of ladies' clothes for a
large department store (doubtless a vocational pun on Eliot's J.
Alfred Pru*frock*), Talliaferro spends his time worrying about
his thinning hair, obsequiously playing bridge with the women
rather than drinking with the men, and creating new means to
increase his sexual frustration. Pathetic and self-deluded, he
seeks an image of wildness in the mirror but finds only the
"customary expression of polite faint alarm." He is a busybody
and a fussbudget whom Eliot defines perfectly:

> Deferential, glad to be of use,
> Politic, cautious, and meticulous;
> Full of high sentence, but a bit obtuse;
> At times, indeed, almost ridiculous—
> Almost, at times, the Fool

Like Prufrock, Talliaferro is ultimately reduced to endlessly
preparing "a face to meet the faces that you meet"—and then
failing to make connections with others.

Perhaps the novel's most unpleasant and unsatisfying relationship is that between Pat and her twin brother, Josh. He it
is who carelessly sets the yacht adrift by clandestinely removing a rod he needs to ream the pipe he carves during the entire
novel. Together the siblings represent both androgyny and
frustration: inexplicably and without affection they call each
other "Gus"; his jaw is described as feminine while hers is
masculine; and she seductively fawns on him as men do on her.
He is clearly long-suffering—at one point she crawls into his
bed and nibbles and moans at his ear—while generally being
as nasty to her as she is to everyone else. They are, alone and
together, so thoroughly self-centered, rude, and dull that it is
difficult to connect this brother-sister pair with those that
Faulkner will later locate at the center of such major books as
The Sound and the Fury, As I Lay Dying, and *Absalom,
Absalom!*

Only two things in the novel—the ubiquitous eponymous
mosquitoes and Gordon's sculpture of a female torso—escape
the general malaise, and both do so through contrasting ironi-

cally with the human sphere to which they might be expected to serve as foils. Both motifs are introduced in the opening scene through Talliaferro who "under the spell put on us by those we admire doing things we ourselves cannot do," returns repeatedly to Gordon's studio to watch him sculpt (even though "he invariably soiled his clothes") and who, while there, "slapped viciously and vainly at the back of his hand . . . slapped his neck savagely." The insects, magical because never actually named or described in the text, yet appear as headnote on every page; they are, further, as pervasive and incorporeal as those in Jean-Paul Sartre's *The Flies,* a far more troubling work that *Mosquitoes* influenced. Faulkner's insects—always present and in motion, always attacking passive flesh that seems as insubstantial as they—represent the lust whose fulfillment is the novel's central nonaction: the pseudophallic in vain pursuit of the nonfeminine, for the women are masculine, resistant, or indifferent, and therefore unattainable even when to hand.

Counterpointing the mosquitoes is the torso, which, though in evidence only in the Prologue and Epilogue, is alluded to throughout as an incontrovertible triumph and a representation of female perfection. It too is oddly negative, a symbolic absence or denial much like the figures on Keats's Grecian urn that it evokes: "As you entered the room the thing drew your eyes: you turned sharply as to a sound, expecting movement. But it was marble, it could not move . . . : motionless and passionately eternal—the virginal breastless torso of a girl, headless, armless, legless, in marble temporarily caught and hushed yet passionate still for escape, passionate and simple and eternal in the equivocal derisive darkness of the world." Gordon, who proclaims the torso "my feminine ideal: a virgin with no legs to leave me, no arms to hold me, no head to talk to me," sees the vacuous Pat—who is also portrayed negatively throughout—as its incarnation in flesh: "Gordon examined with growing interest her *flat breast* and belly, her *boy's body* which the poise of it and the *thinness* of her arms belied. *Sexless,* yet somehow vaguely troubling" (my emphasis). Viewing the torso, "stroking it with slow desire," she herself proclaims that "It's like me," and she longs to possess it as keenly as the sculptor comes to desire her. But in this novel of nonconsummation, neither has the wit to suggest a trade, and so they manage merely to deny each other.

The novel's only fully realized action occurs in its most assured piece of writing, a deceptive preamble on the mosquito's life cycle:

> In spring, the sweet young spring, decked out with little green, necklaced, braceleted with the song of idiotic birds, spurious and sweet and tawdry as a shopgirl in her cheap finery, like an idiot with money and no taste; they were little and young and trusting, you could kill them sometimes. And now, as August like a languorous replete bird winged slowly through the pale summer toward the moon of decay and death, they were bigger, vicious; ubiquitous as undertakers, cunning as pawnbrokers, confident and unavoidable as politicians. · They came cityward lustful as country boys, as passionately integral as a college football squad; pervading and monstrous but without majesty: a biblical plague seen through the wrong end of a binocular: the majesty of Fate become contemptuous through ubiquity and sheer repetition.

The preamble's deceit lies in its implying a pattern—first the young birds of spring, then images of predation and lust, and, finally, Autumnal "decay and death"—that will be repeated in the novel as a whole. But, in fact, the latter offers neither spring's vitality nor its decline. Rather, the lethargy and empty romanticism of its end are established at the very beginning— "summer lay supine, unchaste with decay" and "New Orleans, the vieux carré, brooded in a faintly tarnished languor like an aging yet still beautiful courtesan in a smokefilled room, avid yet weary too of ardent ways"—and sustained throughout. Faulkner's failure to structure *Mosquitoes* on the model of the preamble may well have been purposeful: a way of initiating the novel's theme of frustration, its focus on endless, empty chatter. But as one critic notes, *Mosquitoes* is "a good example of what Faulkner condemns—too much talk and too little art."[2] Faulkner clearly learned a great deal from writing his two apprentice novels—or "foals" as he called them (*Letters*, 38)—for he did not repeat their weaknesses in the works of Yoknapatawpha that his next novel inaugurated. The failures of the latter exist on an entirely different scale of achievement.

Pylon

Faulkner's eighth novel, though far from his finest, has the advantage of *Soldiers' Pay* and *Mosquitoes* in having been written at the height of his powers—in fact, during a break from *Absalom, Absalom!*, that cloister of myth and history whose past obsession serves to displace and deny the present. *Pylon* (1935) exists at the opposite extreme; Faulkner intersperses exposition, but its characters are defined in and by the moment: for them and their book "the past is a nothing—a vacuum."[3] Accomplished with an ease and rapidity second only to that of *As I Lay Dying*, the writing of *Pylon* served first to satisfy a publisher and then to enable Faulkner to complete the stalled *Absalom:* a rare instance of success—albeit a limited one—inspiring return, repetition, and extraordinary achievement for Faulkner.

Like Faulkner's first two novels, *Pylon* takes place over a period of just a few days, though unlike them its focus is intense, violent action: an air show to celebrate the dedication of New Orleans's new airport. The novel counterpoints airmen and reporters—those who participate and those who extract or impose meaning—just as Faulkner himself "inhabited the worlds of both literature and aviation" (Blotner, 869). The rootless, asocial flyers, residents of an alien element, are taken over by an unnamed reporter, assigned to cover the show, who projects onto them "his own aspirations and dreams"[4] and becomes obsessed with them and their lives: "they aint human like us," he insists to his editor; "they couldn't turn those pylons like they do if they had human blood and senses and they wouldn't want to or dare to if they just had human brains. Burn them like this one tonight and they dont even holler in the fire; crash one and it aint even blood when you haul him out: it's cylinder oil the same as in the crankcase."

The novel begins with Jiggs, the airplane mechanic, ogling a pair of cowboy boots in a shoe store window, determined to own them regardless of cost or size. They represent a link to an earlier time, a time of "unblemished and inviolate implication of horse and spur," just as Jiggs himself links the worlds of earth and air by working with and for flyers while remaining both below and indifferent to action aloft. He readies but does not ride, or even watch, the new mounts, which, on the ground, seem "a species of esoteric and fatal animals not trained or tamed but just for the instant inert," as if etherized before the mechanic's skill. With his "bronco legs," Jiggs portrays the anachronism he embodies since he is "a guy that looks like a little horse," or even "the pony man, the manpony" as the two merge and he becomes a "cartoon comedy centaur": "the vicious halfmetamorphosis between thug and horse." The imagery he evokes (like that throughout the novel) is always excessive, more than he seems able to bear, though at times quite fine. After a drunken spree during which he stints his duties and thus causes a plane crash, he is deflated, reduced to a parody of vitality: "The reporter saw now the once raked and swaggering cap crumpled and thrust into Jiggs' hip pocket and that the absence of the raked and filthy object from Jiggs' silhouette was like the dropped flag from the shot buck's—the body still ran, still retained a similitude of power and even speed, would even run on for yards and even perhaps miles, and then for years in a gnawing burrowing of worms, but that which tasted air and drank the sun was dead."

The rest of the group to which the reporter attaches himself includes a pilot, Roger Shumann; his wife, Laverne, for whom he shot dice after she gave birth; a parachutist, Holmes, the other member of the ménage and the loser (or is it winner?) of the craps game; and Laverne's six-year-old son whom she teaches (sadistically or so as to toughen him for living?) to respond with fury to the taunt, "Who's your old man?" The reporter cannot imagine airmen having "kinfolks or [being] descended from human beings"; he sees them as floating free of all earthly connections. Yet Jiggs has a wife and two kids whom he has abandoned, Laverne a sister and a brother-in-law who initiated her into sex, Roger a set of midwest parents disappointed that he did not become a doctor like his father. These characters are, therefore, represented doubly, and as with other exemplars of physical courage—Roman gladiators, medieval knights, bullfighters, mercenaries, and the like— what fascinates is the dichotomy between actor and action, between the valor or courage or pride (or whatever it is) exhibited in performance and the sheer banality of those who so perform. We are told, for example, that during school recess one day Roger suddenly appeared out of the sky and Laverne simply went off with him. And later, about to make her first parachute jump, she climbed onto Roger's lap with "her wild and frenzied body," has sex with him while he struggles to control the plane, and then jumps "not merely naked but clothed in the very traditional symbology—the ruined dress with which she was trying wildly to cover her loins, and the parachute harness—of female bondage." Yet when she expresses her deepest desire it sounds like this: "all I want is just a house, a room; a cabin will do, a coalshed where I can know that next Monday and the Monday after that and the Monday after that. . . ."

It is impossible, in fact, to make anything coherent of her character. Having been literally swept off her feet by Roger, she sleeps indifferently with him or Holmes (the latter a scarcely developed character); gives birth "on an unrolled parachute in a hangar in California"; marries the high dice roller in order to give her son a father; teaches the boy to be obsessed by the incertitude about his father's identity; mourns anguishedly for Roger when he dies in a plane crash; and in the end abandons her son to Roger's parents in order to make a life with Holmes and his baby that she is carrying. This last is especially confused: she refuses to assure the grandfather that the boy *is* his grandson and yet she surrenders him presumably in order to be free of Roger's ghost. The only overt reason

offered—that she and Holmes cannot afford to keep him—is
undercut early on: Roger's income is haphazard, dependent on
prize money, and "when he dont cop they eat on the parachute
guy, which is O.K. because the parachute guy makes almost as
much as the guy at the microphone does." Such contradictions
are left unresolved; they cannot be explained by reference to
clashing perspectives, though much in the novel can.

The book's central perspective is that of the reporter, to
whom everything ultimately refers and who epitomizes all the
qualities he imposes on the flyers: atemporality, ethereality,
spontaneous generation, mechanization. They, after all, have
both family ties and group bonding, while he is not only
unmarried but "a creature who apparently never had any
parents either and who will not be old and never was a child,
who apparently sprang fullgrown and irrevocably mature out
of some violent and instantaneous transition." Despite possessing a mother, a job, and an apartment, he seems far more
devoid of past, purpose, and place than they, far less an
inhabitant of this world. "The reporter had joined the paper
without credentials or any past, documentary or hearsay, at all,
with his appearance of some creature evolved by forced draft
in a laboratory and both beyond and incapable of any need for
artificial sustenance, like a tumbleweed." He passes through
traffic, consequently, "apparently without contact with earth,
like one of the apocryphal nighttime batcreatures whose nest
or home no man ever saw." The flyers fascinate him because of
their constant flirtation with death, but he is death itself: an
apparition, an escapee from a graveyard, "the invoked spirit at
a seance," weightless, a skeleton scarcely held together by his
clothes and always about to disintegrate, a "being beyond all
mere restrictions of flesh and time," an "indefatigable and now
ubiquitous cadaver." He insists that the airmen have no need
for money, food, or sleep, but this is true only of him, as his
actions to assist them indicate. His distorting perspective
falsifies them doubly—into alien beings whose extraordinary
courage sets them apart from mere mortals and also into waifs
for whom, at great cost, he surrenders his bed, apartment, and

such money as he possesses or can claim. In an echo of *Miss Lonelyhearts*, Nathaniel West's fine novel published in 1933, the reporter is represented as "patron (even if no guardian) saint of all waifs, all the homeless the desperate and the starved." But if the airmen are indeed lost souls, the reporter is their Charon:

> they four shades this moment out of the living world and being hurried, grave, quiet and unalarmed, on toward complete oblivion by one not only apparently long enough in residence to have become a citizen of the shadows, but one who from all outward appearances had been born there too. The reporter was still talking, but they did not appear to hear him, as though they had arrived too recently to have yet unclogged their ears of human speech in order to even hear the tongue in which the guide spoke.

He leads them, as this imagery foreshadows, to disintegration and destruction—obtaining the bootleg liquor that reduces Jiggs to drunken incompetence, arranging for the unsafe plane that kills Roger. Not surprisingly, his editor (who has inexplicably assumed the role of father figure to him and keeps "lending" him money he fails to earn) says that he has "an instinct for events" like a crow for carrion, and with analogous purpose: "it's not the living breath of news. It's just information. It's dead before you even get back here with it." It is dead, in fact, because the reporter has touched it.

The reporter's inability to establish vitality or coherence for himself or others is central less to *Pylon*'s story than to its rhythm, for it is one more in a pattern of deflection that continually denies meaning to the novel's characters and action. *Pylon*, then, is *not* about aviation, *nor* about the reporter's romanticization of it, *nor* about his failure to aid the flyers or even to become a whole human being. It is about its own failure to be any—or all—of these things, a failure that permeates not only its action but also its rhetoric. Thus the novel confounds all common categorization by first establishing and then undermining metaphorical meaning. The reporter insists that the aviators "aint human. It aint

adultery; you can't anymore imagine two of them making love
than you can two of them airplanes back in the corner of the
hangar, coupled . . . cut him and it's cylinder oil; dissect him
and it aint bones: it's little rockerarms and connecting rods."
But they are not only machines; they are also angels and beasts
and, according to Brooks, "a wandering tribe of savages."[5]
Their machines are "a species of esoteric and fatal animals not
trained or tamed but just for the instant inert" or, rather,
"creatures imbued with motion though not with life and
incomprehensible to the puny crawling painwebbed globe,
incapable of suffering, wombed and born complete and
instantaneous, cunning intricate and deadly, from out some
blind iron batcave of the earth's prime foundation." The
airplane, its "fabric trembling like a bride," is "a damn gnat
built like a Swiss watch"; it waddles like a duck, flies like a
wasp, and after it crashes its undercarriage projects "into the
air rigid and delicate and motionless as the legs of a dead bird."
Transfixed, the flyers' wives stare at the airshow "like they
might have been stole out of a department store window";
childbirth, on the other hand, combines the bestial and the
mechanical: Laverne's kid "got dropped already running like a
colt or a calf from the fuselage of an airplane, onto something
because it happened to be big enough to land on and then take
off again." It is amazing that the oddly mannish Laverne
manages to give birth at all. The reporter, in addition to being
a cadaver, an escapee of hell, is, variously, Jesus, Dante's
Virgilian guide through *The Inferno*, a "worn and dreamy"
Don Quixote, Macbeth murdering sleep, the vacuous J. Alfred
Prufrock, Miss Lonelyhearts offering fatal succor to lost souls.
By the end, he finds that "it got all mixed up. . . . It started out to
be a tragedy. . . . But it . . . turned into a comedy . . . [though] it's
not that funny."

The eponymous pylons around which the air races turn
would seem to serve as the novel's literal and symbolic fixed
center—representing "speed and sex, the equivalents of God
and love in the waste land of the mechanical age."[6] They are,
moreover, linked explicitly to Roger, who skillfully uses them

to compensate for his plane's slowness. As the announcer, unconsciously punning on the "Chance Specials" flown by Roger's competitors, calls it: "He's beating them on the pylons, folks, because he knows that on the straightaway he hasn't got a chance." But again the reporter—"longer than a lath," so tall that his shadow fell "for an incredible distance eastward along the apron"—himself epitomizes, and thereby confounds, the imagery of the pylons, as he has everything else associated with the airmen. Doubling, or rather anticipating, the announcer, the reporter declares: " 'Look yonder. Roger is going to take that guy on this next pylon,' [speaking as if he] possessed some quality of omniscience beyond even vision." But in imagery evoking Eliot's "Hollow Men," the reporter's pylonic transcendence turns out to be made of straw: he is "a scarecrow weathered gradually out of the earth which had supported it erect and intact and now poised for the first light vagrant air to blow it into utter dissolution."

Faulkner's own attitude toward the flyers, and toward the reporter's obsession with them, is difficult to fathom. In an interview, he speaks of them as "ephemera and phenomena. . . . they were outside the range of God, not only of respectability, of love, but of God too," and therefore beyond ordinary standards of judgment, "almost immoral" (*F in U*, 36). In "All the Dead Pilots," one of the stories that serves as basis for *Pylon*, the narrator says, "I know that no man deserves praise for courage or opprobrium for cowardice, since there are situations in which any man will show either of them."[7] Volpe suggests that "Faulkner was probably fascinated by the type of airmen he described in this novel but that he really did not know them as people,"[8] although he certainly hung around and emulated them (at least until his brother Dean's death in a plane Faulkner had given him). He even proudly wore " 'the modest Q.B. wings' worn by veteran aviators"—the letters standing for "Quiet Birdman," though a mocking flyer said that "It means Bill is a queer bastard" (Blotner, 898). In a review of *Test Pilot*, by Jimmy Collins, Faulkner writes of flyers in the same breathless hyperbole he uses in *Pylon*:

"These would be a species and in time a race and in time they would produce a folklore.... the little puny mortals, vanishing against a vast and timeless void filled with the sound of incredible engines, within which furious meteors moving in no medium hurtled nowhere, neither pausing nor flagging, forever destroying themselves and one another" (*ESPL*, 191-92). Simultaneously anachronistic and heroes of the future, these suicidal conquerors of the air inspire neither respect nor sympathy but perhaps something of the sense of wonder we reserve for holy fools.

Faulkner's uncertain or double attitude toward them may be most fully expressed in *Pylon*'s enormous use of allusion: never had Faulkner borrowed more heavily from literary sources, never had he created a work more apparently distinct and yet more deeply rooted in his other writings. For example, *Pylon*'s radical denial of context for the present contrasts sharply with the past-ridden *Absalom, Absalom!*, yet it employs several of that book's images and motifs, perhaps most notably the shifting and troublesome question of who it is—which story—occupies the novel's center. At one point, the reporter's pylonlike height means that "he seemed doomed to look down at everyone... until that day when time and age would have thinned still more what blood he had and so permit him to see himself actually as the friendly and lonely ghost peering timidly down from the hayloft at the other children playing below"—a slightly comic echo of the scene, early in *Absalom*, of Judith and Clytie, peering down from the hayloft at their father's brutal wrestling with his black slaves. Later on, the blustery but soft-hearted editor, Hagood (his name—presumably pronounced "ha' good"—bespeaks his moral worth) explodes over the reporter's extraordinary self-revelations: "'Get out of here!' he screamed. 'Get out! Out.'" —evoking not only Shreve's frenzied and repeated "Wait!" as he struggles to contain and comprehend Quentin's story, but also the Old Justice—"I cant stand no more!"—who presides at the trial over the spotted ponies in *The Hamlet*.

Analogues and allusions to other Faulkner novels abound. Wishing to join the airmen's ménage, the reporter imagines his role as dealing with the "burnt coffee and dead shrimp"— like Horace Benbow in *Flags in the Dust* and *Sanctuary*. He parallels not only Horace but also Gavin Stevens in his quixotic championing of lost causes. Filled "with tragic and passive clairvoyance," he sounds like Temple being raped in *Sanctuary:* "Something is going to happen to me. I have got myself stretched out too far and too thin and something is going to bust." His name (which for no apparent reason we are never told) evokes the same response as Joe Christmas's in *Light in August:* "it must be his; I never heard of anyone else named that and so no one intelligent enough to have anything to hide from would deliberately assume it." And for all his frenzied activity, he slips at times into a "peaceful and serene waiting" suggestive of the Ratliff of the Snopes trilogy, just as his desperate need to validate Laverne's behavior regardless of facts—"It's all right.... I would believe you even if I knew you had lied"—anticipates Ratliff's refusal to believe the worst about people: "I dont know as I would believe that, even if I knowed it was true" (*H*, 83).

Laverne herself, whom Brooks finds most like Charlotte Rittenmeyer in "Wild Palms" in her wild and willful self-determination,[9] repeats a more central Faulknerian pattern— that of *The Sound and the Fury* and *Light in August*—in abandoning her son to the same stern and delegitimizing upbringing that produces Quentin II and Joe Christmas. One can imagine no more radical attack on continuity and historical meaning; perhaps the very extremity of this pendulum swing compelled Faulkner back to the richest of all his worlds: that of the family- and past-obsessed *Absalom, Absalom!*

A Fable

A Fable, Faulkner's final and furthest foray into worlds elsewhere, was the major work of his later years—a book that he loved because he "gave ten good years of my life to it" (*Letters*, 361-62). The writing of it was slow and difficult, for he felt tired, old, stale, obsessed with money worries, and constrained by an unfair Hollywood contract from which he had to contrive repeated leaves. It was also, as its title implies, being written to a thesis rather than from an image or motif, and it changed constantly in size and shape as it evolved. Variously conceived as a film script, a magazine story, and a play, *A Fable* soon and for years became "the mss.," "the big book," "my magnum opus." Though he sometimes expressed doubts about his work in progress, Faulkner considered it monumental: "It is either nothing and I am blind in my dotage, or it is the best of my time" (*Letters*, 352). Writing it, he saw himself besieged, "crouching in a Mississippi hole trying to shape into some form of art his summation and conception of the human heart and spirit in terms of the cerebral, the simple imagination" (quoted in Blotner, 1242). Based on what he considered "a tremendous idea" (*Letters*, 258), *A Fable* was to be "my epic poem" (Blotner, 1180), "a War and Peace close enough to home, our times, language," his "last major, ambitious work" after which "I shall be through, can break the pencil and cast it all away" (*Letters*, 238, 348, 314). For no other book did Faulkner make such claims or, despite winning both the Pulitzer Prize and the National Book Award, fall so short of achieving what he intended.

In an unusual departure from normal practice, *A Fable* derived from others' ideas rather than from Faulkner's imagination, from concept rather than from perception: "The notion occurred to me one day in 1942 shortly after Pearl Harbor and the beginning of the last great war . . . who might that unknown soldier be? Suppose that had been Christ again, under that fine big cenotaph with the eternal flame burning on it? That He would naturally have got crucified again, . . . that was an idea and a hope, an unexpressed thought that Christ had appeared twice, had been crucified twice, and maybe we'd have only one more chance" (*F in U*, 27). So in the midst of yet another conflagration in which he was not to participate, Faulkner thought himself once more into the war he missed, and which had already served as backdrop for *Soldiers' Pay* and *Flags in the Dust*. Patterns of repetition between Faulkner's first novel and *A Fable* are striking and substantial: the young soldier who complains bitterly that the war has been stopped on him; drunken raucous soldiers on a train at war's end; the soldier so damaged as to be literally only half a man, yet who serves not only as archetypal victim but also as the novel's moral focus; temporal brevity (as in all the novels discussed in this chapter), as if, outside the world and material he knew best, Faulkner could work only within delimiting structural constraints. The similarities, however, serve also to highlight the uniqueness of the later work—not only its allegorical nature but also its European setting, its foregrounding of war, and especially its grandiose intention: to rewrite the story of Christ's Passion as "an indictment of war" (*Letters*, 178).

The time of the novel is a week in May 1918, the place Verdun, the front lines during the latter stages of the debilitating, dehumanizing war. Ordered to launch an attack "already doomed in its embryo" (the reason is obscure, but it seems intended to weaken the Germans—as all their victories do), General Charles Gragnon discovers that "he didn't have a failure. He had a mutiny." Or, rather, he had an unauthorized ceasefire, somehow arranged between the soldiers, that he denounces as a plot to ruin him, and that results, among other things, in his reiterated demand that his entire regiment of three thousand men be executed, his own assassination in prison as an embarrassment, a clandestine meeting of Allied and German generals in order to negotiate not peace but war, and finally the execution of the corporal responsible for what, retrospectively, becomes "the false armistice in May, that curious week's holiday which the war had taken which had been so false that they remembered it only as phenomenon."

Like most Faulkner novels, *A Fable* begins in medias res, with reaction rather than action—here, astonishment and disbelief, "dread and anxiety," provoked by the sudden peace— followed by indirect and multifarious revelations of the initiating action: a regiment's courageous and contagious refusal to fight. The wide-angle opening resembles that of Greek tragedy as the people of the city gather "in an inextricable mass like victims being resurrected after a holocaust" not only to bear witness but to participate in the next suffering, for the "original regiment had been raised in this district . . . by one of those glorious blackguards who later became Napoleon's marshals. . . . most of these old men were not only veterans of it in their time, and these male children already dedicated to it when their time should come, but all these people were parents and kin, not only the actual old parents and kin of the doomed men, but fathers and mothers and sisters and wives and sweethearts whose sons and brothers and husbands and fathers and lovers might have been among the doomed men except for sheer blind chance and luck." The doomed regiment—doomed by peace rather than war—undermines the amalgamation of contrarieties implicit until now in the regiment's history. For both the impotent citizenry and the suddenly irrelevant army, represented by Faulkner as natural forces flowing in and around each other without touching or merging, are bereft of purpose and direction by the unexpected peace that causes the regiment's demise, a peace that seems far more ominous than war's familiar devastation.

Similarly meandering for all its a priori purposefulness, *A Fable* divides uneasily into two. The first part—primarily concerning responses to the cessation of action and to the sudden silence filled, as if miraculously, by cicadas, an occasional lark, and hesitant expressions of hope—depicts the various participants and their backgrounds, but reveals none of their inner workings. The second half, which begins with an overt analogy between the corporal and Christ—both born in a stable Christmas Eve thirty-three years before their deaths—and "continues on, through the Three Temptations, the Crucifixion, the Resurrection" (*Letters*, 179), replays the initiating act—the never-depicted mutiny—by focusing on the immediacy of its consequences. Yet like the act itself, its meaning emerges only through reduction and deflection, an allegorical and contrived replay of the Passion Week replete with twelve disciples, the Judas betrayal for thirty coins, the

Last Supper, the denial by Peter, the temptation in the wilderness, Golgotha, execution between two thieves, a crown of thorns ("a tangled mass of old barbed wire"), the corpse's disappearance, and so on. While telling its central story—that of the mysterious corporal who, by imposing peace, so threatened military authority and purpose that it rose up to destroy him as though he were Christ—*A Fable* expends much time and energy telling other stories. At one point Faulkner said: "What I was writing about was the trilogy of man's conscience represented by the young British Pilot Officer, the Runner, and the Quartermaster General. The one that said, This is dreadful, terrible, and I won't face it even at the cost of my life—that was the British aviator. The Old General who said, This is terrible but we can bear it. The third one, the battalion Runner who said, This is dreadful, I won't stand it, I'll do something about it" (*F in U*, 62). *A Fable* also expatiates on the corporal's three women (Mary, Martha, and Mary Magdalen); the unlamented General Gragnon; his assassins; David Levine (the David Lowe of *Soldiers' Pay*), the British pilot who commits suicide because of the shattered peace; the men sent to retrieve an unknown soldier for ceremonial burial and who, through an incredible series of events, unwittingly procure the corporal's body.

The longest, least integrated, and most famous digression is an epic journey through the American South: a fifty-page flashback about a stolen racehorse that, with only three good legs, impossibly beats all competition and then disappears— with local assistance—whenever his owner's agents close in. His handlers are an English groom—an extreme version of *Pylon*'s Jiggs in terms of both his depravity and his skill at his trade—and a black Baptist minister who, "peaceful and serene," suggests the moral certitude of Ratliff as well as, in his "innocent and invincible affirmation," the simple wordless faith of *Requiem*'s Nancy: "Believe and hope," he tells the initially cynical Runner who comes to him in quest of truth. Despite the legends surrounding their adventure, the minister (called Tooleyman in France—"Tout le Monde"—presumably, Everyman) insists that they made no money because they never gambled. The implication is that the union of this odd couple produced not material gain but something mystical that led to the groom's becoming both a Baptist and a Mason, and to his shooting the horse rather than allow it to be retaken and put out to stud. When we first meet the groom, however, he is surly and manipulative, satanically preying upon the soldiers' fear of death: he gives each of them ten shillings on the first of each month, which they pay back at the rate of six pence per day—thus making a 50 percent profit on those who survive the month—while also having them name him as beneficiary on their life insurance policies in case they die. In his first action, he savagely beats the Runner who, seeing his power, nags him to lead the unarmed soldiers across no-man's land to the unarmed Germans in order to prevent the revival of the war. But 250 pages later—after the implications of the armistice have begun to sink in, after the Allied Air Force has been equipped with dummy shells in order to disguise the arrival of a German general to arrange the war's resumption (the act that impels Levine's suicide), after "the obscure corporal whose name few knew and even they could not pronounce it" comes into focus as "a protagonist for anguishment, an object for execration," after the racehorse flashback, after we meet the corporal's women and learn of their suffering, after the story of the old marshal's career ("he was *the* golden youth" who had graduated with the finest record ever from the military academy and who seemed destined to become mankind's savior), after the confrontation between the marshal and the threee women (during which we learn that he is the corporal's father), after the meeting between military leaders when they demonstrate the validity of the Runner's assertion that generals transcend both nationality and the human race—the aroused Runner and Tooleyman coerce the groom into leading the solidiers, "as though up out of hell itself," to a momentary transformation, "that look of amazed incredulity fading with one amazed

concert into dawning and incredulous hope." And then, as they
and their German counterparts are slaughtered to prevent
their meeting and reifying the peace, " 'No!' he cried, 'no! Not
to us!' not even realising that he had said 'we' and not 'I' for the
first time in his life probably." The groom's death, then, as the
racehorse episode is meant to foreshadow, is simultaneously
failure and triumph, repetition and breakthrough, loss and
finding of self and meaning in an act of denial and transcendence.

At the heart of the novel is the climactic confrontation
between the French marshal, commander of Allied Forces, and
the young corporal; between, as the General puts it, "two
articulations [of] inimical conditions. . . . I champion of this
mundane earth [and] you champion an esoteric realm of
man's baseless hopes and his infinite capacity—no: passion—
for unfact"; between, as it happens, father and illegitimate son.
The meeting is inevitable from almost the novel's beginning
when, in the first appearance of each, the two "stared full at
each other across the moment." Much has been revealed about
the marshal—his brilliant record at the academy, his subsequent and oddly obscure career in the African bush (climaxed
by his betrayal of one of his men—guilty of murdering a
native—to a besieging tribe in order to save the rest), his stay
in "a Tibetan lamasery," his intelligence, power, and dis-
illusionment: "the old gray inscrutable supreme general with
the face of one who long ago had won the right to believe in
nothing whatever save man's deathless folly." He is alternately
a godlike figure, mankind's savior (with "the golden destiny of
an hereditary crown prince of paradise"), and Satan proffering
him the choice between moral and physical destruction—or an
amalgam of the two. Thus, despite his introspection and
quietism he reigns supreme over the allied forces defending
Western values from Eastern invaders and he speaks, virtually
unchanged, Faulkner's Nobel Prize speech; yet he also
personifies militarism and authority, refusing to countenance
peace that begins in the ranks rather than from above and that
does not result in the enemy's total capitulation. Faulkner

speaks of him as "the dark, splendid, fallen angel," but with the fateful twist of his being the corporal's father as well as tempter and executioner: "That was what made him so fearsome and so powerful, that he could usurp the legend of God and then discard God. That's why God feared him" (*F in U,* 62-63). Perhaps even more frightening, he offers, as the corporal's ultimate temptation, something virtually unique in Faulkner: a father's public acknowledgment of a son.

The representation of the corporal, the marshal's echo and opposite, is far more fragmentary. We learn little of his background except some of its details, nothing of how or why he came to be in the French army or the source of his authority over others. Rather than shown, his charismatic moral power is merely asserted, and we are asked to take much on faith: that the men do indeed respond automatically to his extraordinary goodness, that he managed to go among the German troops and persuade them to lay down their arms on cue, that his very existence threatens the pursuit of war. Faulkner renders him mysterious by withholding him from us for the first half of *A Fable,* but his passive self-assuredness when he does appear—more posture or formula than convincing characterization—falls far short of our expectations of him. Further, in the case of neither the marshal nor the corporal—in fact, nowhere in the book—does Faulkner's narrator penetrate to a character's inner working—to psychology, motivation, intention. They must always be inferred from without.

Much of the problem with *A Fable*—both Faulkner's in writing it and critics in evaluating it—concerns its conception as a *roman à thèse.* Early on in its writing, Faulkner expressed his concern that the allegory not overwhelm the fiction: "I will smooth it out, give the characters names, remove the primer-like biblical references and explanations, and let the story reveal its Christ-analogy through understatement" (*Letters,* 179). But for all the book's digressions and indirections—many of them excessive for their purposes and poorly integrated into the whole—this is exactly what Faulkner failed to do, so that in the end the book became no one thing but rather a generic jumble with an ill-fitting title; for as Irving Howe puts it, "the one quality it most conspicuously lacks is the unilinear directness of the fable."[10]

Brooks, who begins his discussion of *A Fable* with "It is not easy to be fair to this novel,"[11] defends his second Faulkner study (largely concerned with the works I treat in this chapter) with this truism: "However limited, however perfunctory, the works of a man of genius are rarely completely unrewarding. After all, they are the product of the same mind, even if it is running at only half-throttle, that produced the master-pieces."[12] In these works, then, we see Faulkner exploring, with mixed success, other places, other contexts, other ways of being, other styles—while repeating, often more immediately and overtly than in his "Faulknerian" fiction, his central concerns. Thus, the oddly deformed and well-intentioned *Fable*—deformed, in fact, *by* its good intentions—deploys the Christian symbology used more organically in *The Sound and the Fury, Sanctuary, Light in August,* and *Requiem for a Nun;* the moral debate about the efficacy of human action that grows out of character and history in *The Sound and the Fury, Absalom, Absalom!,* and *Go Down, Moses;* the eloquent romanticizing and denunciation of war of *Flags in the Dust, Light in August, Absalom, Absalom!,* and *The Unvanquished;* the brilliant father/son dynamics in such novels as *As I Lay Dying, Light in August,* and *Absalom, Absalom!;* the haunting vision of the antagonist as Satan in *The Hamlet;* the Southern tall-tale beast fable handled with a lighter and defter touch in *The Hamlet* and, later, *The Reivers.* Above all, Faulkner sought yet again to tell his basic story—that of the human heart in conflict with itself—by juxtaposing the inescapability of his-torical patterns and the inherited sense of doom overlaying the present with the categorical imperative to say no to quiescence and despair, and yes to moral initiative. Such a notion and belief are central to the entire corpus, the works within and without Yoknapatwpha: Faulkner's worlds, for all his failures and repetitions, are ultimately one.

Notes

I. WILLIAM FAULKNER: FAILURE AND REPETITION

1. Edmond L. Volpe, *A Reader's Guide to William Faulkner* (New York: Farrar, Straus and Giroux, 1964), p. 6.
2. As Faulkner did, according to his brother; see Murry C. Falkner, *The Falkners of Mississippi: A Memoir* (Baton Rouge: Louisiana State University Press, 1967), p. 6.
3. Blotner, in *Letters*, p. 213.
4. David Minter, *William Faulkner: His Life and Work* (Baltimore and London: Johns Hopkins University Press, 1980), p. 8.
5. Ibid., p. 7.
6. Ibid., p. 17.
7. *Letters*, pp. 212-13. The reason was drink.
8. Blotner, in *Letters*, p. 310.
9. *Harper's Magazine*, 211 (July 1955), 33-38. Reprinted in *ESPL*, pp. 62-75.
10. In *Letters*, p. xiii.
11. A. I. Bezzerides, *William Faulkner: A Life on Paper* (Jackson: University Press of Mississippi, 1980), p. 110.
12. See *William Faulkner's Library: A Catalogue*, compiled by Joseph Blotner. Charlottesville: University Press of Virginia, 1964.
13. Robert Coughlan, *The Private World of William Faulkner* (New York: Harper & Brothers, 1954), p. 25. Minter offers a similar summary (pp. ix-x and passim).
14. I should indicate from the outset that by "failure" I do not mean precisely what Walter J. Slatoff does in his provocative *Quest for Failure: A Study of William Faulkner* (Westport, Conn.: Greenwood Press, 1976 [1960]). Slatoff offers much excellent

analysis of the Faulkner canon, especially his verbal, thematic, and structural complexities and irresolution: "Virtually all of Faulkner's experiments with form and style—his rapidly shifting points of view, his disordered time sequences, his unsyntactical marathon sentences, his oxymorons, his whole method, as Conrad Aiken puts it, 'of *deliberately withheld meaning,* of progressive and partial and delayed disclosure'—have one effect in common: tension and frustration in the reader" (75). This strikes me as true to a large extent, but Slatoff goes much further than I would in taking Faulkner to task for his "failure": "My irritation comes, I believe, from my feeling that Faulkner's fictional world is in many respects even more ambiguous and complex than the real one and that this is, in part, the result of a deliberate quest for failure" (264). My own approach to Faulkner's "failure" stresses something different: the dichotomy between the Faulknerian urge to encapsulate meaning precisely in every word, phrase, and sentence and the connotative dissonance in language itself. This gap does much to create the dynamic instability inherent in Faulkner's fiction.

15. Minter, p. x.

16. Meta Carpenter's word for Faulkner's habitual indifference to factual accuracy. See Meta Carpenter Wilde and Orin Borsten, *A Loving Gentleman: The Love Story of William Faulkner and Meta Carpenter* (New York: Simon and Schuster, 1976), p. 10. For a discussion of Faulkner's attitude to such discrepancies in the Snopes trilogy, see Blotner, pp. 1721-41 passim.

17. Irving Howe, *William Faulkner: A Critical Study* (New York: Vintage, 1951), p. 160. Jean-Paul Sartre, or his translator, also uses the word "suspension" (for *l'enfoncement*) in discussing "a kind of arrested motion in time" in Faulkner's novels. "Time in Faulkner: *The Sound and the Fury,*" trans. Martine Darmon, in *William Faulkner: Three Decades of Criticism,* ed. Frederick J. Hoffman and Olga W. Vickery (New York and Burlingame: Harbinger, 1963), pp. 225-32. Another translator uses the expression "a sinking in . . . to indicate a kind of motionless movement." "On *The Sound and the Fury:* Time in the Work of Faulkner," trans. Annette Michelson, in *Faulkner: A Collection of Critical Essays,* ed. Robert Penn Warren (Englewood Cliffs, N.J.: Prentice-Hall, 1966), p. 88.

18. See, for example, *GDM,* pp. 296-97.

19. Cleanth Brooks, *William Faulkner: Toward Yoknapatawpha and Beyond* (New Haven and London: Yale University Press, 1978), p. 101. Hereafter cited as *TYB*.

II. "I'VE SEED DE FIRST EN DE LAST": *Sartoris/Flags in the Dust, The Reivers*

1. See Brooks, "The Relation of *Flags in the Dust* to *Sartoris*," in his *TYB*, pp. 388-91.
2. Douglas Day, "Introduction" to *Flags*, pp. x-xi.
3. *F in U*, p. 285. Faulkner was actually referring to *Sartoris* since no one then knew about *Flags*, but the comment applies even more to the original version.
4. See John Irwin, *Doubling & Incest/Repetition & Revenge: A Speculative Reading of Faulkner* (Baltimore and London: Johns Hopkins University Press, 1980), pp. 55-59 for a discussion of Faulkner's doubling and repetitions of Civil War and World War I Sartorises.
5. James B. Carothers, "The Road to *The Reivers*," in *"A Cosmos of My Own": Faulkner and Yoknapatawpha 1980*, ed. Doreen Fowler and Ann J. Abadie (Jackson: University Press of Mississippi, 1981), p. 102.
6. Faulkner, letter to Albert Erskine (August 1961). Quoted in Blotner, p. 1800.
7. Faulkner's own view, an accurate one, was that "Usually I puzzle readers with what's inside my books. This time I just puzzle them with the title" (quoted in Blotner, p. 1801). For his working title, *The Horse Stealers: A Reminiscence* (Blotner in *Letters*, p. 455), Faulkner substituted an obsolete word with the same meaning but with an anachronistic flavor to match that of the book.
8. Bruce F. Kawin, *Faulkner and Film* (New York: Ungar, 1977), p. 60.
9. Despite Faulkner's intention, Irving Howe not unreasonably maintains that "The Bear" is his *Huckleberry Finn*, while *The Reivers*, tonally far less somber, is his *Tom Sawyer* (cited in Blotner, pp. 1826-27).
10. Brooks goes so far as to suggest "that *The Reivers* is a sort of latter-day 'courtesy book.' " *William Faulkner: The Yoknapatawpha Country* (New Haven: Yale University Press, 1963), p. 351.

11. Brooks, *Country*, pp. 365-66.
12. See Brooks, *Country*, pp. 364-68, for a discussion of similarities and differences between *The Reivers* and *Light in August*.
13. Blotner, pp. 66, 99-100, 111.
14. Quoted in Blotner, p. 6.

III. "DARK HOUSES": *The Sound and the Fury, Absalom, Absalom!*

1. Quoted in Blotner, p. 578.
2. Minter, p. 158.
3. Ibid., p. 94. Blotner also stresses the personal significance: "As the elder Falkners could provide models for the Sartorises, so the younger ones could sit for the Compsons" (p. 566).
4. William Faulkner, "An Introduction for *The Sound and the Fury*," ed. James B. Meriwether, *The Southern Review*, NS VIII, 4 (Autumn 1972), 710. See André Bleikasten, *The Most Splendid Failure: Faulkner's "The Sound and the Fury"* (Bloomington and London: Indiana University Press, 1976), for an interesting discussion of Faulkner's urn imagery in this passage, especially the notion that "the aesthetic is made one with the erotic" (p. 46).
5. Quoted in Blotner, p. 586.
6. Sartre, in Warren, p. 87.
7. Edmond Volpe, in his *Reader's Guide,* usefully outlines the temporal and scenic shifts in these two sections (pp. 353-77).
8. Lawrance Thompson, *William Faulkner: An Introduction and Interpretation* (New York: Holt, Rinehart and Winston, 1967), p. 36.
9. James B. Meriwether, "The Textual History of *The Sound and the Fury*," in *Studies in "The Sound and the Fury,"* compiled by James B. Meriwether (Columbus, Ohio: Charles E. Merrill, 1970), p. 29.
10. Bleikasten, p. 57.
11. Sartre, in Warren, p. 92.
12. Sartre discusses how the second fight repeats the first and how it gets told only "because it has become a story" and not "while it was unfolding in the present" (ibid., pp. 89-90). More generally, as Bleikasten sees it, Quentin's present "is a reenactment of his past; his future is past in waiting" (p. 94).

13. Faulkner said that this dialogue occurs only in Quentin's imagination (*F in U*, 262), but the internal evidence is ambiguous.
14. Bleikasten, p. 55.
15. See Warwick Wadlington, "*The Sound and the Fury:* A Logic of Tragedy," *American Literature*, 53, 3 (November 1981), 409-23, for a good discussion of this concept.
16. Faulkner had, of course, confused the two youngest brothers, Joseph and Benjamin, though in answer to a question he said that he used them interchangeably because the latter was held hostage for the former (*F in U*, 18).
17. See Bleikasten (pp. 56-57, 217) and Joseph Reed, *Faulkner's Narrative* ([New Haven: Yale University Press, 1973], p. 76) for further discussions of these names.
18. Bleikasten, p. 65.
19. Faulkner, "Introduction for *The Sound and the Fury*," 710.
20. Bleikasten, p. 66.
21. Ibid., p. 52.
22. For a relevant discussion of "the three aspects of fiction, story, narration, and narrative," see Francois L. Pitavy, "The Gothicism of *Absalom, Absalom!:* Rosa Coldfield Revisited," in "*A Cosmos of My Own,*" pp. 199-226.
23. Brooks emphasizes "how little hard fact there is to go on" and "how much of the story of Sutpen and especially of Sutpen's children has been spun out of the imagination of Quentin and Shreve," as well as its other narrators (*Country*, p. 311; see also pp. 312-15 and 429-36). Brooks rightly adds that "The conjectures made by Shreve and Quentin... render the story of Sutpen *plausible*" (p. 315; my emphasis).
24. Minter, p. 154.
25. See Irwin for a discussion of Quentin's double role—he plays both defender and seducer of his sister—projected onto Henry and Bon, respectively (pp. 28-29).
26. For a full-scale treatment of this subject, see Eric J. Sundquist, "*Absalom, Absalom!* and the House Divided," in his *Faulkner: The House Divided* (Baltimore and London: Johns Hopkins University Press, 1983), pp. 96-130.
27. Faulkner expressed his own attitude toward the South in Quentin-like terms: "I love it and hate it. Some of the things there I don't like at all, but I was born there, and that's my

home, and I will still defend it even if I hate it" (*Lion,* 101). The bases for both the love and hate are explored at some length in his fictional essay, "Mississippi" (*ESPL,* 10-43).

28. For a discussion of Coldfield's failings, see Arthur F. Kinney, *Faulkner's Narrative Poetics: Style as Vision* (Amherst: University of Massachusetts Press, 1978), pp. 198-200.

29. Estella Schoenberg suggests another possibility: that the cry "in the book's title [is] Jason Richmond Compson's grief for his son Quentin." *Old Tales and Talking: Quentin Compson in William Faulkner's "Absalom, Absalom!" and Related Works* (Jackson: University Press of Mississippi, 1977), p. 4. See Ilse Dusoir Lind, "The Design and Meaning of *Absalom, Absalom!"* in *Three Decades* (pp. 278-304), for a good discussion of the novel's literary, mythical, and historical analogues and echoes.

30. Irwin sees Bon as also playing "the role of shadow" to Henry and to Quentin (pp. 30-35).

31. Irwin convincingly argues that Quentin's narration is central "because the other three only function as narrators in relation to Quentin." Further, since all the other narratives come through Quentin, they tend both to sound alike and to bear "a striking resemblance to Quentin's own personal history and that of his family" (p. 26).

32. See Sundquist (p. 130) and also Donald M. Kartiganer, *The Fragile Thread: The Meaning of Form in Faulkner's Novels* (Amherst: University of Massachusetts Press, 1979), p. 103.

33. Brooks nicely sorts out the discrepancies (*Country,* pp. 424-26).

IV. VISIONS AND VERSIONS: *As I Lay Dying, Light in August*

1. Minter, pp. 117-18.
2. Michael Millgate, *The Achievement of William Faulkner* (New York: Vintage, 1966), p. 110.
3. William Faulkner, "Introduction for *The Sound and the Fury,"* 709.
4. Partly, as Brooks points out, it is a matter of convention that the characters, "when they speak their inmost thoughts, shift from the north Mississippi hill dialect in which they ordinarily address one another into a diction far beyond their actual cultural level" (*TYB,* p. 105). But some characters do so far more than others, and the differences are revealing and instructive.

5. The relationship between Darl and Dewey Dell is, if anything, even more intense, if also less hateful, in an excised passage from Faulkner's manuscript. Not only has Darl silently communicated his prescience about Addie's imminent death to Dewey Dell, who instinctively believes him, but his knowledge of her pregnancy is imaged in sexually charged language: "Because there is something between Darl and me. It was outside of me at first, and Darl was outside of it. But now it is inside of me and I am inside of Darl. Like I was inside a wall made of little rocks, the little rocks Darl's eyes, not looking at me any more now the wall is sealed up, the gap in it sealed. And the thing inside of me and Darl's eyes looking through me at it. And so that's where I want it to be, hid from seeing with sight. And so I can never be mad again at Darl because" (quoted in Blotner, p. 637).

6. Brooks, *Country,* p. 143.

7. Ibid., p. 148.

8. Ibid., p. 149.

9. Homer, *The Odyssey,* trans. W. H. D. Rouse (1937). According to Blotner in *Faulkner's Library* (p. 80), Faulkner owned two editions (1935 and 1950) of the S. H. Butcher and A. Lang translation (originally published in 1879), but of course he may have used an earlier edition when seeking his title. Their version of the first part of this passage reads: "I strove to raise my hands as I was dying upon the sword, but to earth they fell." Perhaps Faulkner's title influenced subsequent translators such as Rouse.

10. Brooks, *Country,* pp. 141, 165-66; Minter, p. 118.

11. See Minter, pp. 94-98, for a discussion of how parents fail children generally in Faulkner's fiction, and especially in *The Sound and the Fury.*

12. See Irwin, pp. 61-63, for a discussion of the grandfathers in *Light in August.*

13. Alfred Kazin, "The Stillness of *Light in August,*" in *Twelve Original Essays on Great American Novels,* ed. Charles Shapiro (Detroit: Wayne State University Press, 1958), pp. 263, 264, 276.

14. Ibid., p. 268.

15. See, for example, Howe, pp. 200-202, 209.

V. ERRORS AND TRIALS: *Sanctuary, Requiem for a Nun*

1. See Linton Massey, "Notes on the Unrevised Galleys of Faulkner's *Sanctuary*," *Studies in Bibliography*, 7 (1956), 195-208, and Noel Polk, ed., *Sanctuary: The Original Text*. New York: Random House, 1981.

2. The intense sexuality of this passage, as well as the conflation of characters and actions, is far more representative of *Sanctuary's* original style than of its published version. See Gerald Langford, *Faulkner's Revision of "Sanctuary": A Collation of the Unrevised Galleys and the Published Book* (Austin and London: University of Texas Press, 1972), pp. 15-20.

3. R. P. Adams, *Faulkner: Myth and Motion* (Princeton: Princeton University Press, 1968), p. 157.

4. Quoted in Blotner, p. 1506.

VI. TWICE-TOLD TALES: *The Unvanquished, The Wild Palms, Go Down, Moses*

1. This notion is central to Edward M. Holmes, *Faulkner's Twice-Told Tales: His Re-Use of His Material*. The Hague: Mouton, 1966. See also Joanne V. Creighton, *William Faulkner's Craft of Revision: The Snopes Trilogy, "The Unvanquished" and "Go Down, Moses."* Detroit: Wayne State University Press, 1977.

2. Marshall J. Smith, in *Lion*, p. 13.

3. Leslie A. Fiedler, "William Faulkner: An American Dickens," *Commentary*, 10 (October 1950), 385.

4. Harvey Breit, Introduction, *AA*, p. v.

5. As per Faulkner's instructions, as discussed below.

6. Brooks, *Country*, p. 82.

7. Ibid., p. 84.

8. See *A Loving Gentleman* for her generally reliable account of their relationship.

9. Faulkner himself, according to Meta Carpenter, spoke this line to her on more than one occasion before it became part of *Wild Palms*. He was, however, not above self-parody, even on such a subject. When asked how fussy he was about what he drank, he said, "Between scotch and nothing, I'll take scotch" (*Lion*, 240).

10. William Faulkner, "Lion," *Harper's Monthly Magazine*, 172 (December 1935), 67-77.

11. Gary Lee Stonum, *Faulkner's Career: An Internal Literary History* (Ithaca and London: Cornell University Press, 1979), p. 38.

12. Quoted in Cynthia Grenier, "The Art of Fiction," *Accent*, 16 (Summer 1956), 175. Faulkner reiterates this point in a subsequent interview: "McCaslin ... says, This is bad, and I will withdraw from it. What we need are people who will say, This is bad and I'm going to do something about it, I'm going to change it" (*F in U*, 246).

VII. "JEST ANOTHER SNOPES": *The Hamlet, The Town, The Mansion*

1. Certainly Faulkner intended it as such (see *F in U*, 96 and 193, and the author's note to *The Mansion*). Yet Faulkner himself is the first to acknowledge that there are discrepancies as well as purpose behind the form and conception of the trilogy; for he came, as he puts it, to know "more about the human heart and its dilemma" during the thirty-odd years of its composition (see also *F in U*, 107-108). For a sampling of those who see the trilogy as un-unified, see Howe (282-92), Volpe (317-43), Adams (158-61). Minor discrepancies have been noted by Brooks (*Country*, 412), Volpe (402-403), Steven Marcus ("Snopes Revisited," in *Three Decades*, pp. 387-88), and Robert W. Kirk and Marvin Klotz (*Faulkner's People* [Berkeley and Los Angeles: University of California Press, 1963], pp. 309-13).

   Many of the substantive arguments raised in these works are considered here. The strongest, and perhaps the strangest, position is that of Irving Howe, ordinarily a perceptive and rational critic: "One can anticipate scores of essays which will trace the ways in which each incident or episode in the trilogy contributes to the total scheme and which will thereby create the false impression that a satisfying congruence exists between the conceptual design and the novels as they actually are. Yet, as regards both *The Town* and *The Mansion*, such a congruence is not to be found, for only fitfully do those novels realize the needs and possibilities of Faulkner's over-all design"

(285). I will be arguing the opposite view, but beyond mere disagreement, Howe's position seems to me *fundamentally* unsound and intellectually suspect. It is one thing to demonstrate and maintain one's own approach and evaluation; it is quite another to damn in advance all attempts at a different one. Howe's discussion of *The Town* and *The Mansion* is also undercut by its condescension: "Faulkner never seems able to face up to . . ." (289, 292, etc.). Brooks offers effective repudiation of much of Howe's interpretation (on the trilogy, see especially *Country*, 234-35, 369-70, 412-13).

The opposite extreme to Howe may be represented by Steven Marcus who, asserting an analogy with "the post-Homeric fragments," subsumes and exalts even trivial discrepancies: "in those almost entirely lost cyclic poems the stories of *The Iliad* and *The Odyssey* were recreated and amplified with the same character of variation that one finds in *The Town* and in parts of Faulkner's other works. As one reads about them one gets a renewed sense of how one of the primal powers of literature is to raise mythology to the level of history, to treat the material of the imagination as if it were indistinguishable from the actuality it invades and transcribes" (388). Marcus's statement may be largely true, but no more than its opposite does it follow from the fact that the trilogy contains discrepancies. Warren Beck argues more convincingly that the discrepancies are both minor and a successful part of the scheme (*Man in Motion: Faulkner's Trilogy*. Madison: University of Wisconsin Press, 1961).

2. Minter, p. 72. For a discussion of this early draft, see James B. Meriwether, *The Literary Career of William Faulkner: A Bibliographical Study* (Princeton: Princeton University Library, 1961), pp. 40-44, 69-73; Millgate, pp. 24, 180-83; and Blotner, pp. 526-31.

3. Beck, pp. 31, 43.

4. Brooks seems to me convincing on the moral praiseworthiness of this action (*Country*, 407-10).

5. Both Brooks (*Country*, 209-10) and Faulkner (*F in U*, 195), on the other hand, offer strong argument for accepting Eula's motivation at face value. (Adams, who finds Eula a generally unconvincing character, offers a third view: he maintains that the suicide is illogical because useless and ineffective [161]. But

our knowing the consequences gives us an advantage, allowing us to be coolly reasonable where the emotionally trapped Eula cannot be.) Ratliff's explanation of Flem's "suicide" stands up better—perhaps because we know so little of Flem's inner workings that no evidence contradicts it.

6. Howe, p. 284.
7. Brooks, *Country*, p. 194.
8. Ibid., p. 196.
9. Ibid., pp. 196-204. See Denis de Rougemont, *Love in the Western World*. New York: Anchor Books, 1957.
10. Brooks, *Country*, pp. 200, 203
11. Somehow missing this, Volpe makes much of Linda's "undying love" for Barton Kohl (337). Beck similarly speaks of "Linda's inconsolable grief for her lost husband" (108).
12. Howe is understandably upset by Gavin's obsessive puritanism, and he rightly notes the lack of sensuality in this trilogy of passion. Yet Howe condemns Faulkner for Gavin's lack of sexual candor though it is surely untenable to blame an author for the failings of his characters. Beck, though praising Faulkner for it, also sees Gavin as mouthpiece (51). Michael Millgate has a brief discussion of Gavin's impotence—expressed in "his adolescent sexual attitudes and behavior" (247)—that parallels mine in several respects; and, along with Marcus (386-87), Millgate compares him to Eliot's J. Alfred Prufrock—a character I presume no one takes as speaking his author's voice.
13. Howe, who condemns Faulkner for being only rarely aware "that Stevens is very far from what he has tried to persuade us he is" (287), considers Chick even more of a failed authorial speaker: "Nothing in the text, so far as I can see, provides any ground for supposing that Faulkner takes a caustic view of [his] sophomoric wisdom, or that he wishes us to see Mallison in any but a sympathetic light" (288). Marcus is equally patronizing toward Stevens: Faulkner is "too involved with him personally to admit that Stevens never was and never could be that fountainhead of moral enlightenment and of a gallant, embattled tradition which in the crisis of his culture and therefore of his art Faulkner needs to portray." Unlike Howe, though, Marcus sees Chick as simply "a decent and perspicacious young man" in *The Town* and, therefore, as a generally

successful Faulknerian speaker (386-87).

   Brooks, however, is correct when he says that anyone making
the mistake of taking Gavin as mouthpiece in *The Town* "is
very likely to miss the tone and even the basic meaning of the
novel. For if any one thing about this novel soon becomes clear,
it is that Gavin, and not for the first time in Faulkner's fiction,
is treated as a figure of fun—almost as the butt of the author's
jokes" (*Country,* 194). And in response to Marcus's view that
Chick's comments on the South are Faulkner's, Brooks adds:
"The novels of Faulkner can tell us a good deal about the quality
of Southern culture, but the way to read them is not to seize
upon remarks made by the characters to support our own
conceptions or preconceptions. We compound the folly involved
in this kind of reading when we decide hastily that this or that
remark made by a character bears the stamp of Faulkner's
personal approval" (*Country,* 370). The point is that Faulkner,
like any good artist, does not use characters to make authorial
statements in the simplistic manner implied.

14. Faulkner himself, though at one point he says that Chick had
    more judgment than Gavin (*F in U,* 140), was fully conscious of
    the limitations of Chick's narration: "I though it [*The Town*]
    would be more amusing as told through the innocence of a child
    that knew what he was seeing but had no particular judgment
    about it. That something told by someone that don't know he is
    telling something funny is sometimes much more amusing
    than when it's told by a professional wit who is hunting around
    for laughs. Also, to have it told partly by a child, partly by a
    grown man. It's to hold the object up and look at it from both
    sides, from two points of view" (*F in U,* 116).

15. *Tristram Shandy,* a book ostensibly about its title character,
    similarly focuses on events largely occurring before its
    protagonist-narrator's birth. If Sterne's book is the influence
    on Faulkner's comic vision that it seems to be, then Chick's
    distance from the events he recounts and judges may be seen as
    all the more intentionally comic.

16. See Robert Penn Warren, "William Faulkner," in *Three
    Decades,* p. 124.

17. Brooks, *Country,* p. 220.

18. Leslie A. Fiedler, *Love and Death in the American Novel*
    (Cleveland and New York: Meridian, 1962), p. 447.

19. Howe, p. 289.

20. Leslie A. Fiedler, *Waiting for the End* (New York: Delta, 1965), p. 10.

21. Fiedler, *Love and Death*, p. 447.

22. Beck, p. 91.

23. D. H. Lawrence, letter to Edward Garnett (5 June 1914), in *The Selected Letters of D. H. Lawrence*, ed. Diana Trilling (New York: Farrar, Straus and Cudahy, 1958), p. 75. Walter Allen, who quotes this same passage, adds this reminder: "Any method of character-creation is a convention" (*The English Novel* [London: Pelican, 1963], p. 346).

24. Beck, p. 106.

25. Howe gets into some difficulty when he takes Ratliff's anecdote literally and maintains that its country humor clashes tonally with the moral danger that Snopesism represents. Such a view makes a number of assumptions whose invalidity I have tried to demonstrate: that Snopesism is monolithic and simply external, that it can be confronted and defeated only by heroic actions, that, in fact, it really *can* be defeated and eliminated, and so on. See also Brooks (*Country*, 234-35) for a reading of the Clarence episode that undercuts Howe's position.

26. Beck, p. 116.

VIII. WORLDS ELSEWHERE: *Soldiers' Pay, Mosquitoes, Pylon, A Fable*

1. See Volpe, pp. 50-56, for a good summary of the emptiness and frustration in *Soldiers' Pay*.

2. Volpe, p. 66.

3. Brooks, *TYB*, p. 205.

4. Ibid., p. 181.

5. Ibid., p. 400.

6. Volpe, p. 176.

7. *CS*, p. 513. Brooks, *TYB*, pp. 401-405, discusses "Faulkner's Attitude toward Fighter Pilots and Aerial Acrobats" in *Pylon* and other works.

8. Volpe, p. 184.

9. Brooks, *TYB*, p. 400.

10. Howe, p. 269.

11. Brooks, *TYB*, p. 230. Brooks is generally excellent on all that is wrong with *A Fable*; see *TYB*, pp. 230-50.

12. Ibid., p. 101.

Bibliography

Items in I and II are listed in order of date of initial publication. See Chronology for original publication dates.

I Works by Faulkner

Soldiers' Pay. New York and Toronto: Signet, 1968.

Mosquitoes. New York: Dell, 1965.

Sartoris. New York: Random House, 1956.

The Sound and the Fury. New York: Modern Library, 1956.

As I Lay Dying. New York: Vintage, 1957.

Sanctuary. New York: Vintage, 1967.

Light in August. New York: Modern Library, 1959.

Pylon. New York and Toronto: Signet, 1968.

Absalom, Absalom! New York: Modern Library, 1951.

The Unvanquished. New York: Vintage, 1965.

The Wild Palms. New York: Vintage, 1939.

The Hamlet. New York: Vintage, 1964.

Go Down, Moses. New York: Modern Library, 1942.

Intruder in the Dust. New York: Modern Library, 1948.

Collected Stories of William Faulkner. New York: Random House, 1950.

Requiem for a Nun. New York: Random House, 1951.

A Fable. New York: Random House, 1954.

Big Woods: The Hunting Stories of William Faulkner. New York: Random House, 1955.

The Town. New York: Vintage, 1957.

The Mansion. New York: Vintage, 1959.

The Reivers: A Reminiscence. New York: Vintage, 1966.

Flags in the Dust. New York: Random House, 1973.

Sanctuary: The Original Text, ed. Noel Polk. New York: Random House, 1981.

II COLLECTIONS, INTERVIEWS, LETTERS

The Portable Faulkner, ed. Malcolm Cowley. New York: Viking, 1967.

Faulkner at Nagano, ed. Robert A. Jelliffe. Tokyo: Kenkyusha Press, 1956.

Faulkner in the University: Class Conferences at the University of Virginia, 1957-1958, ed. Frederick L. Gwynn and Joseph L. Blotner. New York: Vintage, 1959.

Essays, Speeches and Public Letters, ed. James B. Meriwether. New York: Random House, 1965.

The Faulkner-Cowley File: Letters and Memories, 1944-1962, ed. Malcolm Cowley. New York: Viking, 1968.

Lion in the Garden: Interviews with William Faulkner, 1926-1962, ed. James B. Meriwether and Michael Millgate. Lincoln and London: University of Nebraska Press, 1980.

Selected Letters of William Faulkner, ed. Joseph Blotner. New York: Vintage, 1978.

III SECONDARY SOURCES

Adams, R. P. *Faulkner: Myth and Motion.* Princeton: Princeton University Press, 1968.

Bassett, John, ed. *William Faulkner: The Critical Heritage.* London and Boston: Routledge & Kegan Paul, 1975.

Beck, Warren. *Man in Motion: Faulkner's Trilogy.* Madison: University of Wisconsin Press, 1961.

———. *Faulkner.* Madison: University of Wisconsin Press, 1976.

Bezzerides, A. I. *William Faulkner: A Life on Paper.* Jackson: University Press of Mississippi, 1980.

Bleikasten, Andre. *The Most Splendid Failure: Faulkner's "The Sound and the Fury."* Bloomington and London: Indiana University Press, 1976.

Blotner, Joseph. *William Faulkner's Library: A Catalogue.* Charlottesville: University Press of Virginia, 1964.

———. *Faulkner: A Biography.* New York: Random House, 1974 (2 vols.).

Brooks, Cleanth. *William Faulkner: The Yoknapatawpha Country.* New Haven: Yale University Press, 1963.

———. *William Faulkner: Toward Yoknapatawpha and Beyond.* New Haven and London: Yale University Press, 1978.

Coughlan, Robert. *The Private World of William Faulkner.* New York: Harper & Bros., 1954.

Creighton, Joanne V. *William Faulkner's Craft of Revision: The Snopes Trilogy, "The Unvanquished" and "Go Down, Moses."* Detroit: Wayne State University Press, 1977.

Falkner, Murry C. *The Falkners of Mississippi: A Memoir.* Baton Rouge: Louisiana State University Press, 1967.

Faulkner, John. *My Brother Bill: An Affectionate Reminiscence.* New York: Trident Press, 1963.

Fiedler, Leslie A. "William Faulkner: An American Dickens," *Commentary,* 10, 4 (October 1950), 384-87.

————. *Love and Death in the American Novel.* Cleveland and New York: Meridian, 1962.

————. *Waiting for the End.* New York: Delta, 1965.

Fowler, Doreen, and Ann J. Abadie, eds. *"A Cosmos of My Own": Faulkner and Yoknapatawpha 1980.* Jackson: University Press of Mississippi, 1981.

Hoffman, Frederick J., and Olga W. Vickery, eds. *William Faulkner: Three Decades of Criticism.* New York and Burlingame: Harbinger, 1963.

Holmes, Edward M. *Faulkner's Twice-Told Tales: His Re-Use of His Material.* The Hague: Mouton, 1966.

Howe, Irving. *William Faulkner: A Critical Study.* New York: Vintage, 1951.

Irwin, John. *Doubling & Incest/Repetition & Revenge: A Speculative Reading of Faulkner.* Baltimore and London: Johns Hopkins University Press, 1980.

Kartiganer, Donald M. *The Fragile Thread: The Meaning of Form in Faulkner's Novels.* Amherst: University of Massachusetts Press, 1979.

Kawin, Bruce F. *Faulkner and Film.* New York: Ungar, 1977.

Kazin, Alfred. "The Stillness of *Light in August,*" in *Twelve Original Essays on Great American Novels,* ed. Charles Shapiro. Detroit: Wayne State University Press, 1958.

Kinney, Arthur F. *Faulkner's Narrative Poetics: Style as Vision.* Amherst: University of Massachusetts Press, 1978.

Kirk, Robert W., and Marvin Klotz. *Faulkner's People.* Berkeley and Los Angeles: University of California Press, 1963.

Langford, Gerald. *Faulkner's Revision of "Sanctuary": A Collation of the Unrevised Galleys and the Published Book.* Austin and London: University of Texas Press, 1972.

Massey, Linton. "Notes on the Unrevised Galleys of Faulkner's *Sanctuary*," *Studies in Bibliography*, 7 (1956), 195-208.

Meriwether, James B. *The Literary Career of William Faulkner: A Bibliographical Study*. Princeton: Princeton University Library, 1961.

————, ed. *Studies in The Sound and the Fury*. Columbus, Ohio: Charles E. Merrill, 1970.

Millgate, Michael. *The Achievement of William Faulkner*. New York: Vintage, 1966.

Minter, David. *William Faulkner: His Life and Work*. Baltimore and London: Johns Hopkins University Press, 1980.

Reed, Joseph. *Faulkner's Narrative*. New Haven: Yale University Press, 1973.

Schoenberg, Estella. *Old Tales and Talking: Quentin Compson in William Faulkner's "Absalom, Absalom!" and Related Works*. Jackson: University Press of Mississippi, 1977.

Slatoff, Walter J. *Quest for Failure: A Study of William Faulkner*. Westport, Conn.: Greenwood Press, 1976.

Stonum, Gary Lee. *Faulkner's Career: An Internal Literary History*. Ithaca and London: Cornell University Press, 1979.

Sundquist, Eric J. *Faulkner: The House Divided*. Baltimore and London: Johns Hopkins University Press, 1983.

Swiggart, Peter. *The Art of Faulkner's Novels*. Austin: University of Texas Press, 1962.

Thompson, Lawrance. *William Faulkner: An Introduction and Interpretation*. New York: Holt, Rinehart and Winston, 1967.

Vickery, Olga W. *The Novels of William Faulkner: A Critical Interpretation*. Baton Rouge: Louisiana State University Press, 1959.

Volpe, Edmond L. *A Reader's Guide to William Faulkner*. New York: Farrar, Straus and Giroux, 1971.

Wadlington, Warwick P. "*The Sound and the Fury*: A Logic of Tragedy," *American Literature*, 53, 3 (November 1981), 409-23.

Warren, Robert Penn, ed. *Faulkner: A Collection of Critical Essays*. Englewood Cliffs, N.J.: Prentice-Hall, 1966.

Wasson, Ben. *Count No 'Count: Flashbacks to Faulkner*. Jackson: University Press of Mississippi, 1983.

Webb, James W., and A. Wigfall Green, eds. *William Faulkner of Oxford*. Baton Rouge: Louisiana State University Press, 1965.

Wilde, Meta Carpenter, and Orin Borsten. *A Loving Gentleman: The Love Story of William Faulkner and Meta Carpenter*. New York: Simon and Schuster, 1976.

Index